INCHWORM, INCHWORM:

PERSISTENT PROBLEMS
IN READING EDUCATION

Constance M. McCullough, Editor
San Francisco State College

INTERNATIONAL READING ASSOCIATION
800 Barksdale Road   Newark, Delaware 19711

Copyright 1980 by the
International Reading Association, Inc.

Library of Congress Cataloging in Publication Data
Main entry under title:

Inchworm, inchworm.
    Bibliography: p.
    1. Reading—Remedial teaching—Addresses, essays,
lectures.   2. Reading disabilities—Addresses, essays, lectures.
I. McCullough, Constance Mary, 1912-
II. International Reading Association.
LB1050.5.I46   428'.4'2   79-17125
ISBN 0-87207-937-6

Contents

115300

The Reading Consultant

Foreword

The history of progress in reading instruction can be measured, in part, by the careers and commentaries of various individuals. As they have progressed in their perceptions and applications of reading processes, so has the field. This progress has been slow but steady, moving at a measured pace—even as the title of this volume suggests.

We are fortunate to have this collection of papers from individuals who have contributed to the progress of our profession. They share their insights on issues of importance to professionals in reading. The issues are broad ranging and the presentations are varied but all are interesting and worthy of our consideration.

Dr. McCullough is to be congratulated for compiling this volume. It is a useful additon to the literature and one that you should enjoy reading and rereading.

Harold L. Herber
Syracuse University

The International Reading Association attempts, through its publications, to provide a forum for a wide spectrum of opinion on reading. This policy permits divergent viewpoints without assuming the endorsement of the Association.

Introduction

At the Miami Convention of the International Reading Association in May 1977, the Reading Hall of Fame and IRA presented a cosponsored symposium on Current Issues in Reading. Eight members of RHF participated in expressing their views of present priorities, from their long perspective of leadership and contribution to the field of reading improvement, well over an aggregate of 320 years of dedication. Nearly a thousand people occupied the chairs and floor and lined the walls of the auditorium to listen, and their enthusiastic response and participation encouraged the publication of what they had heard and said.

The unity in the papers lay in the conviction of the speaker, in each case, that his topic—his suggestion for caution or reform—was of utmost importance to the improvement of reading. The lure for the audience was the eminence of the speakers and the privilege of hearing so many of them in one session. Several generations of their colleagues, students, coauthors, editors, readers, and critics-gone-mellow composed that audience.

George Spache, with his characteristic candor, irony, and flawless logic, dealt with the fallacious assumptions underlying the design of some current programs for instruction, the materials, the authorship, and the evaluation instruments.

Both Albert J. Harris and Sterl Artley addressed the current reading disabilities/learning disabilities controversy. In his review of current political, diagnostic, and remedial issues, Harris drew attention to new research, some of it in support of old neglected recommendations. Artley proposed in considerable detail a practical solution of the RD/LD dilemma, which is well-illustrated in his own institution.

1

After years of scholarly research and arduous authorship, Donald Durrell urged professional preparation for authors, and proposed to set an example of a more direct way to design and publish pretested, useful classroom materials, by involving publishers, authors, teachers, librarians, supervisors, administrators, and curriculum directors in a workshop for the purpose.

Four discussants were scheduled to comment on the papers presented. The first was Emmett Betts, whose conviction that laboratory experiences are the real teachers, moved him to doubt whether anything would be changed in classrooms on Monday by what had been said on this particular Wednesday. Gertrude Whipple advised the audience to become acquainted with the writings of these speakers, and the speakers to update their writings. In the interest of saving time for audience participation, she did not comment further. Edgar Dale, having been quoted in some length by Durrell and also being concerned for time, declined the invitation to speak. Helen Robinson directed her remarks to teacher education in learning disabilities and reading disabilities, to the percentage of children with learning disabilities, to the importance of good instruction for clinical cases, and to a comment on Betts's remark about the value of a lecture.

The meeting proved so stimulating that the Publications Committee encouraged some of its presentations into print as a collected volume. It further suggested augmenting the volume with other papers that address current issues in reading, papers not presented through the auspices of the Reading Hall of Fame but, nonetheless, papers of strength and clarity on topics of vitality, stance, and to some extent controversy.

As the moderator of the original Hall of Fame meeting and as compiling editor for this volume, I commend the experience of reading the ideas of people who know well what they are talking about.

CMM

Section One
TOWARD A MORE LITERATE SOCIETY

The End of Optimism?

David B. Tyack
Stanford University

I am one of those historians who are paid for looking backwards. I believe that history can help us to look at our present realities in a new light, just as a visit to another region or country helps us to see familiar sights with new eyes. In recent years in education we have been on such a roller coaster of hope and despair, of reform and disillusionment that this seems to me an appropriate time to stand back and look at the present mood and temper in a longer historical perspective.

My major theme is that the mood of pessimism about schooling that has emerged in the past decade is quite unprecedented in this country. Americans of all political persuasions and walks of life have traditionally had a deep and lasting faith in education. I will argue that this optimistic belief has itself been a major reason for the rapid expansion and improvement of our schools. Attitudes do influence behavior. A belief that something *can* be done spurs effort. When one athlete ran a mile in four minutes, others promptly found that they could do it too. Conversely, when people lose confidence, they can readily find excuses for not doing the possible. I will surely *not* be saying that our problems would be solved if we simply became Pollyannish optimists. Much of my own writing has stressed the gap between our aspirations and our performance. But I do believe that much of the current pessimism is mistaken in its premises, sometimes self-serving, and often destructive in its consequences. We need instead a realistic hope that does not demand panaceas or rely on illusions.

Let me indicate, then, the direction of my argument. First I will examine briefly some of the reasons for the current atmosphere of gloom and doom in education. Then I pose the question, "Are things now really worse objectively than they were at the turn of this century?" We will call to witness some scenes and voices from the past, the voices of people who lived at that time. Next I will ask where this traditional American faith in schooling came from and suggest how that conviction influenced our educational history. Finally, I plan to return again to the present and to ask if that traditional faith is really outmoded and to ask what are the major tasks we face.

First, the Bad News

If one looked only at some titles of recent muckraking books on schools, one would be likely to believe that we are attending the funeral of public education: *Death at an Early Age, Our Children Are Dying*, or simply *School Is Dead*. Other titles are hardly more cheerful—witness *An Empty Spoon, The Twelve Year Sentence,* and *Compulsory Miseducation*. In addition to the writers who exposed conditions in ghetto schools and the social philosophers who advocated deschooling, we have also seen dozens of scholarly books pour off the presses which documented the failures of compensatory programs, the injustices of school finance, and the overwhelming importance of social class in explaining school performance. In his overpublicized book *Inequality*, Christopher Jencks argued that schools could not do much to alter the gross maldistribution of wealth and income in this country. It was only a matter of time before a writer would ask the obvious question: "Do Schools Make a Difference?"

Some of these books were sensational and full of animus toward teachers, some were setting up straw men, some evaluated education by irrelevant criteria but, surely, there was fire under all that smoke. There *are* serious problems with American schools. One is functional illiteracy. Schools have rarely given good or even adequate education to the poor or to minorities, and these are the groups worst off today. Not long ago school systems refused to release the achievement scores of children; but, increasingly, states, cities, and the federal government have forced disclosure. As ghetto parents have learned about the low achievement scores and continued failures of their children, they increasingly have lost faith in the expertise of the professionals. What they had thought was simply a personal misfortune—that their child could not read—has now been revealed to be a public problem of epidemic proportions. Tyler (5) has estimated that about 20 percent of students leave the classroom without "learning the basic abilities, skills, and knowledge that the elementary school seeks to teach." A recent University of Texas study found millions of American youth unable to perform basic tasks required in a complex society, such as reading job advertisements or making simple calculations. In my opinion, this is a far more important problem than falling SAT scores.

Both educators and the general public have become aware of other real educational problems. During four of the past five Gallup Polls Americans have rated poor discipline as the number one problem in schools. Surveys have shown that vandalism, violence, and intimidation have grown alarmingly. Senator Birch Bayh's subcommittee recently reported that school vandalism in 1976 cost over $600,000,000, that there were more than 70,000 physical assaults on teachers, and that hundreds of thousands of children were physically attacked.

While this violence multiplies in classrooms and corridors of schools, in many communities the relationships among teachers, parents, administrators, school boards, and community interest groups have become increasingly hostile. An older consensus style of governance has given way to an adversary tone. Teachers go on strike, aggrieved parents bring suits in court, voters increasingly turn down school bond levies, and school boards seek ways to distance themselves from even their closest agents, superintendents.

Finally, as if these problems were not enough, education is in some respects a declining industry. When the number of pupils drops—as sharply as 15 to 20 percent in some states—

teachers and administrators are fired or reassigned, school boards get embroiled in controversy over closing schools, and districts find it ever harder to hire new staff or promote from within. We educators are now competing for jobs and scarce resources. We can no longer expect the constant growth fueled by the baby boom following World War II.

So, in many ways, the picture *is* grim. Is not pessimism a realistic response? To this question I will return shortly. But for now, let us take a look at the problems and attitudes of educators at the turn of this century. Were the issues they faced any less daunting?

The problems educators faced at the turn of this century were at least as staggering as any we face today, although in some ways they were different. Most of the educators of that period had a deep and sustaining faith in what they were doing, a sense of optimism that impelled them to great effort. Perhaps the most impressive expression of that hope came from an obscure superintendent in Collinwood, Ohio, after a disastrous elementary school fire had claimed the lives of 162 students and two teachers in that community. Despite that terrible tragedy, he wrote in his autobiography that "just to be alive in that period and to have a sense of sharing even in some small way...in the great adventure called education was a privilege beyond all price." Schooling "seemed indeed to be at the very heart of all progress. It was the key of the future. It was the focus of all those wild and entrancing dreams of what seemed the coming golden age, no longer dim and remote but just around the corner" (6).

Such a faith and commitment to work for progress was, of course, not restricted to educators but was deep in the American grain. Take out a dollar bill. On the back side, opposite George Washington, you will find the Great Seal of the United States. Note the mottoes. They translate "He Prospered Our Undertakings" and "New Order of the Centuries." Over all the land there looks out the all-seeing eye of God. This conviction that Providence had destined the United States to be a model for the rest of mankind, a redeemer nation, was an old idea even before the country became independent. John Winthrop had told his fellow Puritans in 1630 that "wee must Consider that wee shall be as a Citty vpon a Hill, the eies of all people are vppon vs." Thomas Jefferson expressed a similar idea in the midst of the Napoleonic wars: "The eyes of the virtuous all over the earth are turned with anxiety on us, as the only depository of the sacred fire of liberty" (4). This strong sense of providential intent and manifest destiny inspired men and women to action, not fatalistic observation on the sidelines of history. Like other crusaders for a common school system, Horace Mann had a strong sense of the cosmic importance of his work. Schooling for him was the hub of a great wheel of social reform that might one day abolish poverty, intemperance, and the inhumanity of mankind. Missionaries took the gospel of public education to the distant frontiers of Oregon and Alaska.

By the end of the nineteenth century, the United States led all other nations in providing schooling of all kinds to its children and youth. One of the most striking features of this educational expansion was that it happened without the powerful apparatus of a centralized state. Especially in the small towns and rural areas it was a grass roots enterprise. The United States Office of Education was essentially powerless, composed of a commissioner who sometimes made speeches and a handful of clerks who collected statistics. As late as 1890 the average size of state departments of education was two— *two*, including the chief state school officer. The famous promoters of the common school—people like Horace Mann and Henry Barnard—had almost no formal power; basically, they could only try to persuade people to invest their taxes and place their children in public schools. Thus, the effective decisions lay with the hundreds of thousands of school trustees and many millions of school patrons. It was they who had faith enough in schooling to create the largest free system in the world.

I do not mean to suggest that only hope and a sense of manifest educational destiny underlay this massive achievement. Fear of cultural differences and anxiety about the stability of the capitalist order also motivated both leaders and followers. The people who did most to create the public school system were quintessential Victorians: British-American in ethnic origin, bourgeois, and evangelical Protestant. As Daniel Howe has observed, American Victorian culture was profoundly didactic, confident in its own superiority, aggressive in extending its boundaries. Consequently, Victorian educators were often intolerant about cultural differences and sought to homogenize all children to their own standards. They also shared many of the prevailing notions about racial and sexual inferiority. School leaders regarded themselves as an aristocracy of character and shared a vigorous faith in common Victorian values.

During the early twentieth century, as we have seen, this aggressive optimism continued, but new elements of culture merged with the older evangelical legacy. In particular, school leaders added to their ideological baggage a faith in what they called "science." They also began to find ways to administer schools in a more "businesslike" manner, seeking thereby to ciothe themselves also with the prestige of corporate managers. Historian John Higham (3) has said that the distinctive feature of the early twentieth century "is not the preeminence of democratic ideals or of bureaucratic techniques, but rather a fertile amalgamation of the two.... For a time it seemed that a modernized Americanism and a social gospel could be the moving spirit of a technical society."

This note of heroic confidence continued to ring loud and clear in the yearbooks of school superintendents. The 1933 volume said leaders in education had no lesser task than "to mold human character and to ameliorate the whole intellectual, moral, social, civic, and economic status of their fellows." As late as 1952, this heroic image was still alive and well in the yearbook: "Today's mid-century attacks upon the schools and school leaders are not more powerful nor more vicious than those of 100 years ago. The Horace Manns and Henry Barnards had to win school support by sheer missionary zeal and convincing logic." Now as then, "it is the superintendent of great heart and courageous spirit, possessed of sound judgment and deep understanding, who will carry the profession and the schools forward.... His world will be immeasurably enriched by his service and leadership" (1). The days of low profile had not yet arrived.

Rhetoric like that now sounds either quaint or like a parody from the pages of the *Harvard Lampoon* or *Mad Magazine*. Now we live in an age of deflated hopes and perhaps see more clearly than they did the dangers of educational oversell. As a result of a decade or more of muckraking tracts and scholarly studies, we can see, more clearly than ever before, certain major problems in our educational ideology and practice:

1. Schools *alone* cannot abolish poverty or create equality of opportunity for outcast groups.
2. Schools have often been insensitive to the cultures and needs of non-middle-class and non-Anglo groups.
3. The idea of "keeping schools out of politics" and leaving most decision making to the professionals has often disenfranchised parents and community groups.
4. The search for a *one best system* of schooling, either based on Victorian values or on the new science of education, is probably misguided. Since different people learn in different ways, since tastes and philosophies of citizens are varied, and since no one approach fits all pupils, it seems best to search for several acceptable alternative kinds of schooling rather than to try to find one best system for all. Panaceas do not exist in schools any more than in any other institution.

Improvements Have Been Made

Still, the problems we face hardly justify unmitigated gloom any more than earlier successes justified euphoria. It is interesting to speculate what William Maxwell or Ella Flagg Young would have to say now if we could bring them in a time machine from their superintendencies in New York and Chicago in 1910. They would doubtless be delighted with the tremendous improvement in school buildings and with our achievement in cutting the pupil-teacher ratio to less than half what it was in 1910. They would also probably be amazed by these facts: that secondary education has become nearly universal; teachers now almost all have at least B.A. degrees; and it is routine to find special classes for handicapped children, differentiated curricula, and all kinds of educational specialists—changes they were struggling to achieve in 1910. Perhaps they would be most surprised to find that people now define *declining* enrollments as a serious problem, since they were constantly struggling to build new schools and to find teachers to staff them.

Indeed, without being Pollyannish, I think it is accurate to say that for the great majority of American children and youth, schools are now more humane places than they used to be and teach as effectively as they did in the past. The 1973 Gallup poll on education shows that most Americans think so too. Eighty-two percent said yes to the question "Do you think your child is learning what you believe should be learned?" Eighty-three percent said that their children attended school because they wanted to, not because they were required to do so. And 69 percent of parents of public school pupils said that they thought that their children were getting a better education than they did. On the critical issue of the age limit for compulsory schooling, only 3 percent said it should be less than sixteen years; 50 percent said it should last until age eighteen and nineteen.

My own view, then, is that in the present time there are grounds for asserting modest hope and for regaining some of that older idealism that argued that schooling could improve the lives of those on the bottom of society. Indeed, for me the truest test of any reform or any institution is: what will it do for the outcasts and the losers, for the rejects and casualties, for the victims of poverty and discrimination? Now, I do not believe that schools by themselves can erase inequality. Only massive social, political, and economic change can do that. We as teachers have a special stake in making those larger changes come about, for we encounter every day in our classroom the problems that this larger social injustice creates. We have just as much interest in creating a full employment economy as an earlier generation of educators had in creating a school lunch program, for we can see all around us the results of our scandalous rates of unemployment of youth. But we can also act directly every day to lessen social injustice through our own work as teachers—we can, as Booker T. Washington urged, cast down our buckets where we are.

Focusing on the Job Ahead

I am convinced that we could make of the next decade a major period of reform in American education, if only we have the wisdom and the will. The main reason I believe this is that we have a moratorium on growth, now that the pupil population is declining. Now for the first time in history we have enough space and trained teachers to do our work really effectively. We could—and might—go the way of other declining industries like the railroads and insist on feather-bedding and let facilities and morale run down. We might continue to chew each other up in our adversary relationships and argue about who is to walk the plank first in these hard times. But with the right kind of leadership we can focus our own and the public's attention on the unfinished business of American public education. There is more than enough for all of us to do.

What, then, might be some of the items on this agenda? I will briefly mention only two. The first is the problem of functional illiteracy. It is both a pedagogical problem and a matter of urgent public policy. There is abundant evidence that the general public is aroused. State legislatures have mandated minimum standards of intellectual competence for graduation. Parents have begun to sue schools for malpractice for failing to give children basic skills. In my view the answer to the problem does not lie so much in the courts or in state mandates as in providing the resources, the skills, and the expertise to identify learning problems early and to help those students.

In most schools these children will be a small minority, but in some they may even constitute a majority because of residential segregation by class and because of long term patterns of discrimination. I believe that a consolidated attack on the problem of functional illiteracy will attract the public support necessary to provide the research, the retraining of teachers in service, and the employment of experts that will be necessary to ensure success.

The second item on my agenda is to try to create alternative forms of education within the public school systems. For too long we have been bewitched by the panacea mongers who promised that they had the one best way; much of the recent disillusionment with schools has stemmed from the disappointment we experienced as one highly touted reform after another failed to deliver on exaggerated promises. Why not offer parents and students a greater variety of kinds of schooling, for not all people want or need the same thing? Already, prosperous parents have such choices, for they can move about from district to district or pay for private schooling for their children. But the ordinary working class family has little choice. At present the only alternative to violence ridden, ineffective innercity schools is usually just truancy. The growing surplus of classrooms and higher ratio of teachers should enable imaginative principals and teachers to create alternatives and to give greater power to parents and students to control their own educational destinies.

These are only two possible approaches to the long and difficult task of reform in education. The key test of reforms, I have suggested, is what will it do for people on the bottom of society, those who need effective schooling the most. It is easy to convince ouselves that problems are insoluble and to find alibis. But we have a long tradition of hope and effort to sustain us in our work. It was that tradition that led the slum school teacher Leonard Covello (2) to say this in his autobiography:

> There are those, I am sure, who will argue that I have painted too glowing a picture of the boys whose lives began in the slums of Manhattan, that I should have made more of the violence, of juvenile delinquency, and of social chaos. It is so easy to concentrate on the sensational events in the life of a community and to ignore the everyday pattern of living of the thousands of families that struggle to raise their families decently amid tremendous odds.... This is not and never was the way I looked on my job as a teacher. My approach was determined by the fact that beneath the rough, defiant, and cynical attitude I saw the yearning for appreciation, understanding and the willingness to struggle....

His was an idealism that did not demand panaceas or rely on illusions. We need such an idealism today.

References

1. American Association of School Administrators. *The American School Superintendent*, Thirteenth Yearbook. Washington, D.C.: AASA, 1952, 63, 437, 444.
2. Covello, Leonard. *The Heart Is the Teacher.* New York: McGraw-Hill, 1958, 269-270.
3. Higham, John. "Hanging Together: Divergent Unities in American History," *Journal of American History*, 61 (June 1974), 24.
4. Tyack, David (Ed.). *Turning Points in American Educational History.* Greenwich, Connecticut: Xerox Publishing, 1967, 14, 90.
5. Tyler, Ralph W. "Universal Education in the United States: Milestone Influences on the Past and Future," *Bulletin*, 51 (March 1975). Bloomington: Indiana University.
6. Whitney, Frank. *School and I: The Autobiography of an Ohio Schoolmaster.* Yellow Springs, Ohio: Antioch, 28, 30-31.

The Status of Reading Achievement: Is There a Halo Around the Past?

Leo Fay
Indiana University

When I first considered this topic, I had a clear idea of what the presentation would be. In fact, I gathered a vast amount of data concerning the status of reading achievement in the United States and, with Roger Farr, systematically tested 10,000 sixth graders and 10,000 tenth graders in Indiana using the same tests given to comparable groups in 1944. It all seemed so straightforward, but then some unusual things happened that changed the nature of this presentation in some significant ways.

I received and accepted an invitation to serve as a consultant to the Institute of Education and Research at the University of Punjab in Lahore, Pakistan. The institute faculty is divided into two parts—a teaching faculty offering the master's and Ph.D. degrees to prepare a cadre of educational leaders and a research faculty engaged in attempting to develop a research and development base for education in the country. Pakistan is both an old civilization with a history extending beyond 2500 B.C., and a new country having been formed by the partition of the Indian subcontinent in 1947 into two independent countries—India and Pakistan. The development needs of the country are tremendous—almost overwhelming—in agriculture, commerce, health, and education. Unesco, the U.S. Agency for International Development, and the Institute are all working to strengthen the educational base upon which all other development depends. Recently the World Bank provided Pakistan with a 50 million dollar loan to develop a better base of literacy in the country. Think what it must be like to try to develop anything if your labor pool is over 85 percent illiterate.

Later, I received an invitation from Unesco to serve as a consultant to the Ministry of Education in Saudi Arabia to establish a system to evaluate their five year plan for educational development. I could not accept this invitation but did stop by Unesco in Paris to meet the head of the Arab section and several others concerned with educational development in the Arab nations. When I walked into the office of the head of the Arab section, he asked me what I thought a certain sign in his office meant. It was a strange question because the sign was in Arabic, but he went on to say, "Those are the first words of the Koran. They say, 'Read what God has revealed to you.' Our holy book tells us to read and yet we are the most illiterate people on earth."

The Importance of Education for Everyone

The following conversation made a deep impact on me. I saw how blessed we are and have been as a people. How wise our early leaders had been in emphasizing the importance of education for everyone. To read is to possess a power for transcending whatever physical power humans can muster. And we, my friends, have been blessed with this power in ever increasing measure throughout our history. We have enjoyed the presence in our past of the halo referred to in the title of the paper; it is here in our present; and it will continue into our future.

The development of literacy in our country is interesting to trace. At the time of the first census in 1790, the estimate was that 15 percent of the people were literate in that they could read and write their own names. It was not until after World War I that half the people were literate, defined in terms of having attended four years of school. As late as 1943, 750,000 men had been rejected for military service because of illiteracy. Most of these young men were from remote rural areas and were predictors of the postwar problems that urban areas experienced with the mass movement of people out of rural areas to the large cities. By 1960, 75 percent of the children who were in fifth grade went on to complete high school; today, over

50 percent of our youth go on to postsecondary education and by some definitions we are 90+ percent literate. This is a truly phenomenal accomplishment. But too often we simply do not appreciate the significance of the contribution that schooling of *all* of our youth has made to the well being and power of this nation.

In his "A Letter to the President-Elect" (*Change* magazine, December 1976), Wilbur Cohen reminded Mr. Carter that "Education has been a critical key to our national development and the quality of our life." Edward Denison (in a Brookings Institution report) found that the biggest single stimulus of our economic growth during 1962-1969 was increase of knowledge. Another major source was the increased education of our labor force. Fourteen percent of our economic growth during this period came from increased education per worker and 41 percent from advances in knowledge.

"According to Denison, educational background decisively conditions the type of work individuals can perform as well as their proficiency." Cohen then comments about the upward shift in the educational background of the labor force from 1929 to 1969 and concludes his letter with the observation that "Nothing is more important [than education of the people] for the fulfillment of the nation's goals." The truth is schools and teachers have served the nation well.

Achieving our Literacy Potential

Having said this, let us look at the present state of reading achievement and try to determine where we are now. As we do this, I would also like to comment about some potential dangers on the horizons that we can and must avoid if our literacy potential is to be achieved.

It is a difficult if not impossible task to pick a particular moment in time to understand the status of any social phenomenon. This is certainly true of school achievement data. Usually it is more useful, in attempting to make judgments about the present, to look at trend lines over some span of time. Fortunately, various researchers have done this. In their study, "Reading: Then and Now," Farr and Tuinman and Rawls reported a compilation of studies which over the span of time from about 1920 through the middle sixties showed a continuing improvement in reading achievement. More recently, in their report, "The Decline in Reading Achievement: Need We Worry?" Harnischfeger and Wiley presented additional data that supported the same findings.

But then something seemed to happen, at least as far as test scores were concerned, from the middle grades through college levels. From about 1967, reading test scores for people beyond the age of nine, started to drift down. This drift continued into the 70s, and at best is only now beginning to level off. The magnitude of this drop is such that one can say that while today's students perform better than their parents did at comparable ages, they are not doing as well, at least on standard tests, as their older siblings.

The evidence for this conclusion is found in two sets of data. The first, from the Iowa statewide testing program, shows the following drops in grade scores over the decade from 1965-1975:

	Grade 5	Grade 6	Grade 7	Grade 8
Reading	1.9 mo.	2.5 mo.	5.2 mo.	5.5 mo.
Vocabulary	.5 mo.	1.4 mo.	3.9 mo.	4.3 mo.
Math Concepts	3.1 mo.	4.8 mo.	6.5 mo.	7.0 mo.
Math Problem Solving	3.2 mo.	5.0 mo.	7.4 mo.	7.3 mo.

The second set of data is derived from a comparison of 1945 with 1976 reading achievement for a systematic, statewide sampling of sixth and tenth grade children. (Farr, Fay, Negley, *Then and Now: Reading Achievement in Indiana, 1944-1945 and 1976* [1978].) Because 1976 sixth grade students were ten months younger than their 1945 counterparts and 1976 tenth graders were fourteen months younger than the 1945 students, comparisons were adjusted by age. These comparisons resulted in a superiority of eight months for the 1976 sixth grade students and a superiority of ten percentile points for the 1976 tenth grade students. The marked reduction in dropout rates over this period suggests that the difference was, in fact, substantially larger at the tenth grade level.

It should also be noted that the National literacy assessment data for seventeen year olds showed an increase of 2 percent over the period of 1971-1974. The NAEP data reported for nine year olds also showed an increase. The Iowa and

NAEP data are based upon very different kinds of instruments and as a consequence are not directly comparable. The Iowa tests show a lower mean performance over the span of time whereas the NAEP shows an increase in the percentage of a given group that can perform successfully on the instruments. One interpretation is that NAEP data show that the percentage of functional literates has increased while the Iowa data show that the average performance of students has decreased.

Data from the city of Minneapolis and the state of Minnesota show patterns comparable to the above. Standardized tests show an improvement in the early elementary grades with some drop after the fourth grade, and National Assessment data show a high and increasing level of functional literacy within the state. Data from other communities indicate that this is a general pattern across the country, although actual levels of performance may differ.

In essence, then, on the long term, achievement has gone up. On the short term, achievement has appeared to have dropped. At this time there is no research to justify a stronger term than *appears* in this context. While there is no hard evidence, however, there is much speculation as to whether the observed change is real and, if it is real, what the reasons for the change might be.

At first glance, it would appear that there has been a real change. After all, the same instruments were used and the difference without question is there. This conclusion, however, assumes that conditions have remained constant enough for the instruments to remain valid. You could also speculate that the nature of literacy itself has broadened over the past decade to the extent that it can no longer be assessed by reading tests that are based upon models of forty or more years ago. The recent activities of the Association for Visual Literacy and the most recent definitions of literacy appearing in IRA publications would suggest this might be a distinct possibility. Badly needed are studies to determine the dimensions of reading and literacy in our society at this time.

The research is yet to be done. Perhaps it can be structured by speculation as to possible causes relating to the apparent drop in achievement in reading as well as the other school subjects. Strong opinions exist in regard to this matter.

In the eighth annual Gallup Poll on Education (*Phi Delta Kappan*, October 1976), it is reported that 59 percent of the population believes that the quality of education today is declining as evidenced by the decline in national test scores. Furthermore, the poll revealed that the public places the greatest blame for declining scores on parents, on society, on children's lack of motivation, and too much viewing of television. Others blame the schools. The Hudson Institute Report by Frank Armbruster and others (*Wall Street Journal*, July 23, 1976) concluded that schools are deteriorating everywhere and that teachers and administrators are the ones primarily responsible. In both cases, the assumption is accepted that school achievement was, indeed better in the past. School people have had to live with that contention probably for as long as schools have existed. Will Rogers used to comment that, "The schools ain't as good as they used to be—and they probably never were." In an address on April 21, 1932, Arthur Gates observed that teachers and schools were not responsible for the great depression.

Today's Schools

Schools do not exist in a void. They are a basic institution and in many ways reflect the society they serve. The period from the mid-sixties to the mid-seventies was not the most tranquil decade in our history. It was a time of conflict and of loud and serious questioning of our basic institutions. The home, church, state, and schools have all felt the negative impact of this period. Interestingly, this period was marked by a significant drop in the productivity of the American worker as measured by output per hour of work. Could this phenomenon bear any relationship to the apparent drop in school achievement? Is it reasonable to expect the school to run counter to a major opposite force in the society?

Look again at the American family. The children in school during this period were the later children of the relatively large postwar families. For some reason, later children tend toward lower achievement in school than their older siblings. This is the period when large numbers of women joined the labor force and family patterns started to change. Drug and alcohol abuse had a devastating effect on middle class America with the eight to fourteen year olds becoming the fastest growing group of drug users. Last year there were 300,000 births to unwed mothers ages fifteen and less. While not exactly a new phenomenon, the rate of increase is up more than 300 percent over a decade ago. In the report, "Greening of the High School—A Look at the Clients," the conclusion is documented that today's youth is far different from his parents and grandparents.

The school became the battleground for desegregation and racial balance which is but another societal problem cast upon the school. Yet, in spite of these changes in society, critics maintain that teachers and administrators are primarily responsible for the deterioration of school achievement. That is like saying that doctors and hospital staffs are responsible for the frightening trends in the increased incidence of cancer.

During this period, the value of schooling has been questioned in the various media. The lower economic payoff of education has been so publicized that there is a growing drop in enrollment in higher education among middle class families. Related is a change in values concerning work with a consequent drop in purpose for education. In a 1973 Gallup Poll, over one-third of the eighteen to twenty year olds did not consider education as important as success. Older populations had a much higher percentage of positive response, thus reflecting a major change in attitude between the two groups.

Patterns have shifted in school as well. Retention rates have increased during this period but, unfortunately, attendance has dropped significantly. A group of Illinois teachers reported to me that when students were in school they attended fewer classes. A typical pattern was a work study assignment, study halls, and only two academic classes a day. Courses in English, foreign languages, and general mathematics all show drops in enrollment. The anti-schooling, anti-intellectual attitudes commonly held in our society apparently are having their impact.

One could hardly comment about school achievement without commenting about television. TV appears to be a positive force for the young learner up to ages eight and nine. After that age, TV begins to detract from reading and home study. Furthermore, TV watching may result in changes in thinking patterns that may affect school performance and performance on tests. This is another area for further research.

If you reflect upon these factors that may impinge upon school achievement, you realize that we must know much more before we can interpret what the nature of reading achievement really is. However, in spite of all the problems, the school has remained a viable institution. It continues to serve large numbers of people well. The Minnesota assessment revealed that the vast majority of students reacted very positively to their schooling and, furthermore, that this attitude is a positive force for higher achievement—more important than amount of money spent or various types of school interventions. Judging from past performance, the schools will be a major factor in building a better future for our nation.

New Developments to be Considered

There are two major current developments, however, that need to be dealt with cautiously. One is the back to basics movement and the second is the trend toward forcing equal expenditures for the education of all children. On the surface, both developments appear attractive. Both, however, can result in mediocrity. The March 1977 issue of the *Phi Delta Kappan* features a series of articles discussing the back to basics movement and its meaning. This issue merits careful review. "Back to" suggests to the practices of some golden period, and "basics" needs definition as well. As Farr and his colleagues suggest, there was no golden period of American schooling. Rather, the schools have generally successfully adjusted to changing conditions and will most likely continue to do so. Basics or fundamentals as the terms are generally used mean a restriction of the curriculum to the teaching of skills that can be easily measured. This is a sure route to mediocre performance as has been demonstrated over and over again in American education. Superior performance is not achieved this way. Basics can be defined differently to mean the development of high levels of performance in the skills of communicating, of problem solving, and of creative behavior. A broad and demanding curriculum is essential if students are to come anywhere close to achieving their potential. I can agree that education should be concerned with the basics, but I further believe that professional teachers should be deeply involved with the definition of what this means in school practice.

The second condition currently being legislated in many places, that of necessity will lead schools to mediocrity, is the move to force the same level of expenditure on all schools within a state. No more, no less. Even if a district wanted to add to the support of its schools, it is not permitted to do so. Where are the centers of excellence to come from that test out the adaptations to changing conditions or that attempt to find the better way to provide schooling? American education sorely needs to encourage centers of excellence and this of necessity involves differential funding.

In conclusion, American schools have long merited a halo for their contribution to the strength of the nation. That halo is still merited, for the school continues to perform well in spite of the massive changes and problems that have characterized our recent history. In regard to reading achievement, the picture is anything but bleak. Basic functional literacy has increased particularly among our younger people. This is not to deny that a literacy problem exists. The recent IRA publication, *Adult Literacy Education in the United States*, by Wanda Cook, documents the problem thoroughly. However, as we study the ways to help our students become increasingly effective, let's do so with the confidence and pride that come from a solid record of accomplishment.

Who is Literate?

J.E. Merritt
The Open University

This question is rather ambiguous and it can be approached in a number of ways. One way to begin is to look at the problem from a developmental point of view. For example, we can look at those groups in our society whose work does not demand a high level of literacy and examine the achievements of their children. This is what I propose to do first. Later, however, I shall look at standards of literacy in the general population.

Diagram 1 is taken from the National Child Development Study (9). As you can see, there is a massive difference in the attainments of children whose parents have jobs which demand some reasonable degree of literacy and those whose parents have jobs which make minimal demands on literacy. These differences bear little relation to differences in measured intelligence and they show quite clearly the influence of the home on educational attainment. One of the most important factors involved here is language.

Now we all know that some linguists are skeptical about the idea that children can be "linguistically deprived." They argue, quite reasonably, that the language of the socially deprived can be very rich in its own way and perfectly adequate for the purpose of communicating ideas. They argue that it is different, rather than inferior.

This paper was originally published as Occasional Paper Number Three, Queensland Department of Education, Professional Development Centre, Bardon, 1978.

Diagram 1. Southgate Test Score and Occupational Group of Father

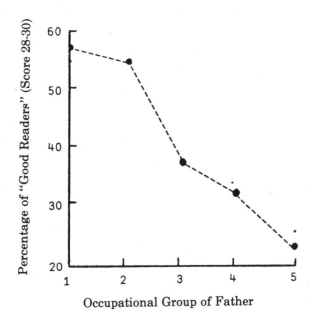

Occupational Group of Father

Key 1 = Professional and Technical
2 = Other Nonmanual
3 = Skilled Manual
4 = Partly Skilled Manual
5 = Unskilled Manual

This may very well be so. The fact of the matter is, however, that the language of the socially deprived is not the language that is found in textbooks. And there is now a fair amount of evidence (8, 10) that reading is significantly easier when the linguistic patterns in the text bear a reasonably close relationship to the oral language patterns of the learner. I would certainly agree, therefore, that we must respect the child's language and take this as our starting point. And we must try, in the early stages, to provide material which matches the child's own language—hence the value of a language experience approach. On the other hand, as children get older they will need to cope with the conventional patterns of written English and if they are going to cope with this efficiently they must become effectively bilingual. It is perfectly clear, therefore, that we must pay a great deal of attention to the development of language in those children who come from what I will continue to call "linguistically deprived" homes. Otherwise, this group will continue to provide a very large number of illiterates.

Let us look at some of the evidence on present day standards of literacy. It is interesting, first, to have a look at the evidence that has sparked the current debate about whether standards are falling.

Diagram 2. Attitudes and Standards
Scores in the reading tests of 1948-1970 inclusive
(eleven year old pupils in maintained schools)

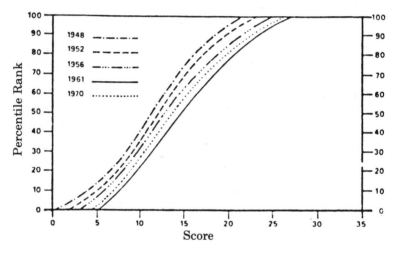

From "The Trend of Reading Standards," N.F.E.R.

Diagram 3 shows that even in 1948 some fifteen year old pupils were scoring the maximum. In succeeding years the "top of the S" has almost disappeared and "bellying" has increased as the distortion of the distribution of scores has become more marked. There is a definite ceiling on the W.V. at age fifteen, a fact which has been known since the early 1950s.

Diagram 3. Scores in the reading tests of 1948-1971 inclusive
(fifteen year old pupils in maintained schools)

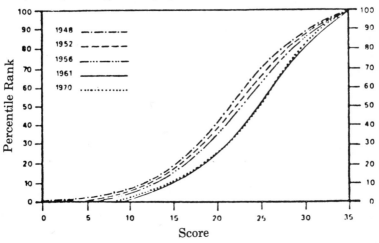

From "The Trend of Reading Standards," N.F.E.R.

These graphs summarise the results of national surveys conducted since the war. Look at the steady march along the line of achievement of those scores at each percentile. These improvements in achievement between 1948 and 1964 were certainly very gratifying. But now look at the latest results shown in Tables 1 and 2.

Table 1. Fifteen Year Olds
Comparable mean scores with standard errors for pupils aged 15.0 years. Watts-Vernon Test (maintained schools and direct grant grammar schools).

Date of Survey	1948	1952	1956	1961*	1971
Mean score	20.79	21.52	21.71	(a) 23.6 (b) 24.1	23.46
Standard error	0.37	0.20	0.26	0.14	0.26

*Although only secondary modern and comprehensive children were tested in 1961, these figures are estimates of total school populations: a) taking other schools at the 1956 level, b) supposing other schools made the same advance as secondary modern schools between 1956 and 1961.

From "The Trend of Reading Standards," N.F.E.R.

Table 2. Eleven Year Olds
Comparable mean scores with standard errors for pupils aged 11.0 years, since 1948. Watts-Vernon Test (maintained schools only).

Date of survey	1948	1952	1956	1964	1970
Mean score	11.59	12.42	13.30	15.00	14.19
Standard error	0.59	0.30	0.32	0.21	0.38

From "The Trend of Reading Standards," N.F.E.R.

Diagram 4. N.F.E.R. Survey: Watts-Vernon Test
Based on Start and Wells (*11*)

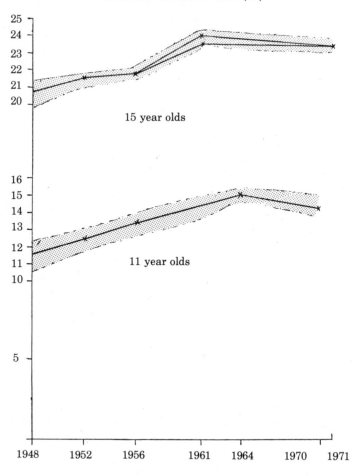

In Diagram 4, instead of providing a cumulative frequency graph, I have plotted the means using the figures provided by Start and Wells (*11*) which are also shown. As you can see, instead of there being a further increase, there seems to have been a decline. And this has caused great alarm and despondency. But now look at the shaded area on each side of the figures for eleven year olds and fifteen year olds. This shows the area of uncertainty based on the standard error of measurement. We can be 95 percent confident that the averages obtained on another occasion using a similar sample would have fallen within this shaded area. Now it's quite possible that in 1964 the true means for eleven year olds and fifteen year olds respectively were at the tops of the shaded portions and that the true means in 1971 were at the bottom of each shaded portion. If so, there has been a much more serious decline than people realise. On the other hand, the true means in 1964 might have been at the bottom of the shaded portions and at the top in 1971. If so, then reading standards have actually improved! In other words, we can say without any shadow of doubt that in the past ten years reading standards have either declined or improved! So much for the results of surveys of this kind as a means of assessing trends.

There are many factors that may have affected these results in varying degrees. First, it may be that standards declined significantly during the war when classes were over-crowded and many teachers had to be brought back from retirement to fill the gaps left by those who were doing National Service. The improvements since 1948, therefore, may simply represent a return to prewar normality. The changes in the past ten years may simply represent random fluctuation.

Second, tests become increasingly out-of-date as our language changes. Many of the words that were common ten or twenty years ago are no longer in use, so this makes the tests significantly more difficult for children today and this must be allowed for in interpreting any results.

Third, although every effort is made to achieve a sensible matching between the different samples over the years there are, inevitably, some significant population changes in the interim as a result of immigration.

The more closely we look at our efforts to assess changes in reading standards over the years, the more we realise how difficult it is. Certainly, it would be very simpleminded to draw any firm conclusions from these figures. Yet, in spite of this, there are many people who are using this kind of evidence to suggest that standards have declined and who are arguing that we ought to return to some mythical golden age when teachers paid more attention to basic skills. Personally, I do not believe there was any such golden age. If you go back to earliest writings of ancient times you will find each older generation saying, "The younger generation ain't what it was." If all these pundits were correct, by now we should be back swinging by our tails from trees.

Naturally, there are people in industry and commerce who would point out that they are now having to accept staff whose academic standards are much lower than they were. And I think they're right. What they do not seem to realise is that the demand for literacy has increased. In the period they are talking about only a small proportion of jobs demanded any great standard of literacy. Those who were appointed to such jobs were naturally those who had attained high standards. But if standards are held constant, and you increase the demand for literacy, then it is inevitable that the standards of achievement of those obtaining such employment will be lower than in a previous age—even if the overall level of educational achievement remains constant.

The real trouble is that standardized tests tell us nothing at all about the standards that are needed in everyday life. So in one sense, our critics are right. They may be wrong about the past, but they are right about the present. If they say standards are not good enough for their requirements, then I think we should take that as a fact. Or if we do not take it as a fact, then we must come up with some very good reason for disputing this opinion. After all, if we simply look at our norm based test results, we have no means of knowing whether the standards they reflect are very much higher than are needed or the best we can reasonably expect of our pupils—or whether they are very much lower than are needed, and than are arguably attainable. It could be that we are spending vast amounts of money on teacher training, and vast amounts of effort on testing reading, when standards are really so high that we would do better to spend more energy on other aspects of the curriculum. Alternatively, it could be that standards are so desperately low in terms of what is needed, and in terms of what children could potentially achieve, that we need to make a vastly greater effort than hitherto. Standardized tests simply do not provide the kind of information that is needed.

I have already indicated that we must either take notice of our critics or find some other kind of evidence on which to base a judgment. Fortunately, the sort of evidence we need is now beginning to accumulate, and the picture it presents is not very rosy.

I am now going to examine three different kinds of evidence. First, I will look at some evidence on the ability of students to comprehend newspaper articles. Next, I will present some information about the reading levels demanded by different kinds of reading material. And finally, I shall look at some interesting evidence based on a wide range of reading materials, and the effectiveness of a wide range of readers in tackling this kind of material.

The cloze procedure consists of deleting every nth word from a text, say every seventh word, and inviting subjects to try to complete the passage by using all the context cues available to identify the missing words. To demonstrate any reasonable level of comprehension, a subject should be able to replace correctly at least 35 percent of the missing words. Bormuth (1) used this method in schools in a middle class residential suburb of a large midwestern city. He used extracts from newspaper articles. Diagram 5 shows the results for twelve and eighteen year old students.

You will see that two-thirds of the twelve year olds fell below the 35 percent success mark. Now, if the average twelve year old is not capable of achieving any reasonable level of comprehension on everyday newspaper articles, then a reading age of twelve must be regarded as a totally inadequate baseline for functional literacy.

Now look at the eighteen year olds, and here you must bear in mind that many students will already have dropped out of the system so this is a fairly highly selected population. Nevertheless, *one-third* of these students failed to achieve any

Diagram 5. Levels of Literacy: Achievement levels of children from middle class homes in a residential suburb of a large midwestern city in the United States. Based on Bormuth (*1*).

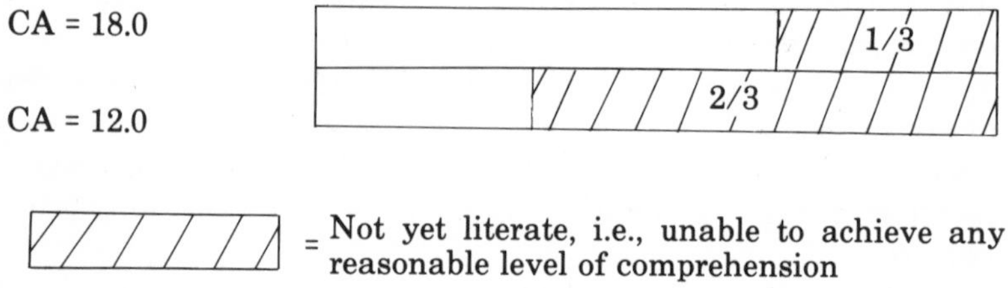

CA = 18.0

CA = 12.0

///// = Not yet literate, i.e., unable to achieve any reasonable level of comprehension

reasonable level of comprehension, according to this criterion. I don't know how you react to these figures, but I regard this as a pretty sorry state of affairs. It doesn't say very much for our efforts to develop competence in functional reading.

It would be easy, of course, simply to blame the teacher. Many teachers in infant schools can be heard saying, "Oh yes, my children can read by the time they go up to the juniors." As if a reading age of seven or so represented competence in reading. After all, you might say, they know perfectly well that a child's reading age improves significantly during the school years so such a statement is obviously foolish. What they mean is that their children can pronounce the words they encounter in their textbooks and in their tests. And the position is no better higher up in the school. Here, children improve in terms of ability to answer comprehension questions. You know the sort of thing: "Was the little boy's hat red, green, yellow, pink or purple—answer yes or no." But what is the value of what is currently practised in developing comprehension if one-third of eighteen year old students cannot achieve any reasonable level of comprehension on a simple newspaper article?

Before we blame the teachers for having such limited perspectives, I think we should look more closely at the training they receive. Can we expect much more even of the most outstanding teachers given the gross inadequacy of their initial training and subsequent inservice provision (6)?

Perhaps we should look at the evidence that comes to us from studies of the readability of different kinds of reading material, and I draw on some evidence produced by the British Association of Settlements Literacy Group (2). The illustrations they provide as typical examples include an article from the *Sun* newspaper which demands a reading age of fourteen and an article from the *Times* which requires a reading age of sixteen and a half. But what about the reading in the home? Here, even a simple pastry mix was found to demand a reading age of fourteen. A similar reading age was required for one part of an official form, a Department of Health and Social Security Income Supplement. Another part of the form required a reading age of fourteen and a half, and yet another part demanded a reading age of seventeen. That's the bit where it tells you how to make a claim. If you had a reading age of seventeen you probably wouldn't need to make a claim. The safety instructions on a bottle of household bleach demanded a reading age of seventeen. Is it any wonder that we get so many accidents in the home through people who ignore makers' instructions?

Finally, let us consider some more direct evidence. Just suppose that you were to keep a record of all the things you read in everyday life, starting with the packet of breakfast cereal you look at in the morning. Your reading might include recipes, instructions for the use of household adhesive, a medical prescription, a delivery note, a bill, a guarantee form, a hire purchase agreement, a technical journal, a works notice, a selection of adverts, a political tract, or a variety of other printed formats.

A formal investigation of everyday reading materials was conducted some years ago in the United States. Over 5,000 people were interviewed and a structured questionnaire was used to find out about all the reading carried out on the day prior to the interview. The investigators then designed a large number of test items based on the various kinds of materials which they had found were widely read in everyday life. They constructed ten tests, each consisting of seventeen items. Each item was specially designed to elicit the kind of reading behaviour normally required in handling that kind of material in everyday life. For example, an item based on a railroad timetable would not ask, "What is the conventional sign for *dining car*?" because this would not make a realistic demand of the reader. A much more appropriate question would be, "You need to travel from A to B with two children and a fair amount of luggage. You wish to get there before x p.m. in the evening. What is the most convenient train?" In practice, the items had to be specified rather more simply, but this example gives you some indication of what is needed if we are to get any kind of valid estimate of adult reading standards.

Now we must bear in mind that tests of this kind really demand 100 percent correct solutions. After all, it is no good saying, "Oh well, I did not actually catch the train—but I was only two minutes late!" or "Well, I read that insurance policy very carefully and got most of it right. There is just one small problem—I am not covered against this particular kind of damage so I now have to pay out $500 for storm damage to my fences." In real life, we do not just lose Brownie points when we make a mistake in reading—some mistakes cost us time, others cost money—and some even cost lives. Some of you may have read about a disaster in Michigan a few years ago when someone misread a word on some sacks and a chemical that was designed to make materials fire resistant was put in sacks intended for foodstuffs for animals. The chemical got into the food chain and literally millions of people have been affected to some degree, some of them very seriously. This was blamed on a reading error. At the Open University, a student took a whole foundation course—that's the equivalent of one semester of full time study—because she hadn't read the instructions correctly.

Now, just think for a minute what it would be like if you were to track your own reading every minute of the day and if someone else monitored the accuracy of your reading. How many errors do you think you would make? I am not really talking about dramatic errors, although I am sure we make quite a number of these. I am really talking about all of the inconveniences that we cause ourselves and others through failing to read accurately, sometimes through carelessness, and sometimes by merely projecting onto the material what we want it to say instead of reading what is actually there.

This is the kind of perspective we need when we look at the results of the American study. Unfortunately, the statistics were not produced in a way that would enable us to arrive at a meaningful interpretation in terms of the levels of functional literacy of the adults studied. It would be interesting, for example, to know what percentage of adults made what percentage of errors. I suspect the figures were not produced in this way because the results were politically unpalatable. I constructed a graph based on the figures that were presented (Diagram 6).

Diagram 6. Error Rates in Normal Reading
Items in order of difficutly based on Murphy (7).

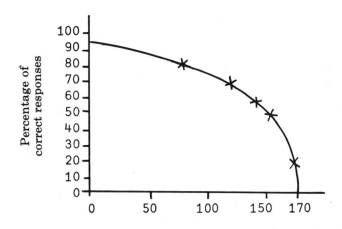

We can see from this that even on the easiest item the error rate was 10 percent, i.e., one person in ten got it wrong. The hardest item in each test was answered incorrectly by more than 50 percent of the population, and half of the items were answered incorrectly by more than 20 percent of the population. That's a lot of missed trains, lost jobs, poisoned children, and garments spoiled through washing incorrectly. Just in case you think these figures only relate to America, I should remind you of the survey of functional illiteracy in Sydney reported by Judith Goyen (4). In this investigation, half the population were found to be recording errors on 10 percent of the items. Those who recorded errors on more than one item in four were classified as illiterate. Just think of the errors being made by all of those people who are below average as readers yet not classified as illiterate. I might add that the 25 percent error level was regarded as being equivalent to a reading age of ten years, two months. Compare this figure with the readability levels quoted earlier. Who, indeed, is literate?

I suggested earlier that it would be interesting if each one of you could monitor your own reading throughout a day and if someone else could make a note of all the errors that arise through your own misreading. But you are all professional people and your own reading standards are very high. Just think what the result would be if we could monitor the reading effectiveness of the rest of the population.

The trouble is, there is no automatic feedback when we make mistakes in our reading. We misread or misinterpret a report and in a subsequent discussion we can all too easily get at loggerheads with someone else who has misread the article in a different way. I doubt whether such mistakes are often traced back to their origin. Or we may misread an advertisement and think we are getting superior value by buying a particular automobile, not realising that a lesser priced model also contains most of the features we thought went only with the model we had purchased. How often do we draw up an attributes matrix to check this kind of information? So we pay more than we would have if we had made a correct appraisal in the first place, but we may never find out that we have done so.

How often do we read a newspaper article and form an opinion without taking the trouble to consider all the additional factors that need to be taken into account before forming such an opinion? If you read one newspaper account of a political or industrial incident you may feel a certain amount of self righteous indignation at the iniquities of one of the parties. If you happen to read an account in a different newspaper first, however, it is equally possible to feel quite the reverse. But because we tend to read the same newspapers, we have little opportunity to check on the extent to which we are simply building up our own prejudices.

A further problem is that once our prejudices are formed, we tend to interpret whatever we read in accordance with our previous convictions no matter what evidence is presented. Naturally, we all flatter ourselves that we can read objectively, but I don't think that any of us would come out too well on a wholly objective assessment. The problem with misreading is that there is so rarely a check on its effects, and these, in my view, can have insidious and cumulative effects on our lives.

In the light of these three kinds of evidence, I suggest to you that assessments of the adequacy of current reading standards by means of traditional tests are completely valueless. They may be of some value in helping a headmaster to decide which class, or class teacher, needs extra assistance. They may also be of value in making decisions about which schools need extra support. In terms of their contribution to an understanding of what is required in the community, however, they tell us absolutely nothing. They serve only to mislead.

It really is quite extraordinary that, after decades of intensive research in the field of reading, we still do not have tests that can provide us with valid estimates of levels of functional literacy in our community. We are only now beginning to identify the kinds of tests needed and only now are we beginning to get a rough idea of the enormity of the problem that faces us in developing adequate levels of functional literacy.

Up to this point, we have been looking at some of the evidence about other people's reading. Now, I would like to tackle this problem of reading from a quite different point of view. In fact, I would like you to look at your reading and your own reading comprehension. I would like you to read this text in order to understand it and, as you do so, try to imagine what it feels like to be a child presented with a textbook in which there are a number of unfamiliar words.

Comprehension Process

The zobins are usually vimbole—like most rengles. They often evimber, but not many of them do so in grent. Those that do are naturally estingled. Most zobins glake slibdoms, but if they use dekinants they normally redintepone. It takes a real blegan to glake slibdoms, although they are often thought to be yive.

Now you may think that you have not really understood very much from this passage because of the strange words that you encountered. In fact, I am going to show you that you have achieved a very considerable level of comprehension, if we are to place any reliance on typical comprehension questions. Indeed, the questions I shall set are not really very typical because they demand a much higher level of comprehension than is often demanded by the comprehension questions you find in textbooks or in comprehension tests. If you haven't already done so, you should try reading comprehension questions in textbooks and answering them before looking at the text. It's amazing how many you can answer even though you don't have any knowledge of the subject. The answer is so often obvious from an examination of the question and the alternative answers that are provided. Now try these questions:

1. What is a Zobin?
2. What do Zobins do?
3. Which Zobins are not estingled?
4. Is it true what they say about Zobins?
5. How satisfactory is this text in terms of its presentation of ideas about Zobins?

First, what is a Zobin? A rengle; a thing that is usually vimbole; thing that often evimbers.

This is a mere *literal* question, yet notice that the first answer was of a very high standard for it answered the question by providing a higher order classification, i.e., Zobins are a member of the more general class of "rengle." The other answers are also highly satisfactory for they represent the various attributes of the Zobin.

What do Zobins do? They usually vimbole; they often evimber (many of them do so in grent); they glake slibdoms; and if they use dekinants, they normally redintipone.

Here, the response to the question represents a certain degree of *reorganisation* of the text. A literal question calls for a more or less thoughtful selection from what is actually in the text, whereas a reorganisation question goes a stage further in demanding not just a simple selection but the extraction of a number of items which may then provide a summary (as in this case), a reclassification, or a synthesis of some kind.

Which Zobins are not estingled? There are some people whose minds go blank if they are presented with a mathematical problem in public. This question calls for a logical *inference* and I find it tends to have much the same effect. It is tempting to say that all Zobins who do not evimber in grent are not estingled. Logically, however, one cannot draw this conclusion, even though it looks rather plausible. It is certainly plausible enough for many casual readers to make this kind of inference even when they are reading texts in which all the words and ideas are very familiar. Naturally, you did not fall into this trap. It would have been easy to structure this text so that you could, in fact, draw a valid inference, and I am sure that you would have had no difficulty with this question had I done so.

Is it true what they say about Zobins? This question calls for some sort of *evaluating* process. For this kind of question you would often draw upon your previous experience, although you cannot do so in this particular case. You might also check the text against other written sources, or against the observations of others. You might examine the text to see how much is fact and how much is opinion. In this particular case, one hopes you will reserve your judgment about Zobins unless you can find some internal inconsistency within the text which might, in your view, make a whole paragraph rather suspect. Certainly, you can consider the possibility of using a number of evaluation processes even though in this case your efforts are abortive and you have to reserve judgment.

How satisfactory is this text in terms of its presentation of ideas about Zobins? As the author of this rather strange text, I hope you will spare my embarrassment by not answering this particular question, but I am sure you will have no difficulty in making such an *appreciation*—another aspect of the comprehension process.

At this stage, you will appreciate that you have engaged in all of the comprehension processes represented in the Barrett Taxonomy (*3*). As I said earlier, this is a much more sophisticated series of questions than you are likely to find in most textbooks.

In spite of your success, what do you actually comprehend about the Zobin? This passage demonstrates that you possess a tremendous linguistic facility. You have learned to answer questions in many subjects and give the impression that you fully understand them, when all that you are doing, in many cases, is manipulating words. This is what we teach children to do for a large part of the time they spend in schools, and this is what they learn to do for a large part of their time even at college. In fact the "helpful" tutor actually encourages this by giving help and advice in "examination passing techniques." You can confirm this for yourself if you reexamine some of the examination papers you mark from time to time and ask yourself whether you really think the writers understand what they are writing. Very often, you will look at an answer and, when it does not hang together very well, you will tend to say, "Oh well that's just examination nerves; look, he's mentioned such and such, so he probably really understands it and just did not get it down." Frankly, I think that throughout our schools, colleges, and universities, we are perpetuating mediocrity and semiliteracy through our failure to diagnose linguistic facility when it masquerades as comprehension. Indeed, I think we need first to diagnose ourselves because I am quite sure we are often misled by our own linguistic competence into thinking that we understand what we are saying when, in fact, we understand as little about the particular topic as we do about the Zobin. It is only when we are really pressed by a critic who wants to achieve a much deeper level of comprehension that we begin to develop a real appreciation of our inadequacies. And the teacher or lecturer is rarely put in this position by a captive audience. Those who are linguistically competent learn to play the education game and duly glake their slibdoms. The others are all too often rejected by the teacher as being of modest intelligence and are then presented with an even more inferior diet.

An even greater tragedy is that many of the textbooks we use in schools, colleges, and universities show signs of a rather limited level of comprehension on the part of the writers; and here, I wonder if I might perhaps be permitted an anecdote. I went on holiday two or three years ago to Weymouth in Dorsetshire and visited Chesil Bank. This is a sort of spur made up of small stones which stick out from the coastline. On my return home, I discussed this bank with my niece, a teacher who took geography as her main course. I asked her how long it would be before this bank eroded but she told me that, far from being eroded, it was steadily being built up. I asked what caused this and when she explained, I thought at first that I understood, realised that I did not, and asked exactly what her explanation meant. She then explained again, and once again I realised that I didn't really understand the process in spite of her explanation. Her response to my next question was "Good gracious, we didn't go into it as far as that." We then consulted the textbook she had used at college and which is also used by sixth form students in English schools. Once again, I found words manipulated in ways that seemed to be meaningful, but there was no way in which individuals who did not understand the process in the first place could possibly improve their understanding. All they could learn was how to repeat, and even reformulate, certain forms of words. Further examination of textbooks leaves me with the impression that all too many make little or no contribution to the development of comprehension and independent thought. Unfortunately, this criticism also applies, in my opinion, to many books of education, and not least to books on the philosophy of education, sociology of education, and educational psychology. Word spinning is the name of the game.

A Curriculum Strategy

What this all means is that if we are concerned with reading comprehension we must start by thinking about the curriculum; reading cannot be developed adequately unless we ensure that all students have an adequate range of concrete experiences to which they can relate what they read. They will not develop the ability to process print effectively unless we ensure that each time they read they do so for a well defined purpose—a purpose which has some immediate reality for them. And if we wish them to develop competence in reading the wide range of texts which they are likely to encounter in everyday life, then we must give them experience of those kinds of texts during the school years.

The following list gives some indication of the kinds of printed text adults encounter. The first level gives a very crude classification by format. The second level provides a starting point for listing these various kinds of materials in relation to the purposes for which they may be read within our various everyday life roles.

TEXTS AND FORMATS
Books
Fiction: Novels, plays, anthologies
Nonfiction: Textbooks, monographs, biographies, autobiographies

Periodicals
Journals, magazines, digests

Newspapers
Local/national, daily/weekly

Regulations
Guarantees, insurance policies, credit agreements, employment contracts, bylaws, rules, constitutions

Forms
Application: Jobs, credit, insurance, clubs
Returns: Income tax, census, car tax
Questionnaires: Medical, political, psychological

Reference Material
Catalogs, guides, quotations, invoices, statements, brochures, timetables, manuals, encyclopaedia, dictionaries, abstracts, indexes, minutes, diaries

Correspondense
Letters, greetings, postcards, telegrams, invitations (official/personal, formal/informal)

Notices
Directions, labels, safety, store signs, bus, indicators, facilities, traffic sign symbols

TEXTS AND ROLES
Home and Family
School reports, circulars, health leaflets, rent books, cook books, letters, postcards, invitations, DIY booklets

Employment
Job adverts, application forms, job particulars, T.U. literature, safety regulations, sick pay information, work notices, instruction manuals

Consumer
Advertising, labels, guarantees, credit agreements, discount house catalogs

Leisure
Sports news, travel brochures, customs regulations, club rules, recurrent education lit

Community
Newspapers, political pamphlets, local government notices, community association literature, charity appeals.

Clearly, there is no point in introducing income tax forms to sixteen year olds. So what can we do? Somehow or other we have to introduce a wide range of role purposes into the curriculum and help children to use materials which serve as an effective introduction. For example, an activity that relates to the home and family role might be achieved by means of an investigation of school meals by children of almost any age. This might include the preparation of a questionnaire on preferences for completion by all the children in a class, an age group, or even a whole school. Both the preparation and the completion of the questionnaire can provide invaluable experience in judging how best to handle that particular type of text format, with all its potential uses and limitations. Similarly, the selection of school equipment, purchased by money raised through various functions, can provide an incentive to engage in the comprehension processes required of the intelligent consumer. Another starting point for consumer reading might be some need that arises among the pupils themselves—an interest in stereo to engage in the comprehension processes required of the intelligent consumer. Other starting points for consumer reading might be some needs that arise among the pupils themselves—an interest in stereo equipment, motor bikes, calculators, transistor radios, or Christmas presents. Within the leisure role there is all the reading of tourist agency literature—and, of course, geography textbooks—which can lead to the better selection of holiday venues. In addition, there are rules and regulations for the various games that children play, or watch on television, that could be more closely studied. Then there are surveys to be made of local leisure facilities and resource units to be developed for storing this information for regular access by the children themselves, by parents, or by visitors.

It is not enough for people to say that we are educating children for life unless we take the trouble to examine all that life entails. It is not enough to say that education consists of providing experiences that are most worthwhile here and now unless we can also demonstrate that they provide an adequate basis for the years that follow. Why must educational theorists argue as if these were alternatives? If we cannot achieve both goals, then we are failing in our educational responsibilities. And it is only within the context of an effective curriculum that we can cater effectively for the development of reading comprehension.

References

1. Bormuth, J.R. "Reading Literacy: Its Definition and Assessment," *Reading Research Quarterly*, 9, 1 (1973), 7-66.
2. British Association of Settlements Literacy Group. *A Right to Read*. British Association of Settlements, 1974.
3. Clymer, T. "What is Reading? Some Current Concepts," in A. Melnik and J. Merritt (Eds.), *Reading: Today and Tomorrow*. London: University of London Press/The Open University Press, 1968.
4. Goyen, J. "Interim Report on Survey of Functional Illiteracy in Sydney," *Language in Focus Literacy Issue*, National Committee on English Teaching, Newsletter No. 2, 1976.
5. HMSO. *Progress in Reading*, Education Pamphlet No. 50, 1966.
6. Merritt, J.E. "Standards of Reading and Inservice Education: Some Harsh Realities," *Reading Education—U.K.* Special Edition, Bullock, "Two Years On," *UKRA Journal*, 2 (March 1977).

7. Murphy, R.T. *Adult Functional Reading Study*. Princeton, New Jersey, Educational Testing Service, 1973.
8. Peltz, F.K. "The Effect Upon Comprehension of Repatterning Based on Students' Writing Patterns," *Reading Research Quarterly*, 4 (1973), 603-619.
9. Pringle, M.L.K., N.R. Butler, and R. Davie. *Eleven Thousand Seven Year Olds*. Studies in Child Development, Longmans Limited, 1966.
10. Ruddell, R.B. "The Effect of Oral and Written Patterns of Language Structure on Reading Comprehension," *Reading Teacher*, January 1965, 270-275.
11. Start, K.B., and B.K. Wells. *The Trend of Reading Standards: (1970-1971)*. National Foundation for Educational Research, 1972.

Bilingualism: Where to Draw the Line

Keith J. Henderson
The Christian Science Monitor

When the press began to take note of the growing presence of bilingual education on the American educational scene a decade ago, stories were prone to open with dramatic reports of social studies being taught in Spanish, arithmetic in Eskimo, and history in French.

The phenomenon was brand-new to most Americans, who probably assumed that English was—and always had been—the sole language of instruction in U.S. schools. At that time, perhaps, people were more inclined to blink in wonder than to raise eyebrows and start posing questions. But for many, that has changed.

In the decade since the federal Bilingual Education Act was passed in 1968, the number of bilingual programs in the United States has leaped from 72 to more than 500, with a corresponding jump in federal appropriations from $7 million to $150 million. The programs serve nearly 290,000 children, most of them from the nation's burgeoning Spanish-speaking, or Hispanic, community which, at latest count, numbered some 11.1 million.

The increasing government commitment to bilingual education has now spawned a flood of questions, among them:

• Are bilingual programs neglecting the teaching of English in favor of increased emphasis on the student's native language and culture?

• Has the federal government's role in promoting bilingual education been a costly mistake?

• Are there other, perhaps more effective ways to meet the admittedly urgent educational needs of the estimated millions of children in this country who may have only a limited grasp of English?

That first question—whether students in bilingual classes are adequately learning to use the English language—strikes to the heart of the current debate over the role of bilingual education in the American educational system.

On one side of the issue are critics—journalists, teacher groups, some university professors—who argue that bilingual programs in which students are allowed to learn in their native tongues may be working against the interests of the very children they are designed to help. The better route, they urge, would be to give children the earliest and fullest possible exposure to English, with perhaps only very limited initial classroom use of the native language.

Opposing Views

Proponents of bilingual education take quite a different view. "I don't think anyone is against learning English," says Dr. Maria Brisk, a bilingual specialist with Boston University's School of Education. "You need a common language, but it doesn't have to be either/or," she adds.

The point made by Dr. Brisk and other advocates of bilingual education is that English-language acquisition is an important part of the program, but not its one paramount goal. There's also the matter of imparting an understanding of other subjects—from such basics as math to classes on Hispanic culture, for example.

This position is challenged by journalist Noel Epstein, whose book, "Language, Ethnicity, and the Schools," (published by George Washington University's Institute for Educational Leadership) has become something of a cause celebre in bilingual education circles.

Mr. Epstein, and others, see the attainment of competency in English as the specific purpose of bilingual programs, at least those set up under the federal Bilingual Education Act (Title VII of the Elementary and Secondary Education Act). The failure of some programs to adhere to this purpose was the theme of a recent hard-hitting segment on CBS TV's "60 Minutes" program.

Much criticism zeroes in on what is seen as the questionable philosophical underpinnings of bilingual education. A number of critics see the trend toward bilingualism as an outgrowth of the ethnic-awareness movement that has swept the country in recent years. They see the need of the individual student to learn English so that he can successfully function in American society being sacrificed on the altar of group identity and group interest.

The "bicultural" aspect of many programs—intended to offset the cultural bias supposedly found in much regular classroom material and boost a student's self-image—comes under particularly heavy fire.

But proponents argue that language and culture go hand-in-hand. A Hispanic or Indian child's education problems, they say, can't be traced solely to his inability to understand what's said by an English-speaking teacher. Much of what confronts him in the classroom is culturally foreign, they contend, and this can present an equally difficult hurdle.

You can't deny the cultural richness in a child's background, declares Maria Swanson, president of the National Association for Bilingual Education. "Our function is to equip the student to be able to function in the English society," but, at the same time, to allow him to "feel positive about his own identity."

Dade County Beginnings

Many experts set 1963 as the inaugural date for the current interest in bilingual education in the U.S. That year Dade County, Florida—faced with a heavy influx of Cuban refugees—set up the first bilingual program in the country since World War I.

(Dr. Brisk points out, however, that instruction in languages other than English far predates recent decades.

"During most of the 19th century," she writes, "multilingual education and cultural diversity enjoyed considerable tolerance." Only with the huge European migrations near the turn of the century, she says, did "Americanization" become the byword and English take firm hold as the sole language of instruction.)

The civil-rights activism of the 1960s gave rise to a number of lawsuits aimed at improving the educational lot of non-English speakers. At the same time, political pressures were being applied on behalf of these children, whose school dropout rates were (and remain) far higher than average.

One 1975 Census Bureau study indicated a high-school dropout rate of just over 38 percent among non-English speakers, predominantly Hispanics. Other estimates go even higher.

These pressures led to the passage of the Bilingual Education Act in 1968 and the first federal funding for bilingual education. The act (often referred to simply as "Title VII") was amended in 1974, with new emphasis on teacher training, program evaluation, and assessing the needs of the children.

1974 also brought a legal landmark. That year the U.S. Supreme Court handed down its so-called Lau decision. This ruling, involving a suit brought on behalf of Chinese-speaking students in the San Francisco school district, held that children with a limited grasp of English were deprived of equal treatment if schools made no effort to address their linguistic problems.

The court based its decision on the Civil Rights Act of 1964, which bars discrimination in federally supported programs—a category which embraces many local school districts.

But the Supreme Court decision did not specifically endorse bilingual education.

This point has been seized by critics who feel the federal government's investment in bilingual education has lost touch with the basic purposes for which it was undertaken.

Noel Epstein, for instance, argues that techniques other than bilingual education—including what he terms "immersion" methods of language instruction—may be more effective in surmounting the classroom problems of non-English speakers.

Attaining Competence

In this regard, Mr. Epstein finds some support from Orlando Patterson, a Harvard sociology professor who has written widely on ethnic matters.

"It's not doing an ethnic minority any good to advocate a policy that allows them to learn through their own language," according to Dr. Patterson. What must be kept uppermost, he asserts, is the student's need to attain competence in the dominant tongue. Anything less than that, he concludes, is "misguided liberalism."

He concedes, however, that there can be a need for a transitional period during which the native tongue is used in tandem with English.

The trend among policymakers in Washington and in many states has been to emphasize this transitional aspect, sometimes to the chagrin of bilingual advocates.

"Government is focusing on transition," says Boston University's Dr. Brisk. She argues again, though, that it is a "double standard" to say that the only purpose of bilingual education is to teach English. The true purpose, she says, as with all other teaching, is learning—science, math, and other disciplines as well as English.

But what about performance? Has the federally supported bilingual program in the U.S. proved itself an educational success?

Critic Cites Lack of Proof

Reporter Epstein answers with a resounding "no." He cites a lack of research pointing to the effectiveness of bilingual education efforts and sums up: "After nearly nine years and more than half a billion dollars in federal funds ... the government has not demonstrated whether such instruction makes much difference in the students' achievement, in their acquisition of English, or in their attitudes toward school."

Proponents, however, take issue with this assessment.

They insist that the lack of "hard" results from Title VII programs is attributable not so much to a failure of bilingual education, per se, as to a lack of proper assessment methods, faulty research, hastily thrown together programs, and the relative newness of the whole effort.

The well thought out programs, they say, demonstrate their worth.

One such program operates at Boston's Tobin School (K-5), located in an economically depressed part of the city with one of its heaviest concentrations of Hispanic residents. When Principal Charles Gibbons came to the school four years ago, the first thing he did was rethink its bilingual program, which, at that time, conformed closely to the transitional bilingual education law of Massachusetts.

As part of his research, Mr. Gibbons traveled to Puerto Rico in order to gain some understanding of his students' background. What became clear to him, he says, is that Puerto Rican students in Boston schools were a "disenfranchised" group. They felt out of place in the regular classroom. Accordingly, he developed a program that emphasized language maintenance and an appreciation for the Puerto Rican culture.

The response from parents and students has been enthusiastic. While no tests have compared the academic performance of Tobin students with that of Hispanic students in other Boston schools, Mr. Gibbons nonetheless is confident that his program is giving students something they need—and something they might not get elsewhere.

One of the most damaging reports on bilingual education was completed recently by the American Institutes of Research (AIR) for the U.S. Office of Education. It concluded, among other things, that students in the Title VII programs studied were doing comparatively poorly in acquiring English.

But Dr. Jose A. Cardenas, executive director of the Intercultural Development Research Association in San Antonio, Texas, scores the AIR findings as "shallow." He claims the report included such flaws as failure to take into account the inadequate bilingual training given many of the teachers involved.

Teaching Quality Criticized

Indeed, both critics and advocates of bilingual education tend to agree that the quality of teaching in many programs could be better.

Dr. Brisk, for example, notes that untrained people have sometimes been plucked from the community to fill teaching slots in hastily conceived programs.

"It's one of the biggest problems," agrees Dr. Albar A. Pena of the University of Texas. Some programs are badly implemented because schools want them set up as fast as possible, even though trained teachers may not be available. Then, he says, critics look at those programs and say, "See, it doesn't work."

One of the more vocal critics of the quality of teaching in bilingual education programs has been Albert Shanker, president of the American Federation of Teachers. While affirming that the federation does not oppose bilingual education as such, Mr. Shanker says, "We believe that bilingual teachers must truly be bilingual—must know both languages thoroughly." And he takes particular issue with what he sees as a tendency in some quarters to accept only those teachers—regardless of training—whose ethnic backgrounds match that of their students.

The teacher training problem will get increased attention in new bilingual education legislation now before Congress, according to Dr. Thomas Burns, acting director of the federal Office of Bilingual Education. The new bill (a further extension of Title VII) would earmark some $41 million for training, including some $13 million for inservice training for present teachers who want to acquire bilingual skills.

What does the future hold for bilingual education in the U.S.?

The answer to that question may well rest on how the American nation views itself—as the traditional great melting pot in which ethnic differences fade into a common culture and language, or as a land in which cultural diversity is valued, even encouraged.

Section Two
THE MEDIA AND
THE READING TEACHER

Judging the News Media

Edgar Dale
The Ohio State University

Introduction

Evaluating the news media is a part of a larger educational problem. A persistent, perennial problem of all sensitive inquiry is, "How do you separate the true from the false, the trivial from the important, the real from the phony, the transitory from the permanent?"

Many of us would like to rerun a film of our lives and then be able to point with a mixture of pride and adequate modesty at those scenes where we participated in the great social movements that later markedly changed our environment. We want to show others where we stood when the lights were flickering and growing dim. We could also shamefacedly contrast these high moments with the times when we were drifting along without deep concern and appropriate action in following the principles stated by our great leaders: Presidents Washington, Jefferson, Lincoln, Wilson. We judge the news with the background of our past experiences. We see clearly only what we know, and we sometimes suffer from hardening of the categories. Our minds lack flexibility, are not elastic.

By a serendipitous set of circumstances I lived my early life in North Dakota on the Western frontier—physically, spiritually, and politically. I was a witness to epochal industrial and agricultural change. My parents were homesteaders. My home was on the 100th meridian and Pare Lorentz's film, "The Plow that Broke the Plains," was a first hand experience for me. I lived for a short while in a sod house. In 1910, prairie land was broken, harrowed, and seeded by a Big Four Tractor—all in one operation. The Agricultural Revolution had already markedly changed the prairie country of the Midwest.

So I often see the news from the point of view of a North Dakota farmer who grew up in a Populist family, worried about Big Biz and Wall Street, the Minneapolis Millers (not the team). I wanted to see the Big Trusts busted.

I also grew up with the Horatio Alger books and kept looking for a runaway team of horses so I could grab them in the nick of time and save the lovely daughter of the rich man. I read about the Rover Boys, what Charles Henty had to say about Clive in India; read the *Youth's Companion* at almost the same time as I read *The Appeal to Reason* (published at Girard, Kansas) and *The Coming Nation*, the *New Republic* and *The Nation* of that day.

In judging the news today, therefore, I do so with a Duke's mixture of seemingly irreconcilable elements. But I believe I am not alone in my predicament—if it is one. We see what we know, and we know what we see.

I refrain from saying that I am just a country boy, a popular cliche, used by those persons who boast about their humility. The last time I heard this statement it was made by the then treasurer of the United States. All I said then was: "I thought you were a very slick city lawyer." To judge the news we must know the point of view of the writer, the speaker, or the visualizer.

My topic, "Judging the News Media," could be treated in two different ways. First, I might have emphasized the specifics of how to read a newspaper or a newsmagazine, listen to radio or recordings, or how to view a television news program. However, I shall not use this approach. Instead, I shall deal with the broad question of the nature of news, the circumstances today under which news is presented, and I shall note some of the overarching problems relating to the news as furnished by print, picture, or voice.

In judging the important news, foreign and domestic, we can have one of two points of view. We can be either hopeful and optimistic, or cynical and pessimistic. H.G. Wells, for most of his lifetime an inveterate optimist and proponent of the far reaching role of science in improving the quality of our society, became increasingly pessimistic. In his last book titled, *Mind at the End of its Tether* (1946), he raised some critical issues. Here are his general conclusions. Do you agree with him?

> The writer sees the world as a jaded world devoid of recuperative power....The old men behave for the most part meanly and disgustingly and the young are spasmodic, foolish, and all too easily mislead. Man must go steeply up or down and the odds seem to be all in favor of his going down and out.... Ordinary man is at the end of his tether. Only a small, highly adaptable minority of the species can possibly survive. The rest will not trouble about it, finding such opiates and consolations as they have a mind for.

If Wells is right (that there has actually been a gradual erosion of the quality of civilized living), then I think that most of us here would like to be in that "adaptable minority" of which Wells speaks. We are not jaded and we would like to develop the recuperative power he suggests is lacking.

Let's explore this idea a little further. Broadly speaking, there are three kinds of people in this world. There are those who take out more than they put in. These are the greedy, the apathetic, the myopiates, the me-centered people. They certainly aren't going to help us much in solving our big problems. Second, there are those who put in as much as they take out. They are useful people, and we could not exist without them. Third, there are those who put in more than they take out. In H.G. Wells' phrase they are the "adaptable minority," the good citizens.

News means something different for each of these groups. For the group taking out more than they put in, the news is often a sedative, a way of escaping, a way of killing time instead of filling it, a salve for wounded egos, a respite from reality. For those who put in more than they take out, the news is insightful information. It provides hypotheses of what can and what probably can't be done. The news may "instruct with delight," a phrase used by the poet Horace. It may be news which questions some of the assumptions on which our society is based.

For these persons, the news—by radio, television or print—offers some real alternatives to the problems of ignorance, greed, selfishness, apathy, me-tooism. The good news is news which helps us become more we-centered, better socialized, better individualized. It is news which helps us become a part of the adaptable, creative minority.

In this sense, then, the *timeliness* of news is not the critical factor but it is important. Nor is the *timeless* news the only important news. What we should strive for is news which is both timely and timeless. Perhaps news articles, magazine articles, and feature programs on television can create this combination. I think they can. But at any rate, we must not let the everyday duty, the everyday routine, whether it be teaching or whatever the field, overwhelm the innovative, the creative approach to key problems in interpreting the news.

What are some examples of the new and the news in reading?

In our work with the *World Book Encyclopedia* we receive galleys of articles about to be published. We submit these galleys to teachers and to their students for their reactions. One of the clearcut signs of a good, readable, interesting article is one about which the students say, "It was a surprise to me." "I never knew that before." In short, it was news to them. Good news has surprises.

So reaction to "news" is personal. It helps us learn what we need to learn. This doesn't mean that fiction isn't news because Charles Dickens' *Hard Times*, as recently presented over Public Broadcasting System, was news. For me it was news because I had read *Hard Times* (written in 1854) and had been impressed by the sensitivity of Charles Dickens in catching the moods and situations in which the people of the early industrial period in England found themselves, the faceless proletariats.

One of the reasons we sometimes object to the cliche, the platitude, or the aphorism is that it isn't news to us. It is no longer fresh, inviting, and evocative. So one thing we can do as teachers, curriculum makers, and reading specialists, is to help children, young people, and adults see the news inside the news. I am interested in seeing more news about people who are appreciative, about people who have learned to say "thank-you," about people who are trying out some new ideas, about people who can look at the old "news" in a fresh, pristine way.

So much for this broad, general approach. News also presents a problem of values, long term or short term. I think here of the Russian fable by the poet Krylov about a pig who ate his fill of acorns under an oak tree and then started to root around the tree. A crow sitting in the oak tree remarked, "You should not do this. If you lay bare the roots, the tree will wither and die." "Let it die," replied the pig. "Who cares as long as there are acorns?" My comment: No acorns, no roots, no more oak trees. We must plant trees under whose shade we will never sit.

It is symptomatic of a new trend for people to become interested in their *roots* as was Alex Haley in the television program by that name. We want to feel that we are a *part of* a continuous strand of development, not *apart from* it. Our news and our values are inescapably intertwined.

Perhaps there is a clue here, too, as to how we ought to teach. We ought to teach history as news, not as something that has happened and is done with. And we ought also to teach news as history. It was news when it happened and it is still news. I recently read the Lewis and Clark story about their winter stay at Mandan, North Dakota. It was news to me. I once heard a woman say, "Boston has a very historical history." So it does.

Could we possibly teach the subject of English as though it were news? Can reading or listening or viewing help the reader understand news, not just the news that is timely, but timeless? Further, I think that a great deal of apparently not timely news can be made so.

How can one make best uses of newspapers, magazines, radio, television to get a reasonably accurate picture of key events in our history? We cannot always depend upon the combined judgments of daily newspapers. In the election of 1972, 71.4 percent of 1,054 daily newspapers in a poll supported Nixon, 5.3 percent were for McGovern, and 23.3. percent were uncommitted. The great majority agreed upon Nixon as worthy of presidential approval and recommended him to their readers. It was a colossal blunder.

What then can we do when great news events challenge us and difficult choices must be made? We can ask that there be honest reporting, that the treatment of the news be fair. We can ask that candidates and other persons not be bullied by persons thrusting microphones in their faces—"Mrs. Jones, how did you feel when you learned that your daughter had been raped and dismembered?"

One thing we can do is to single out certain reporters, able commentators, and give them public approval based on their track record. My favorite columnist is TRB whose column has appeared in the *New Republic* every week for many years. TRB is a pseudonym for Richard L. Strout (now just turned 80), Washington news editor for the *Christian Science Monitor*. I would give high grades to the McNeil-Lehrer news report on Public Broadcasting, to columnist James Reston, and to many of the broadcasting columnists, including some with whom I disagree. I would praise "60 Minutes" developed by Dan Rather, Mike Wallace, and Morley Safer.

Our Mental Maps

One way to judge the nature and quality of news is by the close-up, the daily flow, the *weather*. We can also judge the news by its long term effects, the situations and settings in which it appears, the *climate*. In 1922, Walter Lippmann wrote a book titled *Public Opinion*. He also wrote the syndicated column, "Today and Tomorrow," which ran for thirty-six years. Now we are talking again about the news climate, long term trends in the news.

The first chapter of *Public Opinion* is titled "The World Outside and the Pictures in Our Heads." The pictures in our heads are the mental maps upon which we base our thinking. Some of these maps accurately delineate the truth. Some of these maps, however, are gross distortions. For example, the history of the black man and woman in the United States illustrates how inaccurate, distorted, stereotyped, and cruel these pictures in our heads can be. Further, these distortions may also operate in creating our own distorted pictures of ourselves. Many students underrate their own worth, their friendliness, their artistic talents, their own individuality.

Why do we get these distorted images? We do it because much of our contact with the world is indirect, symbolic, and indeed it must be because there is so much of it. Here Lippmann says:

> ...the real environment is altogether too big, too complex, and too fleeting for direct acquaintance. We are not equipped to deal with so much subtlety, so much variety, so many permutations and combinations. And although we have to act in that environment, we have to reconstruct it on a simpler model before we can manage with it. To traverse the world men must have maps of the world....

So the news tells us both falsely and truly what the world is like. Sometimes the falsity is unplanned, some is planned (e.g., dirty tricks in politics); sometimes it is innocent of guile, just unreasoning or plain stupid. Sometimes, too, we lie to ourselves because the truth would be devastating.

One of the best ways to get the truth, the real news about ourselves, is not only from the massive mass media, but also from great literature. Dickens, writing in *Hard Times* shows the persisting gulf between worker and owner in his account of the blacklisting of a union member who if "rejected by one employer, he would probably be rejected by all. He would get a bad name, that of being troublesome." It was all right for the owners to unite, but not the workers, as Mrs. Sparsit suggested.

Great literature is prophetic. Poet Ezra Pound has written that "Literature is news that stays news." Any problem treated in depth by a perceptive author contains explicit or implicit forecasts of the future. All great books are salted with a Utopian flavor. Great literature is not nostalgic, it looks toward the future. This prophecy of the future may be explicit. For example, H.G. Wells, in speaking to the P.E.N. club on "The Honor and Dignity of the Free Mind," said:

> Every disastrous thing that has happened in the past twenty years was clearly foretold by a galaxy of writers and thinkers twenty years ago. Our politicians and officials were, relatively speaking, little, purblind, mean chaps.

They weren't in touch with the real news.
How do you judge the news media?

The problems of the press are sharply different from what they were fifty years ago. Then we had no instant news that you could get by reaching inside your pocket or turning a dial on your car radio or tuning in your television set. And with all these sources of news we should all be well-informed, but are we? In one sense, yes, but we have also trivialized the news. We have given people the idea that they know what is happening, and many don't. The news is often presented in bits and pieces, shallow stuff, not deep or penetrating. You can't learn the news by reading TV billboards.

For example, how did you judge the truth and adequacy of the news about the Panama Canal treaties? At first, I felt that we were not being given enough detail about the *two* treaties. But as the debate in the Senate continued, many of my questions were answered by newspapers, magazines, radio, and television. I especially enjoyed the editorial analysis by Richard L. Strout (TRB), whom I mentioned earlier.

The Problem of Credibility

> When we hear news we should always wait for the sacrament of confirmation.—Voltaire

All of us make judgments about the credibility of the news. Unfortunately, our judgments are rarely diagnostic. Instead, many resignedly say, "You can't trust newspapers, newsmagazines, books, radio, and television." This cynical comment is too sweeping.

The terms "true" and "truth" mean "agreeing with fact, not false." It is hard to speak, write, or visualize the truth about a debatable question even though we are doing our best not to falsify. After a war is over we realize that many things were said and written that were clearcut falsehoods. American historians spend their lifetimes trying to discover the truths about the Revolutionary War and find that some English historians do not agree with their conclusions.

In every election the candidates say things that are either partly true or sometimes just plain lies. Sometimes the material presented may be narrowly truthful but the sampling is too meager. Editorialized words may be unwittingly used.

For example, a television news reporter said recently that some House Representatives *stalked* out of a committee meeting. Did he mean to walk with "slow, stiff, or haughty strides"?

The capable consumer of news tries to tell the difference between truth and falsehood, fact and opinion. It isn't so hard when the information presented can be checked as factual or as false. We can easily find a correct baseball or tennis score. But you cannot be certain at first how many people lost their lives in a national disaster such as a flood in India or an earthquake in Nicaragua. Reports in the press say that the body count was 2,000, but the number given by the government, "an official source," may be much higher. Newspapers also make little mistakes. They misspell *seize, supersede, liaison, weird.* The *Columbus* (Ohio) *Citizen-Journal* headlined a story (3/2/78)— "Pact Infuriates Ohio UAW Leaders." They meant UMW.

Over a period of time you can discover those newspapers, magazines, and radio or television stations which make a special effort to be fair. Unfortunately the truth is sometimes dull, and falsehood is highly attractive.

Further, experts sometimes differ, and markedly. You see this in regard to new so-called cures in medicine. You see it in regard to claims on gasoline mileage, etc. Furthermore, we often do not want the truth about ourselves. We do not want the truth about the effect of our smoking on lung cancer. We do not want the truth about our attitudes toward others, our selfishness. We do want the "truth," however, when unusually fine qualities are discovered in us.

I hesitate to make broad accusations about truthfulness and where it is and is not found. On debatable issues we assume that the debate will go on. Here are some comments by newsman Thomas Griffith in his book, *How True—A Skeptic's Guide to Believing the News* (1974):

> So often what television shows you may be "true" as a photograph, while false in what it suggests...(p. 9).
>
> ...the reader who thinks that the news can be delivered untouched by human hands and uncorrupted by human minds is living in a state of vincible ignorance (p. 19).
>
> It is not whether the journalist is objective. That is important of course. But that's not the critical problem. It is whether he is fair...(p. 24).
>
> Griffith quoted Harold Nicolson (British diplomat and author, 1886-

1968) as saying: "There are no solutions in foreign affairs, only adjustments" (p. 96).

...it almost takes a presidential funeral to make station owners momentarily forego their round-the-clock greed (p. 125).

Television has raised a generation inexperienced and vicariously knowledgeable—the perfect audience (p. 126).

Whatever one's own preferences may be among the networks' newscasters, they are as a corps men of competence and integrity (p. 127).

Of all the ways to bring you the news, television is undeniably the best when at its best, that is, when its lenses are open on the actual.

The trouble with the newspaper business is that it is becoming more and more just a business (p. 139).

Asking the Right Questions

I have said that a person who thoughtfully judges the news either overtly or covertly is making a choice. To judge wisely is to make an excellent choice; to judge badly is to make a bad choice.

Indeed, all education as contrasted with training involves the development and refinement of choice, the awareness of alternatives, and the need for studying and mentally rehearsing the consequences of these alternatives before choosing. I repeat: To choose wisely is to live well, and the story of every person's life lies in the big and little choices that he/she has made or failed to make.

The reader, listener, or viewer of news is always looking for answers. To judge the news we must first look for or create the questions. When Gertrude Stein lay dying she called to her companion, Alice B. Toklas, and said, "What is the answer?" Miss Toklas replied, "I don't know." Miss Stein said weakly, "Then what is the question?"

We live in an answer-oriented world. Schools do not usually teach the art of questioning, but expect students to develop skill in answering questions they didn't ask. We need to help students to ask better questions—more profound, more provocative, more worthy of study.

What, then, are some overarching questions that we should carry with us when we are looking at, listening to, or viewing important news?

In *Can People Learn to Learn?* psychiatrist Brock Chisholm says:

The sort of questions an active, free and well-developed imagination will answer truly are, "What will happen if I do so and so?" "What will be the result if I go to such and such a place?" "What will be the effect if I say this or that?" "Will those happenings, results or effects be desirable for me? For others? For my relationship with myself and with others?" "Will they enhance or outweigh and diminish whatever satisfactions I may expect my actions to produce?"

What will happen if...? Here the experience of the individual becomes critical. We operate in the present, but we can either merely exist in a restricted, narrow present or we can act in an amplified present, a present illuminated by our past experiences and our thoughtful hopes for the future. For some, the circle of illumination has a wide diameter; for others this circle is limited, circumscribed.

What choices do I have? Ignorance kills real choice. Education extends it.

News expands choices—is fundamental to democratic rule.

Individuals and their choices do make a difference. It is the informed, uncoerced choices of individuals which should concern us as we try to build a decent world. By making informed choices we widen the area and range of choices open to us. Indeed, in a democracy the only way to safeguard choice is to keep choosing. In short, we might well define an educated person as one who makes informed choices. Again, to choose wisely is to live well.

Harm can come to a society where freedom of choice is reduced. This is the danger of one-newspaper towns, of a one-sided press, or of one-sided teaching, of radio or television limited only to commercial stations. Danger may also arise when we mistakenly believe that there is no choice open to us, that we are fenced in, spiritually and intellectually. The result can be to excuse ourselves from the responsibility of choice or from the discipline of making hard choices. The outcome might be either a cynical apathy or an irresponsible Utopianism. We either think we can do nothing now, or assume that everything will eventually come out all right without our intervention.

The Press Criticizes Itself

One of the activities of the press—print, word, and picture—is to investigate the conduct of business, government, education; to watch for unfulfilled promises; to seek out wastefulness in government; to turn the flashlight of thoughtful investigation into the dark corners. It is an important function if it is done thoughtfully and expertly.

But a problem arises: *Quis custodiet ipsos custodes?* Who's to guard the guardians? Who will watch the watchdog?

The media are not in the habit of judging and evaluating each other. Happily, some great newspapers are employing watchdogs for their own newspapers. Charles Seib of *The Washington Post* is one example. Further, there was established in 1973 the National News Council (One Lincoln Plaza, New York 10023). Its aims according to the Foreword in *An Open Press* (1977) are:

> The National News Council does many things. It has prepared itself to receive complaints about press errancy and to seek judicious answers to the problems posed. At one and the same time, the Council is prime defender of the press's rights and forthright critic of its uncorrected misstatements. Most of the press councils around the world deal with the printed press. However, The National News Council considers all protests made, whether they be about newspapers, magazines or broadcasters....

Further, the Press Council deals largely with national problems not local or regional.

The criticism of the press is an ancient custom. For example, the following account is given of Walter Lippmann's comment about the press in 1920. Does it have a contemporary flavor?

> There is everywhere an increasingly angry disillusionment about the press, a growing sense of being baffled and misled; and wise publishers will not pooh-pooh these omens.... If publishers and authors themselves do not face the facts and attempt to deal with them, some day Congress, in a fit of temper, egged on by an outraged public opinion, will operate on the press with an ax.

Thor Severson, Ombudsman of *The Sacramento Bee*, said that out of 3,900 contacts with the public, he has reached these conclusions:

- Today's readers are sophisticated and informed.
- They are impatient with arrogance.
- They read the paper far more closely than editors and reporters suspect, sometimes to the embarrassment of the newspaper.

- They are impatient whenever they think they suspect manipulation of the news and are as quick to suspect it is intentional.

The National News Council is an attempt to bring critical evaluation to bear on the newspaper itself. It has pointed out that the newspapers and other media are quick to criticize others but are loath to receive criticism themselves.

The New in the News

Our goal in education is learning, and this includes learning to learn and developing a taste for learning. Sometimes we learn better what we have partially learned before. We *re*-view it; that is, we view it again from a different point of view, from a different perspective. Reviewing is re-newing, making life *new* every day. Such a life may have challenge, novelty. It is not dull, not hackneyed, not stereotyped.

We can't thoughtfully judge the news that is beyond our comprehension; hence, to read foreign news we must know the words and idioms commonly used in that news. To read the news in the chemistry textbook we must know the technical terms. News sometimes needs to be simplified but this does not mean that it should be simplistic. It should not be harder than it needs to be; neither should it be easier. Sometimes it should be hard enough to challenge but not to frustrate. Einstein said, "Everything must be made as simple as possible, but not one bit simpler."

The chief characteristic of any communication process where ideas are freely exchanged is a mood of mutuality, of trust. The climate has to be right. Many persons want to speak to us and write for us, but they do not want to listen to us or read what we have written. When the climate for communication is right, there is two-way flow of ideas, interaction. Common interests are being mutually explored. The weakness of a mass medium is the absence of interaction, feedback, discussion. In television, we face the speaker but he does not face us. The process is one-way.

If we are to develop the discriminating listener, viewer, or reader, we need teachers who can be mentors, models, wise and trusted advisors, able exemplars of the goals they are trying to reach. They must bend over backwards to be fair in judging the news. This does not mean they should be without personal values, without points of view. But they would be obliged to make clear their own point of view, not to propagandize but rather to present warnings about their own prejudices and predilections.

If it is true that the unexamined life is not worth living, as Socrates said, then we must critically examine what we read and write, say and hear, visualize and observe. It is hard to do and will keep on being hard to do. But whoever said that maintaining a democracy would be easy?

The Impact of Television on Children's Reading

Nancy Larrick
Lehigh University

Almost any elementary school classroom gives evidence of the television takeover. In one third grade, a six-foot cutout of Big Bird dominates the reading corner. In another, the three reading groups are named for *The Fonz, Six Million Dollar Man,* and *Charlie's Angels.*

As children talk, you hear about *Baretta, Welcome Back, Kotter, The Bionic Woman, Starsky and Hutch, Kojak,* and other TV favorites. But the talk is not simply about these TV heroes. Often a child assumes the role, the swagger, the language—even the intonation of a TV character—and keeps with it for weeks.

A four year old visiting a public library story hour in Oxford, Ohio, refused to wear a name tag until it was made out to "Steve Austin." "Because," he explained, "I'm *not* Peter Smith anymore. I'm Steve Austin." And so he remained for the six week story hour sequence.

An amusing incident—but what about the deeper effect of home television on children's responses to the classroom scene and to reading in particular? Seeking answers to this question, I have interviewed small groups of classroom teachers, librarians, reading specialists, and guidance counselors in twenty-seven communities in the East and Middle West and have received completed questionnaires from other groups in the Far West.

With few exceptions, these observers have painted a devastating picture of the extent of the television takeover in the lives of children.

Elementary school children watch an average of more than 30 hours a week, with some individuals watching 60 to 70, even 80 or 90 hours. The heaviest viewers are watching before and after school, late into the night, and in solid weekend blocks. In school, they are frequently drowsy—or extremely aggressive.

Not unexpectedly, attention spans are short—eight to ten minutes at most. Except with the aid of catchy visuals, listening is an underdeveloped skill.

Language comes slowly from these youngsters except when it is about television programs or modeled on the language of a TV hero. Creative writing is said to be more difficult than it was five or six years ago. "They have nothing to write about except TV programs," said a teacher in a Puerto Rican neighborhood in Bethlehem, Pennsylvania. "That's all they see when they aren't in school."

First and second grade teachers work to overcome the TV child's habit of reporting time without using numbers. Asked when the family eats supper, the youngster may say, "When *The Brady Bunch* comes on." Bedtime is after *Charlie's Angels*. The days of the week also have TV designations: Monday is the night for sports. Saturday is "when we watch all day."

Teachers say that many children consider reading a chore to avoid. Of those who can read and who make good test scores, few turn to reading for pleasure. Wordless picture books are favorites in the early grades. *The Guinness Book of World Records* is the overwhelming favorite in the upper grades.

The multimillion circulation of the new children's magazines—*WOW, Dynamite, Bananas, SuperMag*, and *Pizzaz*—is indicative of children's reading preferences. These magazines consist of exaggerated visuals with only a few words. They are as easy for nonreaders as for good readers, and equally popular with both groups.

Last fall librarians reported demand for books that had been adapted to television production: *Nancy Drew, The Hardy Boys*, and *The Little House on the Prairie*, in particular. But many librarians doubted that the children had actually read the books. "After the television adaptations and variations of *The Little House on the Prairie*," said one, "the book itself is a letdown. It's not a big deal for these kids to read that Mother is spending all day making cheese."

A fourth grader in Buffalo who enjoyed the TV program did not like the book àt all. "The book is all wrong," he said. "I know because I watched it on TV."

From all quarters I heard that the child of television expects instant achievement. If a picture painted in two minutes does not please, it is crumpled into a ball and no further tries are made. If the writer of a story gets discouraged, his paper goes into the same wastebasket. The book that fails to grip the reader at once is dropped.

Often a teacher's directions seem to fall on deaf ears, as though the children have switched channels. "They get that glazed look," said one kindergarten teacher. "You have to use nonverbal directions, body communication. I can't say, 'Let's get in a circle.' I have to lead the way and make the circle."

A school librarian in Wisconsin explained, "They want everything laid out so all they have to do is watch or do what you tell them to do."

Again and again I heard the comment that children come to school expecting to be entertained. As one kindergarten teacher put it, "They expect me to be Big Bird all day!"

Along with these negative reports, there were some encouraging comments on the values of TV. Many of these were from young teachers who had grown up with television but had learned to read and enjoy books anyway. "How did this happen?" I asked. Usually I found that their parents were readers who had read to them as children and provided books at home.

Several of these young teachers sharply defended home television viewing. They cited the opportunity to acquire a larger vocabulary, particularly through the commercials. A second grade teacher said her four year old watches three to four hours of television each day, including two showings of *Sesame Street*. "And that's good," she said. "Later we talk about what she has seen and then she asks questions."

When someone remarked that children come to school knowing TV commercial jingles but not Mother Goose, a young principal asked, "Why should they know Mother Goose rhymes? They'll never need them."

One young man who teaches in a private day care center in Buffalo said: "Television has value in reinforcing the fabric of our society. OK? Violence is acceptable, and kids learn that."

I have come through these conversations about children and television with increasing concern over the frustrations, anxieties, tensions, and misunderstandings that prevail in many classrooms today. We are in the midst of a cultural revolution in which television plays a dominant role. Children are in the eye of the storm.

To reach these children, we must understand the nature of the storm, particularly as reflected in the field of communications. Reading and books are still a part of this field.

Have We Become an Oral Language Culture?

When the boy Abe Lincoln sprawled in front of the open fire to read a book, he had no other way to receive communication from beyond his own neighborhood. The boy of today is in a different world where the electronic communications network reaches into virtually every home, car, truck, and bus—indeed into many a boy's pants pocket. Radios, televisions, movies, record players, tape recorders, and telephones bring the sound of the human voice in a round-the-clock bombardment of information, entertainment, advertising, and general mishmash. Any consideration of reading in this country today must weigh this relentless barrage of sound in either the foreground or background of our lives.

As early as 1958, Canadian anthropologist Edmund Carpenter warned that Western civilization had become an oral language culture comparable to the pre-Gutenberg era, when the only books were those lettered by hand and literacy was extremely limited. History, literature, and news were transmitted by word of mouth.

Now we have literally billions of books, plus newspapers, magazines, and pamphlets, but evidence mounts that the oral language culture has taken over. We hear more than we ever read. There are nearly twice as many TV sets in U.S. homes as the total circulation of daily newspapers, and three times as many radios as television sets. The magazine with the largest circulation in the country is *TV Guide.* Each year the average American watches 1,200 hours of television (the equivalent of

150 working days or 30 working weeks) and spends only five hours reading a book. Near the top of the best seller list is *The Book of Lists.*

The oral language culture dominates the business world as well as family life. Business letters have been replaced by telephone calls. Rap sessions and brainstorming have eliminated the president's position paper. One metropolitan newspaper editor asked a contributor to telephone his column "so it never has to go on paper." Business and professional conferences attract millions who travel long distances at great expense in order to listen—instead of reading books and articles at home by the same authorities. Widely scattered families keep in touch with a weekly audiocassette. "It's the sound of their voices that counts," said a delighted grandmother.

Verbal Stimulation from Television

In the years since the swing to oral language, what has happened to children's learning and, specifically, their progress in reading?

Here, again, the reports of teachers vary. But even those who deplore the new behavior patterns acknowledge that today's youngsters possess more facts and have more mature knowledge of the world than did their predecessors of twenty-five or thirty years ago.

Studies show that IQ scores are rising (4). In the 1972 standardization of IQ tests, the average score for a four year old was 110, based upon 1960 standard scores. The average score of children of five and one half was 111 (on the 1960 scale). Robert Thorndike gives television credit for the rise in IQ. In his 1975 presidential address to the American Educational Research Association, Thorndike spoke of the enormous increase in verbal stimulation that preschoolers are getting from television and from parents who have also been exposed to television. Nothing like this existed in the thirties when the tests were first standardized.

It should also be noted that the 1972 standardization of IQ scores showed that averages begin to slip when children enter school at five and one half or six, dropping one point a year to average about 102 at age ten. There is another rise to about 105 or 106 in adolescence.

Again Thorndike pointed to the influence of television: "We should recognize that with television the world of the child has changed, and that the beneficial aspects are experienced primarily, perhaps exclusively, in the preschool years."

Ironically, in the period when IQ averages appear to be climbing, Scholastic Aptitude Test scores have declined (6). The downward trend began in 1963 for scores on verbal ability and in 1966 for scores on mathematical ability. The drop in verbal scores has been more than double the drop in math.

High school seniors taking the 1963 Scholastic Aptitude Tests were the first of the post-World War II babies, the first generation to have grown up with television as a steady diet.

During the sixties and early seventies, the amount of viewing time among children and young people rose about an hour a day. Thus, as viewing time increased, SAT scores, particularly the verbal scores, went down. It is difficult not to conclude that television caused the decline, yet proof is virtually impossible. Television is so all-pervasive that a control group of nonviewers cannot be found to compare with viewers. Nor can the effects of TV viewing be untangled easily from the influences of home, peer groups, and community in our hyped up society.

Still we wonder, "To what extent has television contributed to the decline in SAT scores?"

Wilbur Schramm, Distinguished Center Researcher of the East-West Center in Honolulu, tackles this question in "Television and the Test Scores," an 18-page report to the Advisory Panel on the Scholastic Aptitude Test Score Decline (7).

While careful to avoid blaming television for the SAT score decline, Schramm reports on a number of studies which throw light on the subject and also raise provocative questions. A study by Schramm and Parker in 1961 (when it was possible to find a control group of nonviewers in Canada for comparison with an experimental group of viewers in the United States) showed that the U.S. children with television experience came into first grade with a larger vocabulary and a somewhat wider spread in general knowledge than their non-TV counterparts in Canada. "However, all the advantage seemed to be lost during the first few years of school," according to Schramm.

A 1970 study in Japan, reporting on fourth, seventh, and tenth graders, goes beyond the 1961 American study to include measures of intelligence, creativity, adaptability, social norm, and parent-child conflicts. At each grade level "the Japanese findings seem to establish a close and consistent relationship between higher than average viewing of television and lower than average school achievement," reports Schramm (7). But when other variables are considered, the director of the study, Takeo Furu, concludes "that the lower achievement of heavy viewers is due not to the direct effects of TV but to the intervening effects of such predispositions as intelligence, creativity, adaptability, and so forth."

Also of interest is Schramm's consideration of the effect of long hours of learning from television pictures. "In their first sixteen years of life," he writes, "and before they take a college entrance examination, they would have spent somewhere between 10,000 and 15,000 hours watching television." He says this means "the shifting of a major part of a child's learning time from the linear digital encoding associated with reading to the iconic simultaneous kind of encoding that is the chief part of watching television." Most achievement tests, he points out, depend upon the former.

The fact that "children are now getting fifteen or twenty more hours a week in learning from pictures than they used to" suggests significant possibilities in an area about which very little is known, Schramm suggests. But "the fact remains that after 300 years of exercising the left hemisphere of the brain (the logical, verbal, linear side) our young people have now reversed the balance and are emphasizing the right hemisphere (the visual, affective, simultaneous one)."

Douglass Cater of the Aspen Institute spells out the contrast between learning from print and learning from the electronic media: "Gutenberg man lived by a communication system requiring laborious coding of thought into print and later decoding by the receiver." (Like loading cord wood on a string of freight cars and moving them cross country for the receiver to unload piece by piece.) "Electronic man communicates experience without the need of symbolic transformation.... The Gutenberg communicator—for the past 500 years patiently transmitting experience line by line, usually left to right, down the printed page—is no longer relevant," says Cater (1).

The average American child comes to first grade with 5,000 hours of TV viewing experience. Each week more time is spent watching television at home than is spent in school. The young viewer is habituated to instant gratification, quick change of scene and situation, sharp emotional impact, continuous sound—all with no effort and little intellectual commitment on his part. Television keeps its viewers passive.

TV programs open with a dramatic hooker even before title and byline are announced. Events happen fast, with a cliff-hanger to hold the reader through each break for a commercial. The two days or evenings once required to read a book are cut to two and one-half hours when the story is dramatized on stage—and less than thirty minutes on television.

In TV programing, events do not follow the step-by-step sequence of linear thinking which is typical of print, but explode in a mighty storm of sound and fury. "This is television," says Howard Luck Gossage, San Francisco public relations consultant, "which is everything happening at once, instantaneously, and enveloping. A child who gets his environmental training on television—and very few nowadays do not—learns the same way the member of a preliterate society learns: from direct experience of his eyes and ears, without Gutenberg for a middle man" (3).

The Slow Pace of Print Oriented Learning

In 1964, before the decline in SAT scores became a trend, Marshall McLuhan said, "the TV child encounters the world in a spirit antithetic to literacy" (5). Yet our schools and colleges, set up by our print oriented forebears, are geared to educating primarily through reading and writing.

Drawn into this dichotomy, children are torn between what comes naturally and what seems awkward, meaningless, even painful. It is no wonder that Dorothy Cohen of the Bank Street College of Education sees an "increase in frenetic aimlessness, high distractability, and inability to focus among many more preschool and primary children than experienced teachers remember" (2).

As I have talked with teachers in the past eight months, I have heard again and again that children seem to be bored with everything at school. And from children comes confirmation: Reading is boring. The teacher is boring. Even recess is boring. (So boring, in fact, that sixth graders in one Long Island school sit on the sidewalk around the playground rather than get involved in games.)

Then I read an essay of Susan Sontag's in which she equates boredom with frustration. I have come to think it is more exact to say that children are frustrated with everything at school. With books and reading. With writing and spelling. With the slow pace of lessons.

A young English lad who had recently dropped out of school put it this way: "They was driving me up the wall. And I was driving them up the wall. 'Twas no use."

In his book, *The Responsive Chord*, Tony Schwartz (8) gives the most precise analysis I have come across under the title, "Education in the Global Village." He comments on "The highly saturated information environment" into which children are born and where they spend the major part of their waking hours.

Because it is high speed information pouring forth "as a continuous stream of fleeting, millisecond events," children become scanners. Their patterns of reacting, feeling, and thinking have been restructured, Schwartz says, and they arrive at school expecting to use these skills and learning habits. They are ready to move ahead in the style to which they are accustomed.

Instead, they face a jumble of contradictions and conflicts. The language of the teacher and the textbook is not the language of the Fonz or Kojak, which has become the children's very own. In the classroom, they are told that people speak one at a time. What's that? It never happened on television.

The teacher's manner seems a little flat after long hours with Farrah Fawcett-Majors. Recess is a nothing time if Kung Fu techniques are banned.

Now, instead of instant impressions, children are asked to ferret them out, step by step, even syllable by syllable. All those thousands of hours of TV involvement are walled off by language, procedures, and materials that seem to make no sense at all.

"A child enters the classroom today with the world stored in him," writes Schwartz. "He possesses more information than any school could ever teach him. As a result, the education process has been reversed. Rather than cram new information into *an empty shell*, the school's function is to *order existing knowledge*" *(8)*.

In my conferences of the past eight months I have found only two schools which have any policy or program dealing with the impact of television on children. Like the family skeleton, the subject is kept in the closet where the rest of the household fervently hopes it will stop rattling.

But the impact of television isn't going away. It is growing year by year. We had better make plans to capitalize on it, if books and reading are to survive.

References

1. Cater, Douglass, and Richard Adler. *Television As a Social Force: New Approaches to TV Criticism*. New York: Praeger, 1975, 6.
2. Cohen, Dorothy H. "TV and the Perception of Reality," *Education Digest*, March 1977, 10.
3. Gossage, Howard Luck. "The New World of Marshall McLuhan," in Gerald E. Stearn (Ed.), *McLuhan Hot and Cold*. New York: Dial Press, 1967, 6.
4. Mankiewicz, Frank, and Joel Swerdlow. *Remote Control: Television and the Manipulation of American Life*. New York: Times Books, 1978, 207-209.
5. McLuhan, Marshall. *Understanding Media: The Extensions of Man*. New York: New American Library, 1964, 291.
6. *On Further Examination: Report of the Advisory Panel on the Scholastic Aptitude Test Score Decline*. New York: College Entrance Examination Board, 1977, 6.
7. Schramm, Wilbur. *Television and the Test Scores*. New York: College Entrance Examination Board, 1977, 7-16.
8. Schwartz, Tony. *The Responsive Chord*. New York: Anchor Books/Doubleday, 1974, 108-135.

The Publisher and the Reading Teacher: Avenues for Alliance

Joanne E. Bernstein
Brooklyn College

In this paper, there are no answers—merely questions and statements of concern. As teachers of reading, we have many areas and projects of joint interest with publishers of children's literature. Many ventures are in full bloom and doing beautifully. Others are new, exciting vistas for exploration. Finally, there are some problem areas.

Item. The New York Academy of Sciences, in an attempt to encourage publishers to keep good children's science books in print, gave an award to John Day Company, thus marking the twentieth anniversary of *Cosmic View*, a classic science teaching book by the late Kees Boeke.

Item. At a recent meeting of the Authors' Guild, agent Kathleen Raines warned that authors will no longer be able to look for steady income from sales of their titles on backlists. The growing cost of reprinting, consumers' reluctance to pay high prices, and the preference of librarians to order current books combine to spell the end for many editions (*15*).

Item. The American Library Association Office for Intellectual Freedom claims that nine-tenths of the pleas for help they receive come from school librarians, most of whom request anonymity.

Item. In an article in *School Library Journal*, Sheila Egoff indicates that youngsters between six and fourteen read about 400 books. Calculating about 41,000 books were in print at the time of writing (1972), Egoff (*7*) claims that children may very well pick up and read nothing but mediocre fare.

Item. Random House executive Jason Eptstein says children ignore the Newbery Medal winners. He is echoed by Dewey Chambers (*19*).

Item. In Michigan in 1974, one million dollars was set aside for a Reading Room Program. Schools were given grants to buy paperbacks of high interest and to set up informal surroundings for reading those paperbacks. A dramatic increase in pleasure seeking through reading ensued.

In spite of such efforts, *a final item.* Fifteen percent of today's children are disabled in reading.

These items stretch far and wide—from the problem of books going out of print, to censorship, to questions of quality in reading, to motivation and reading ability—but each is cause for concern by both reading teachers and publishers of children's literature.

At a session of the 1976 International Reading Association Convention, the old question was asked: "Why can't they read?" The answer, for one respondent: "Because they don't read books." That respondent, Richard Bamberger of the International Institute for Children's Literature and Reading Research, continued: "Why don't they read books? Because they can't read."

In order to become mature, efficient readers, youngsters must read fiction and nonfiction, written because the authors felt a compulsion to communicate. Literature produced out of creative need is flavorful and fosters the *art* of reading, instead of merely the skill.

Out-of-Print Books

For books to be read, they must be in print, and so this discussion of out-of-print books. The growing problem of losing fine materials is sad and frightening. Throughout the land, teachers and librarians have been dismayed, even disbelieving, to find that order lists may not offer the titles they want. Expenses are so high that it is often decided that reprinting, particularly of full color material, is too costly. Then a peculiar cycle takes place. Even if librarians and reading teachers want to pay six to eight dollars, the book is no longer available! Some publishers and teachers may feel that if the title is in paperback, it is not lost. Others differ, pointing to the wonder and pride of book ownership. John Rowe Townsend feels that, in spite of healthy paperback sales, when youngsters locate a book dear to the heart, they will want it in hardcover—a "solid, permanent possession and friend" (21).

Those who tell us of the out-of-print problem also warn that these hard economic times mean the end of the B+ book. If a book isn't topnotch, it hasn't the chance of being published it had ten years ago. I suppose that's a good thing, for we all want fine books for children, but there are attendant problems. These days, if a book isn't reviewed quickly and purchased in large numbers quickly, plans are quickly made to put that volume to rest. Reprinting several hundred copies or even one or two thousand may result in raising the price. Will the market bear the price increase? Too often, the answer is no, and so many of today's A and A- hardcovers are gone—unavailable for permanent possession and friendship. In many cases, such books never did become paperback, so they do not remain in that form either. The A work of the publishing team is simply gone.

Is this our concern as reading teachers? Yes, for more than the reason of losing good literature. Earlier, Kathleen Raines' concern was mentioned that authors would no longer be able to rely upon income from the backlist. Why should reading teachers care about that? Should reading teachers feel sorry for authors who lead so-called glamorous lives? Well, authors of all literature, and particularly those of children's literature, do not lead glamorous lives. It has often been publicized that only about one hundred writers (on all subjects, for all ages) in this country can earn a living from writing literature alone. Most teach, work at other jobs, or work in the home. Even if the one hundred figure is exaggerated, the children's field may well be the orphan of the industry. One author recently told me of her situation. She's written about twenty-five books for young people—almost all of them currently in print. From these books, a lifetime's work, she receives a grand sum of about $12,000 yearly in royalties. That author has recently signed her first contract for an adult book. She was surprised to find the advance to be four times what she receives for children's fare, and the earnings would seem to be likewise.

The author of whom I speak is first-rate—puts out A quality all the time. But I ask you: If good books disappear from the shelves because of economic hardship and an almost pathological societal drive toward having new things, if writers, illustrators, and editors see their work forced into oblivion, *will my friend the author stay in the children's field?*

Yes, we reading teachers should be concerned. The award by the New York Academy of Sciences calls attention to the problem. We, too, can do something about it—by remembering the old as we are admiring the new; by looking for our orders on the back pages of publishers' catalogs, as well as the front pages; by asking to see publishers' catalogs if jobbers tell us certain books are out of print, to check if it is just the editions *they* stock which are gone; by utilizing the enlarged reviews in the journals of IRA, thus encouraging further increase in space; by stopping in at the literature booths at IRA conventions, thereby letting the publishers' promotion people know we think literature is as important as text material; and, finally, by taking time out to think about those books which are popular and which could be reordered, taking nothing for granted in terms of an individual title's supposed immortality. Today *no* title is immortal unless we make it so.

Paperback Books

We must not let hardcovers go but, at the same time, let us celebrate the wonderful paperback revolution. So many wonderful things have taken place.

The joyous act of reading for pleasure has been enriched by the presence of easy to carry, aesthetically pleasing books. The Michigan Reading Room Program is but one means of spreading the word. Also of note is Reading Is Fundamental, in which local participating groups distribute paperbacks given by sponsors. Sometimes, as on television, the books arrive in "Reading Is Fun-Mobiles." Other programs include Project Read, an example of alliance between publishers and reading teachers. One segment of Project Read involves the American Correctional Association and provides teachers with training in diagnosis and remediation of reading problems. As part of the effort, paperbacks are given to juveniles living in training schools and prisons. About 36,000 youngsters have been reached. Sixteen is their average age; fourth grade is their average reading level. The administrators of that program have made the news with their discovery that if the teenagers are interested in the subject matter, they master reading material at a higher level. Seeking books about adolescent problems, minority groups, and women's studies, their success is not limited to high interest, low vocabulary books (14).

Another program is an annual event sponsored by Scholastic Magazines. Called the "Great Paperback Contest," prizes are awarded to teachers, librarians, and school administrators who contribute descriptions of outstanding, original ways to motivate classroom and library reading with paperbacks.

What else can be done? I've touched upon only a few of the many programs, and the paperback has been around schools for more than two decades. I still recall the approximate look of some of the titles I ordered in 1955 as a member of the TAB book club.

But what's in the offing today? In an article in *School Library Journal*, Laskey (11) suggests placing displays just about everywhere. Reminding us that motivation is higher when the full cover is showing and not the spine, he tells us we've overlooked some places for buying and trading, including playgrounds, swimming clubs, beaches, and laundromats.

We've also recently heard of bookstores as part of the daily routine in British elementary schools. Many American high schools sport such enterprises: Let's see more bookstores in elementary schools. One book fair a year is not enough.

And then there has been rumbling about commercial children's bookstores. They are bold adventures, for one can't make enough from sales off the street. To eke out a bare living depends upon sales to institutions. The Toronto bookstore for children has been a model for many, and it can boast many institutional retainers. But some of the cities and states in the United States have been cutting the budgets of schools and day care centers to shreds, especially for items such as books. Bravo and double bravo to those who venture forth anyway, seeking out their dreams and opening bookstores dedicated to the needs and desires of children. As teachers know, most traditional bookstores stock few hardcovers for youngsters, usually limiting themselves to classics, neoclassics, and novelty books. At children's bookstores, if one can find a way around proscriptions of contracts the school system has made with jobbers, one can see and buy some lesser known hard-covers. And there one can see the scope, depth, and beauty of paperbacks, without simultaneously attending to the needs of youngsters, which is the way it would be at a book fair.

Publishers can also assist children's bookstores. At Eeyore's, one such shop in New York, local authors come down for readings. They are paid no honoraria, giving their time simply because they share love of words with the owner and customers. If publishers could take a more active role in supporting activities at these stores—perhaps advertising the dates in trade and public media—more people would gather in the stores, and they would become more than the hand-to-mouth enterprises some of them currently are. They're important and deserve support.

Each year, more hardcover companies throw their hats into the paperback ring. Joining recently were Little, Brown and Parents' among others. Some firms, such as Dell, Avon, and Bantam, have long been aware of the needs of reading teachers for the development of paperback programs to go with the paperbacks. Guides for teaching popular titles have been very useful in schools. It is hoped that some of the firms now joining the paperback circus will also offer the services of educational directors and the benefits of guidebooks. School bookstores and children's bookstores offer another avenue for distribution to teachers.

Censorship

Censorship in the marketplace is a phenomenon faced by publishers of both hard and softcovered books; it is also a problem faced by teachers and librarians. In fact, today the problem is more complicated than ever before. In the tight economic market, publishers looking for quality books are also, of necessity, asking themselves: Are we sure it will sell? Are we sure it will sell at least 5,000 copies? If not, in today's times, publishers are wary of taking a chance. We, the public, are the losers, for is this not (as expressed by Zimet) precensorship? Publishers may be especially unwilling to risk losses because of current efforts to maximize profits (22).

This problem is responsible for the fact that there are two versions of the paperback version of Jean Fritz's biography,

And Then What Happened, Paul Revere? In the first, a police officer shouts, "Damn you, stop!... If you go an inch farther, you are a dead man." A later version altered the accurately recorded words from historical annals, all for the sake of pleasing the masses (*13*).

Censorship can be the quiet removal of books or their nonselection by librarians and teachers, either by outside direction or decision from within. The recent case in Island Trees, New York, where the school board openly refused to allow nine books already on the shelves to remain there, was the exception. Removing titles already purchased was declared unconstitutional by the Sixth Circuit Court of Appeals; cases of open defiance are in the minority. But secret decisions are not rare at all and are easy to conceal. When librarians protesting censorship request anonymity, one wonders how much of the tip of the iceberg is actually seen. How many librarians, teachers of reading, English teachers, and publishers don't complain but are swayed by lists of proscribed books circulated by groups on either the right or the left?

It's frightening, but a recent study of more than 3,000 librarians indicated that only 2 percent of them were strongly against censorship; 64 percent were neither highly favorable nor unfavorable (*3*). Equally frightening is that there is no reason to think librarians are any different from reading teachers or other groups. Many have looked the other way and taken the easy path. Today's problems are made even more complex because sometimes the ones asking us to censor have fine intentions. By now it is well known that the Council for Interracial Books for Children desires that all literature be monitored for evidence of racism, materialism, escapism, sexism, elitism, and other isms—literary qualities of plot and character taking a back seat.

In the booklet on censorship created for Dell to distribute to teachers, Stanek (*20*:10-11) elucidates the positions of many anticensorship organizations. The American Library Association "takes the position that while efforts to counteract injustices are understandable, perhaps even commendable, they are in conflict with the professional responsibility of librarians because intellectual freedom, in its purest sense, promotes no causes, furthers no movements, and favors no viewpoints.... Tolerance is meaningless without tolerance for what some people may consider detestable." Zimet (22:119) agrees with ALA in her stress upon examining an entire collection for tone and broad range or opinion, instead of growing alarmed and overreacting to literature which reflected the time in which it was written or authors' occasional imprudent paragraphs or phrases.

The policies developed by ALA and other groups can be helpful to teachers. ALA recommends maintaining a written policy which is applied to all materials equally without exception. School and faculty libraries can purchase a subscription to the ALA Newsletter on Intellectual Freedom for $6 a year, keeping everyone abreast.

The National Council of Teachers of English also has a policy, most popularly stated in Donelson's *The Student's Right to Read* (6). Therein it is suggested that complainants be required to complain in writing—and only after they have read the entire book and have become acquainted with literary criticism received by the volume. In addition, they must offer advice about substitute titles (20:16). These constraints would put off many a complainant, but Stanek feels that English teachers lack daring, and so many complainants wouldn't even need to pain themselves going through the procedure. She indicates that when teachers buckle under, children learn more of the nastiness of the real world than anything they might find in censored material.

Other publications and groups are available which teachers and publishers may want to rely upon in their fight against censorship. The American Civil Liberties Union has sponsored *The Rights of Students* (12) and *The Rights of Teachers* (17). The National Ad Hoc Committee against Censorship, consisting of professional and citizen's groups, publishes *Censorship News* and fosters coalitions on local levels.

Quality Reading Material

Finally, we turn to our most crucial alliance to provide quality reading material. Recently, the U.S. National Committee for Unesco sponsored an international symposium on "Promotion of the Reading Habit." Symposium members felt that reading in the U.S. "often concentrates too much on skills and techniques and too little on its joys and pleasures" (1). Claiming that concentration upon texts did not allow for development of curiosity, they were concerned about further learning and pleasure through reading. Desiring "an international codification system whereby materials that have proven effective in increasing motivation could be coded by reading level, age level, language, and content," the symposium recommended that executives of extracurricular reading programs meet regularly with school officials in order to mutually learn ways to enhance common goals. Can publishers of literature be considered administrators of extracurricular reading programs? Certainly. And they should, indeed, be encouraged to meet with reading teachers at conventions and in their local districts.

Another recommendation is noteworthy. "The relationship between oral traditions and reading in both developed countries and developing countries should be investigated. Publishers and literacy programs should make more use of folktales and fairy stories for motivating young children to read." Although Newbery winners may be ignored, a look at recent Caldecott winners and honor books indicates an abundance of folklore, some even joking that in order to be considered, the book would have to be a folktale.

A side note about the oral tradition is appropriate. When Tomie dePaola wrote and illustrated *Strega Nona* (5), several people exclaimed, "Oh, you found the Italian version of *The Magic Pot!* I've looked all over!" Acutally, that version comes from dePaola's head, modeled upon his own grandmother. But now, with its popularity, it is becoming part of our own continuing folklore. And so it should be.

If *Strega Nona* enters our folklore, some may consider it unorthodox, but reading motivation often comes about from stressing the unorthodox and moving toward change. An example: Larrick (10) suggests grouping books on various topics along with related filmstrips, maps, and artifacts, instead of using a Dewey Decimal system combined with a vertical file and other systems. Reshelving according to ways which appeal to children may not stress adult, logical order, but circulation and pleasure in reading and learning may result, helping those children who are not up to par. Larrick points to advantages of such a method, including shelving a filmstrip made by children in the school along with other professionally made materials.

As we go along in the publishing and teaching businesses, we seem to be moving toward change in the area of reading levels and readability. If a publisher or teacher relies upon only one method of ascertaining readability, many a fine early reader may be rejected. While these books joyously combine early reading style and good story lines, if one speaks of multisyllable dinosaur names, as happened in Parish's *Dinosaur Time* (16), that book could be doomed on the Fry Readability Graph. Happily, most publishers, reading teachers, and users of graphs realize that no one system is good for all instances—there is more than one way to skin a cat, and it needn't be by strangulation.

It's marvelous to see moves toward change in the giving of awards in children's literature. Recent awards have stressed the inclusion of children's preferences, as exemplified by the Bank Street College of Education Irma Simonton Black Award and the Woodward School Award. IRA is active in this movement, as seen in Children's Choices—the list of trade books published each year and chosen by youngsters in collaboration with children's literature specialists and teachers. The representatives of IRA and the Children's Book Council who formulated the list are right on target when they say "trade books offer curriculum experiences at least as effective and most often more exciting than many materials written expressly for classroom use" (4). One annotation suffices for indication of the tone: Regarding *The Monster Riddle Book* (18), the bibliographers note that youngsters waited eagerly for a turn to read it. They add that the book may be used to "develop awareness of play on words and clever use of double meanings." Perhaps a book display of those given special attention on this list could be exhibited at IRA Conventions— regional, national, and even local.

But awards and listings in bibliographies are too often ignored by publishers. Rarely is a distinction won by a book announced on its jacket. This is cost dependent, of course, but many publishers do not include some minor accolades and awards in their catalogs, keeping news from readers. And rarely is a book in the children's field re-reviewed after its merit is realized. Thus, many a fine book is not even to be found in

Book Review Digest, a primary selection tool. Teachers may not find the book they want—"the book which sends one rushing to share it with anyone one can find, child or adult" (7).

Publishers can play a role in getting good titles to reading teachers, beyond the confines of what their individual houses have published. Along with free posters and bookmarks, it would be good to see more publishers informing teachers about ways to find and use books. Setting up examination centers in school districts is one way. Sending out bibliographic lists to faculty is another, letting people know about the reference tools available. If more people knew about the Children's Book Council Calendar and its low lifetime subscription rate ($5), more would subscribe. Too few teachers are aware of the lists librarians use. Reading teachers need this information, too.

Reading teachers want to know what's going on. They want to know about the things like the Muscular Dystrophy Readathon, in which five million dollars have been collected since 1975 and ten million books have been read in the fight against MS. We can quantify the number of books read and the money received, but no one can estimate the motivation spurred in reading and continuing to read. If publishers would take on the distribution of Readathon materials at conferences and book fairs, all would benefit from their expenditure.

Recently, Frances Henne called for an activist movement of adults to "spread the word of the importance of children's literature." She saw the librarian and publisher as interlocking forces for bringing the best books to children. The reading teacher and the publisher are also interlocking forces. In Henne's words, "If we don't do something, other people are going to sell substitutes for books" (9).

References

1. Academy for Educational Development. *A Reason to Read: A Report on an International Symposium on the Promotion of the Reading Habit.* New York: U.S. National Commission for Unesco, 1976.
2. Bamberger, Richard. "Bridging the Gap: Reading and Children's Literature," paper given at the International Reading Association Convention, Anaheim, California, May 13, 1976.
3. Busha, Charles Henry. "The Attitudes of Midwestern Public Librarians toward Intellectual Freedom and Censorship," unpublished doctoral dissertation, Indiana University, 1971.

4. "Classroom Choices," *Reading Teacher*, 30 (October 1976), 50-63.
5. dePaola, Tomie. *Strega Nona*. Illustrated by the author. Englewood Cliffs, New Jersey: Prentice-Hall, 1976.
6. Donelson, Kenneth. *The Student's Right to Read*. Urbana, Illinois: National Council of Teachers of English, 1972.
7. Egoff, Sheila. "If That Don't Do No Good, That Won't Do No Harm: The Uses and Dangers of Mediocrity in Children's Reading," *Library Journal*, 97 (October 1975), 3435-3439.
8. Fritz, Jean. *And Then What Happened, Paul Revere?* Illustrated by Margot Tomes. New York: Scholastic, 1976.
9. Harper, P. "Henne Calls for More Activism in Children's Book Field," *Wilson Library Bulletin*, 50 (December 1975), 332.
10. Larrick, Nancy. "Setting the Stage for Reading," *Catholic Library World*, 47 (February 1976), 286-287.
11. Laskey, Harold. "The Pull of Paperback Displays," *School Library Journal*, 23 (February 1977), 31-35.
12. Levine, Alan, Eve Cary, and Diane Divoky. *The Rights of Students*. New York: Avon, 1973.
13. Lynch, Priscilla. "The Joy of Paperbacks," comments made at the cosponsored meeting of the Association of American Publishers and the International Reading Association, Miami, Florida, May 4, 1977.
14. Maryles, Daisy. "Educational Paperback Association Seeks Larger Share of the Education Market," *Publishers Weekly*, 211 (March 1977), 84.
15. Meltzer, Milton. "Children's Market Favors Paperbacks, New Sales Shrink Backlist Strength," *Authors Guild Bulletin*, June-August 1977, 13.
16. Parish, Peggy. *Dinosaur Time*. Illustrated by Arnold Lobel. New York: Harper and Row, 1974.
17. Rubin, David. *The Rights of Teachers*. New York: Avon, 1968.
18. Sarnoff, Jane, and Reynold Ruffins. *The Monster Riddle Book*. New York: Scribners, 1976.
19. Shackford, Jane. "Who Reads the Newbery Winners?" *School Library Journal*, 23 (March 1977), 101-105.
20. Stanek, Lou Willet. *Censorship: A Guide for Teachers, Librarians, and Others Concerned with Intellectual Freedom*. New York: Dell, 1976.
21. Steinberg, Sybil. "English Expert Speaks on Children's Books at CBC," *Publishers Weekly*, 210 (November 1976), 24.
22. Zimet, Sara Goodman. *Print and Prejudice*. London: UKRA, 1976. Newark, Delaware: International Reading Association.

Section Three
LEARNING DISABILITIES/ READING DISABILITIES

A History of the Syndrome of Dyslexia with Implications for Its Treatment

E. Jennifer Monaghan
Brooklyn College

It is ironic that most of the advances in our knowledge of the mysterious workings of the human mind have come from the evidence provided by the damaged mind. In particular, the selective damage inflicted by cerebrovascular accidents (strokes) has provided clearcut evidence for identifying those areas in the brain that are intimately connected with separate human functions such as motor movements or the comprehension of language.

Alexia without Agraphia

At the close of the nineteenth century, there was a sense of excitement and discovery among those engaged in studying the mechanisms of the human mind. The medical communities in both Europe and the United States had been tremendously impressed by the historic presentations of Broca in 1861 and Wernicke in 1874. Broca and Wernicke had shown, to everyone's satisfaction, that specific lesions in the brain, as disclosed by autopsy, could be pinpointed as the cause of, respectively, a disturbance in speech and a loss of the comprehension of speech (19). Scientists began to talk of "centers," such as centers in the brain for speech or vision. It appeared that, with time, man would be able to locate in the brain the structural position of all physical and mental functions.

This was the prevailing intellectual climate when, in 1892, the French neurologist Dejerine recounted the case history, with autopsy findings, of a seventy-two year old man named Oscar. The case, claimed Dejerine, was the finest published example of wordblindness (the term then in use for the loss, by an adult, of the ability to read) without agraphia (loss of the ability to write). (A year earlier, Dejerine had published an article on a case of wordblindness accompanied by agraphia.)

At the age of sixty-eight, Oscar, an intelligent and cultured man, had experienced a loss of sensation in his right arm and leg. (These, of course, are the classic symptoms of a stroke located in the opposite hemisphere of the brain—in this case, the left hemisphere.) Two days later, Oscar made an astonishing discovery: He had completely lost the ability to read. When Dejerine examined Oscar, he found that Oscar could not name a single letter. If he copied a letter, he did it in the manner of someone drawing a design. Yet he could write spontaneously, or to dictation, almost as well as before his cerebral accident. Interestingly, Oscar could recognize letters, and even words, by an artifice: If he traced the contours of the letters on the page or in the air, recognition came. He also had totally lost the ability to read music, but not to learn new tunes by ear. Yet his grasp of numbers was unimpaired. Oscar gave a fascinating account of how he managed to write what he could now no longer read. When he thought of anything, he said, he heard the words in his ear. When he concentrated on a word, he saw it mentally after hearing it. "Je vois bien écrit dans mon cerveau le mot que je viens d'entendre et je vais vous l'écrire de suite." "I see the word that I have just heard, written clearly in my head, and I'm now going to write it for you" (11:73). Besides his inability to read, Oscar's only other symptoms were a partial right homonymous hemianopsia (loss of vision in the right half of the visual field of both eyes), and a right hemiachromatopsia (a loss of color vision).

Four years later, Oscar suffered another stroke, which left him with agraphia as well as alexia. He also lost the power to speak, but communicated in mime for the remaining ten days of his life. His power of comprehension was unimpaired. The day after his death, his wife gave Dejerine permission to perform an autopsy. Dejerine found two lesions—one old, and the other clearly a fresh one. The old one, which was readily identifiable as the source of Oscar's four years of wordblindness, was situated in the "cortical visual zone." The recent lesion had occurred in the inferior parietal lobe. Dejerine also reported a small scar on the splenium of the corpus callosum.

Dejerine concluded that the two areas concerned could be pinpointed as the "centers" for reading and writing respectively. He further deduced that, because of his right homonymous hemianopsia, Oscar was no longer able to receive visual impressions with his left hemisphere. (The left hemisphere had long been known to be the site of the language functions.) He still saw letters and words with his right hemisphere, but "they no longer held any meaning for him, because the connection between his two common visual centers and his visual center for words was interrupted." The visual center for words, however, was itself undamaged, as was the pathway between that and the graphic center (*11*:89).

Three years later, the Scots surgeon James Hinshelwood reported a case similar to Dejerine's in all respects. His patient, too, suffered wordblindness without agraphia, and was unable to read any of the languages—English, French, and German—that he had read previously. Like Oscar, Hinshelwood's patient displayed right homonymous hemianopsia. Like Oscar, who had recognized his regular newspaper, *Le Matin*, apparently from the visual configuration of its title, Hinshelwood's patient could still recognize the word "the," seemingly processing it as a unit. Hinshelwood's conclusions followed those of Dejerine: the pathways connecting the primary visual centers in both occipital lobes with the visual word center in the left angular convolution had been cut (*17*).

Subsequent work has elaborated upon the insights of these early speculations, although the concept of a "word

Dyslexia

center" has been discarded, and the role of the splenium of the corpus callosum given greater stress. Relatively few post mortem examinations of patients suffering from alexia have been undertaken—only seventeen by 1969. The results of these few autopsies, however, have been strikingly similar. In all cases there was medial occipital pathology; the left hemisphere was involved in all instances but one. In addition, either the splenium of the corpus callosum was involved or the splenial pathways just to the left of the splenium were disconnected. As Dejerine had suggested, vision itself is not disturbed, but visual information cannot reach the area which processes language. Because of the right homonymous hemianopsia, the language-competent left hemisphere no longer receives visual language stimuli directly. Because of the defect in the corpus callosum, the left hemisphere—which can read—can also no longer receive visual stimuli by transference from the right hemisphere—which cannot read. The patient therefore cannot read by visual means (3).

Congenital Wordblindness

The validity of the condition of alexia without agraphia, as the syndrome is known today, is beyond dispute. Alexia itself belongs to a different channel of history from that of dyslexia. The early definiton of alexia, however, gave rise to another type of identification based, of course, upon the existence of alexia: an alexia that was not acquired by the adult as a result of a cerebral insult but which was inborn in the child. A general practitioner, Pringle Morgan of Seaford, England, read Hinshelwood's 1895 article on wordblindness ("may I call it your classical paper?" he wrote to Hinshelwood) and was inspired to write an article on a fourteen year old boy who had come to him as a patient. Paradoxically, the boy was clearly intelligent but had been totally incapable of learning to read. Indeed, his parents had almost despaired of his ever learning his letters. Morgan believed that his article was the first reference in the literature to the possibility of the existence of a congenital type of wordblindness (21). As a matter of fact, a medical officer, James Kerr, had mentioned the defect in an essay on school hygiene a few weeks earlier (8:6-7).

The notion of a congenital type of wordblindness spread from England to the United States. In February 1906, a New York physician named Schapringer read a paper on the condition to the New York Academy of Medicine. Later that year, Herbert Claiborne, whose contributions would prove influential in the United States, presented a paper on two patients presumed to be suffering from the condition, at the annual meeting of the American Medical Association. Claiborne's first case was a ten year old boy who was unable to name all the letters accurately and whose writing—unlike those of the cases described earlier—exhibited all the earmarks of classical motor aphasia. The child could, however, easily identify numbers. So, too, could Claiborne's second case, a nine year old boy who could identify letters without error, but not words. He read "how" as "you," for example. As a medical practitioner, Claiborne's responsibility to his young patient did not end with diagnosis: he prescribed the whole word approach, then being used in the public schools of New York, as the method of choice for his patient, arguing that "if individual letters can be remembered, words which are composed of letters should be remembered under repetition" (7).

Two decades later, the syndrome variously known as congenital wordblindness or (more commonly, by this time) dyslexia was accepted as a reality by the medical community. United States workers were familiar with the work done in England and with what for many years was regarded as the last word on the subject, Hinshelwood's monograph *Congenital Wordblindness* (18). The condition was believed to result from some congenital deficiency in the "visual center" of the child's dominant hemisphere, a suggestion made by Hinshelwood as early as 1904 (10). The validity of dyslexia as a specific and identifiable syndrome was based on the analogy of its symptoms to those of adults suffering from alexia.

Most of the articles dealing with wordblindness or dyslexia in those years were to be found in American and European medical journals (4). Mentions of the condition in educational journals were not frequent. Characteristic of the latter was Bowers' description of a ten year old boy who could identify only 32 words (5), or the thirteen cases outlined by Schmitt in a 1918 educational journal. As an educator, Schmitt had some suggestions for teaching these children. She advocated phonics, but with the involvement of all the senses, and gave a description of a class so taught. This description of the techniques used by the teacher concerned, however, "only palely portrays," she asserted, "the constant vividness with which sounds and words are associated with experiences and ideas already possessed by the child and the devices for giving the child motor or other experience in connection with the reading to be taught" (27:759).

Approaches for Teaching Disabled Readers

While some educators advocated a multisensory phonic approach for dyslexics (at a time when "look-and-say" was in its heyday), an eminent neurologist was about to reach the same conclusion. Samuel Torrey Orton published the first of a series of articles on the subject in 1925, under the title "Wordblindness in Schoolchildren" (23). In the course of his professional work, Orton had come across a number of children whose massive reading difficulties could not be explained by pointing to emotional or physical handicaps, low intelligence or cultural deprivation. As he studied such children, he became convinced that, while they did indeed form a homogeneous group, their difficulties should not be ascribed to a defective development of the brain. Instead, he suggested that their characteristic errors of direction (the confusion of *b* with *d*, *was* with *saw*), displayed in both reading and writing, came from the failure of one hemisphere of the brain to establish clearcut dominance over the other. He coined the term "strephosymbolia" for this condition. In Orton's view, the child without well-established dominance would receive conflicting signals from printed matter: he would receive "engrams" from both halves of the brain, one the mirror image of the other. In contrast, the child who had unilateral brain dominance "elided," that is, suppressed, the records from the nondominant part of his brain (24).

Orton's treatment for this condition took advantage of the child's grasp of spoken language. "We capitalized," he wrote, "upon these children's auditory competency by teaching them the phonetic equivalents of the printed letters and the process of blending sequences of such equivalents so that they might produce for themselves the spoken form of the word from its graphic counterpart" (25:158). Furthermore, he established the kinesthetic pattern of the letters by having the child trace the letter, or write it, at the same time as he pronounced its phonetic equivalent. Two rather different versions of Orton's approach are in use today (15, 31).

At about the same time that Orton was becoming involved with dyslexic children in the eastern United States, another type of approach was being tried on the west coast. Grace Fernald, with her colleague Helen Keller, became interested in children and young adults with massive disabilities in reading, writing, and spelling. In a discussion in the 1936 *Mental Measurements Monographs* (12), Fernald described the characteristic profiles of these children, who performed adequately in arithmetic, very poorly in reading and composition, and worst of all in spelling, and described her treatment.

In contrast to Orton, Fernald eschewed a phonetic approach. Her pupils learned words as wholes entirely from tracing them with the forefinger. In a detailed study, she described the stages through which a child passed as he followed her technique. First he traced with his finger the word he wished to read, then wrote it from memory. Later he would dispense with tracing but still needed to write the word in order to recognize it. Finally the child could dispense with writing. At no point was the child allowed to sound out the word, as in Orton's approach. The movements of the child's hand, however, were constantly linked to his speech, as he pronounced every word as he traced or wrote it. Again in contrast to Orton, Fernald insisted that the child choose the words he wanted to learn. In this way she guaranteed a high degree of motivation on the child's part (13).

In her early exposition of her method of remediation, Fernald discussed the theoretical rationale for her kinesthetic approach. She noted that the similarity of her cases to the disabilities shown by patients with acquired alexia suggested that some condition of the brain was responsible for the condition. At the same time, she showed that she was well aware of the early literature on wordblindness and pointed out that alexic patients had been able to recognize letters, and even words, by tracing them (12:98).

Changes in the Educational Climate

In spite of these two apparently highly successful types of treatment, evolved from a consideration of the neurology of the child, the history of the syndrome of dyslexia, and of its treatment, was to take a sharply different turn. It is difficult to pinpoint the historical moment at which this occurred. Perhaps it was the 1946 publication of Robinson's *Why Pupils Fail in Reading* (26) that marked the turning point. In any case, there is no disputing the cleavage that occurred between the medical profession (responsible, as we have seen, for the definition of dyslexia) and the educators. The syndrome of dyslexia itself, which seemed to be accepted without question by educators in the 1920s, fell into disrepute. It is a disrepute that has continued to our own day.

For an understanding of how this occurred one must look not only to the professional literature on reading disability of the time, but to the general educational climate. In the late 1920s, the teaching of reading was emerging as a specialty with its own covey of experts. Arthur Gates, working closely with Edward Lee Thorndike and William S. Gray, headed an array of persons across the United States whose chief interests and expertise lay in the area of reading disabilities. While the normal reader was not neglected (basal reading textbooks such as the famous Scott, Foresman series, coauthored by William S. Gray, were the products of this period), the disabled reader seemed to provide more professional challenge. In 1945, Helen Robinson, who worked with William S. Gray at the University of Chicago, assembled an extraordinary battery of medical, psychological and educational experts to examine a number of children who were failing to learn to read. After administering extensive tests, the team concluded that there was no *one* cause of reading disability. The children concerned exhibited a wide array of symptoms, ranging from deficiencies in oral language, defective hearing and vision, to unsatisfactory emotional adjustment. Robinson therefore postulated a theory of multiple causation for reading disability (26). The term "dyslexia" became disreputable, and the attention of the educators turned towards correcting the many defects the child presented.

One rather dramatic result of all this was that the spotlight was turned away from the teacher to the children. It was, as it were, the children's fault (because of their various disabilities) that they had failed to learn how to read. It is ironic that while many educators opposed the notion of a syndrome of dyslexia partly because it seemed to offer such a poor prognosis for children, the alternate hypothesis (that of multiple etiology) left children in no better position. The teacher who had failed to teach children to read could always point to something in their home backgrounds, personalities, or physical conditions that prevented them from benefiting from instruction. The educational psychologists (the experts such as Gates, Witty, and Gray all came from the field of educational psychology, not from the ranks of classroom teachers) had ensured that teachers could all too easily rationalize the children's failures.

A further result was that the medical profession, by now heavily outnumbered, opted out of the discussion, at least in the United States. Meanwhile, educational researchers spent a great deal of time, at no profit to anyone in particular, on what was an attempt to discredit Orton's theory of incomplete lateralization. In spite of the fact that Orton himself had said that where there was no motor disorder (that is, no speech or writing defects) associated with strephosymbolia, the problem of handedness was not important (25:173), many researchers attempted to explore the correlation of eye dominance (itself a most questionable concept), foot dominance and, above all, handedness with reading disability (14). Better constructed modern studies have discredited the importance of handedness in reading disability but found that an immature left-right body awareness is present among a significantly larger number of disabled readers than among normal readers (2).

In Britain, there was a similar disenchantment among British educational psychologists with the whole notion of a syndrome of dyslexia. Thanks, originally, to the work of Burt (6) and Schonell (28), a strong tradition grew in Britain that reading disability was to be regarded as part of a wider syndrome of educational disability, which itself had many causes, some of them deriving from the children's unfavorable home conditions (29).

To be fair to the educational psychologists in both Britain and the United States, there were aspects of the syndrome of dyslexia which justifiably caused some skepticism. Foremost among these was the controversy over the symptoms of the syndrome. Physicians were far from unanimous in their assessment of what was, or was not, a symptom of dyslexia. The World Federation of Neurology's research group on developmental dyslexia (a term that itself implied organic immaturity rather than the Hinshelwood-style organic brain defect) attempted a definition in 1968. (British Neurologist Macdonald Critchley, long interested in the condition, chaired the group.) The 1968 definition ran as follows: "A disorder manifested by difficulty in learning to read despite conventional instruction, adequate intelligence, and sociocultural opportunity. It is dependent upon fundamental cognitve disabilities which are frequently of constitutional origin" (9:11).

Critics have objected to this definition on many grounds, including the point that, if this definition be correct, only intelligent middle class children can be presumed to be suffering from dyslexia. The dull children of the poor apparently must be suffering from something else. Moreover, according to this definition, the only clear symptom is the child's inability to read (29). On the other hand, there were also listings of symptoms of dyslexia that left virtually every child open to being diagnosed as a dyslexic. These ranged from perceptual and motor difficulties to anomalies of development such as late talking or handedness (22).

One of the responses to these difficulties (at least in Great Britain) by some educational psychologists has been to formulate a new definition with no etiological implications. The category of "specific reading retardation" has been established to include those children whose reading scores fall at least two standard errors below the scores predicted by age and intelligence (33). Critics of this new definition point out that no educational implications spring from identifying a child as falling within this "specific reading retardation" group and that the burden of proof still remains with those who wish to distinguish the group from that of children who are merely backward (29).

Neurologists, on the other hand, maintain stoutly that the existence of a syndrome of dyslexia is validated by four components: the persistence of reading and writing disability into adulthood, the peculiar and specific nature of the errors in reading and writing, the familial incidence of the defect, and its frequent association with other symbol-defects (8:11).

Professional Rapprochement

If, in Britain, the current scene is still one of considerable antagonism between educational psychologists on the one hand and neurologists and other physicians on the other, there are glimmerings, in the United States, of some kind of rapprochement. The fresh national conviction that the learning disabled child is as much entitled to education at the public expense as is the normal child has given new life to the interest in dyslexic children. There have been three national conferences on the subject in the past fifteen years: at Johns Hopkins University in 1961; at Philadelphia, under the auspices of the American Committee on Optics in 1966; and at San Marcos, Texas, under the sponsorship of the U.S. Office of Education in 1967. This last conference, incidentally, came to the conclusion that there was no prospect of arriving at a definition of dyslexia that would be generally acceptable (32). The following year, several symposia were devoted to the topic of dyslexia by the International Reading Association at its annual convention (30). So, even if a satisfactory definition of dyslexia still seems remote, the two sides involved are at least beginning to communicate again.

At a recent conference at Johns Hopkins University, this time sponsored by a symposium on research in early childhood education, the theme "aspects of reading acquisition" brought together psychologists, reading specialists, pediatricians, and neurologists. Frank Benson, a highly regarded neurologist and a colleague of Norman Geschwind, devoted his paper to a discussion of alexia (3, 16).

Historically, then, the wheel has gone full circle. Once again the neurologist's expertise in the damaged brain of the adult appears to offer hope to physician and educator alike that more light will be shed on the child who presents so many symptoms resembling those of the adult with acquired alexia. However, just as alexia may be distinguished into types, according to the portion of the brain affected and the symptoms presented, so too have three varieties of dyslexia been identified (*3, 20*).

While the turn of the century belief in "word centers" in the brain has been discredited, it still remains true that lesions in specific parts of the brain may be identified as those which are almost invariably accompanied by a loss in reading ability. It would be rash and unprofitable to speculate upon theoretical damage to equivalent areas in the brain of the child. Even if we could somehow discover that the same areas of the brain are malfunctioning in the child as in the alexic adult, we would be no closer to recommending treatment. It is function, after all, that is the educator's primary concern; structure is of secondary interest. Nonetheless, there are provocative suggestions for remediating dyslexic children—if we accept, as this writer does, the reality of the syndrome—that may be gleaned from the early neurological studies and educational experiments with alexic adults.

Implications for Remediation

The first and most obvious lesson is that remediation must take place through channels other than the visual alone. The child must employ his auditory and tactile senses to compensate for his inability to learn visually in the conventional way. The fully elaborated techniques of Samuel Torrey Orton and of Grace Fernald should be reassessed experimentally. The neuropsychological rationale for the kinesthetic approach (employed in different ways by both Orton and Fernald) derives from the universal testimony of early physicians that their alexic patients could recognize letters and words in this manner. While Dejerine's patient, Oscar, never learned to read again in this way [it took him too long, explained Dejerine (*11*:83)] we have convincing evidence from Fernald's and Orton's case studies that the more adaptable child can learn to read by kinesthetic means, whether it be by Fernald's pure kinesthetic approach (*13*) or by a systematic phonics method kinesthetically fortified by the act of writing (*25*).

Moreover, there is another clue from the early case studies of alexia that has never really been pursued: the ability of some alexic subjects to read by spelling the words syllable by syllable. (Learning to read by spelling was the only methodology in use for centuries in the English speaking nations.) Hinshelwood's patient was able to relearn how to read by going through a child's primer in this way, albeit slowly and haltingly, just like a child learning to read (*17*). The evidence for the ability of alexic patients to recognize words by spelling them (provided, of course, that they can still recognize letters) spans the years from the close of the nineteenth century to modern times. Bastian cited the case of a shipwright with wordblindness and hemianopsia: "Although he names every letter without mistake," his physician had reported, "he is unable to tell or understand a single word, no matter how short, unless he spells it out aloud like a child learning its first lesson" (*1*:196). Similarly, Benson (*3*:13) has noted that patients with pure (primary) alexia can decipher short words by spelling them out in this way. (In fact, a key test of alexia without agraphia is the ability of the patient with pure alexia to recognize words spelled aloud. The patient suffering from agraphia in addition to alexia cannot recognize spelled words.) It is surely no mere coincidence that the Gillingham-Stillman approach (one of the two Orton-derived approaches) is the only teaching method known to this writer that uses oral spelling as a word recognition technique. The technique known as "simultaneous oral spelling," where the child spells a word aloud as he writes it, is said to be very helpful to the severely reading disabled child (*15*).

There are, of course, many hazards in extrapolating from the adult who has lost a language skill to the child who has never yet learned it. But there is a compelling reason to pursue this line of investigation further: quite simply, the insights gained from alexic adults provide the only clues that we have to go on. The practical implications that flow from our accepting the analogy of dyslexia to alexia justify our taking the reality of the syndrome as our working hypothesis. Only by so doing can we once again engage the energies of educators, physicians, and psychologists in a mutual endeavor to assist the reading disabled child. It is not too late for these specialists to pool anew their own particular skills. A crossfertilization of these disciplines must prove beneficial to the children, whose interests we all have at heart.

References

1. Bastian, H. Charleton. *A Treatise on Aphasia and Other Speech Defects.* New York: D. Appleton, 1898.
2. Belmont, Lillian, and Herbert G. Birch. "Lateral Dominance, Lateral Awareness, and Reading Disability," *Child Development,* 36 (March 1965), 57-71.
3. Benson, D. Frank. "Alexia," in John T. Guthrie (Ed.), *Aspects of Reading Acquisition.* Baltimore: Johns Hopkins University Press, 1976, 7-36.
4. Betts, Emmett, and Thelma Marshall Betts. *An Index of Professional Literature on Reading.* New York: American Book, 1945.
5. Bowers, Elmer. "A Case of Congenital Wordblindness," *Educational Research Bulletin,* 4 (November 1925), 344-345.
6. Burt, C. *The Backward Child.* London: University of London Press, 1937.
7. Claiborne, J. Herbert. "Types of Congenital Symbol Amblyopia," *Journal of the American Medical Association,* 47 (December 1906), 1813-1816.
8. Critchley, Macdonald. *Developmental Dyslexia.* Springfield, Illinois: Charles C. Thomas, 1964.
9. Critchley, Macdonald. *The Dyslexic Child* (Second and augmented edition of *Developmental Dyslexia*). Springfield, Illinois: Charles C. Thomas, 1970.
10. deHirsch, Katrina. "Specific Dyslexia or Strephosymbolia," *Folia Phoniatrica,* 4 (1952), 231-248.
11. Dejerine, M.J. "Contribution a l'étude anatomo-pathologique et clinique des différentes variétés de cécité verbale," *Comptes Rendus Hebdomadaires des Séances et Mémoires de la Société de Biologie,* 4 (Sér 9, 1892), 61-90.
12. Fernald, Grace M. "On Certain Language Disabilities, Their Nature and Treatment," *Mental Measurements Monographs,* 11 (August 1936).
13. Fernald, Grace M. *Remedial Techniques in Basic School Subjects.* New York: McGraw-Hill, 1943.
14. Gates, Arthur I., and Guy L. Bond. "Relation of Handedness, Eyesighting and Acuity Dominance to Reading," *Journal of Educational Psychology,* 27 (1936), 450-456.
15. Gillingham, Anna, and Bessie E. Stillman. *Remedial Training for Children with Specific Disability in Reading, Spelling, and Penmanship,* Seventh Edition. New York: Educators Publishing Service, 1960.
16. Guthrie, John T. (Ed.). *Aspects of Reading Acquisition.* Baltimore: Johns Hopkins University Press, 1976.
17. Hinshelwood, James. "Wordblindness and Visual Memory," *The Lancet,* 2 (December 1895), 1564-1570.
18. Hinshelwood, James. *Congenital Wordblindness.* London: H.K. Lewis, 1917.
19. Luria, Aleksandr R. *Higher Cortical Functions in Man.* New York: Basic Books, 1966.
20. Mattis, T., J.H. French, and I. Rapin. "Dyslexia in Children and Young Adults; Three Independent Neuropsychological Symptoms," *Developmental Medicine and Child Neurology,* 17 (April 1975), 150-163.
21. Morgan, W. Pringle. "A Case of Congenital Wordblindness," *British Medical Journal,* 2 (1896), 1378.
22. Newton, M. *Dyslexia: A Guide for Teachers and Parents.* Birmingham: University of Aston, 1971.
23. Orton, Samuel T. "Wordblindness in School Children," *Archives of Neurological Psychiatry,* 14 (1925), 581-615.

24. Orton, Samuel T. "An Impediment to Learning to Read: A Neurological Explanation of the Reading Disability," *School and Society*, 28 (1928), 286-290.
25. Orton, Samuel T. *Reading, Writing, and Speech Problems in Children*. New York: Norton, 1937.
26. Robinson, Helen M. *Why Pupils Fail in Reading*. Chicago: University of Chicago Press, 1946.
27. Schmitt, Clara. "Developmental Alexia: Congenital Wordblindness, or Inability to Learn to Read," *Elementary School Journal*, 18 (May 1918), 680-700; 18 (June 1918), 757-769.
28. Schonell, F. *Backwardness in the Basic Subjects*. Edinburgh: Oliver and Boyd, 1942.
29. Singleton, C.H. "Dyslexia or Specific Reading Retardation: A Psychological Critique," paper presented at the Thirteenth Annual Conference of the United Kingdom Reading Association, University of Durham, 1976.
30. Spache, George D. (Ed.). *Reading Disability and Perception*. Newark, Delaware: International Reading Association, 1969.
31. Spalding, Romalda. *The Writing Road to Reading*, Second Revised Edition. New York: William Morrow, 1969.
32. Strother, C.R. "Minimal Cerebral Dysfunction: A Historical Overview," in Felix F. de la Cruz, Bernard H. Fox, and Richard H. Roberts (Eds.), *Minimal Brain Dysfunction*. New York: New York Academy of Sciences, 1973, 6-17.
33. Yule, W., et al. "Over and Underachievement in Reading: Distribution in the General Population," *British Journal of Educational Psychology*, 44 (1974), 1-12.

Learning Disability and Reading: Theory or Fact?

Robert Karlin
Queens College, City University of New York

On a coast-to-coast TV talk show a well known comedian explained that his son who had been experiencing difficulties in learning to read and adjusting to school requirements was suffering from a learning disability which he believed afflicts many children. He went on to say how well the boy was progressing, now that he attended a special school which specialized in the treatment of learning disabilities. He did regret that many parents of children so afflicted were not able to afford the expense of obtaining this specialized help.

The belief that children who are doing poorly in reading (and possibly other areas) suffer from a learning disability is reflected in policies adopted by some schools. Where in the past they have employed reading teachers to help children overcome difficulties in learning to read, now they seek teachers trained in special education to teach learning disabled children. We assume such schools believe the latter practice is in the best interests of the children. We do know that federal and state monies are available to support the teaching of children who are identified as learning disabled. If we believe that learning disabilities are entities in themselves and that reading teachers are less well prepared to work with learning disabled children who are reading disabled, it makes sense to take advantage of the financial support available to school districts which support learning disability programs conducted by learning disability teachers. But are there justifications for concluding that the rationales underlying learning disabilities are sound and that they ought to be applied to reading disabilities which might be described as one manifestation of learning disabilities? Should we view the concept of learning disabilities as theory or fact?

To be certain that we are thinking of the same population considered to be *learning disabled*, the following description is generally accepted by specialists in the field (*18*):

> Children with special learning disabilities exhibit a disorder in one or more of the basic psychological processes involved in understanding or using spoken or written language. These may be manifested in disorders of listening, thinking, talking, reading, writing, spelling, or arithmetic. They include conditions which have been referred to as perceptual handicaps, brain injury, minimal brain damage, minimal brain dysfunction, dyslexia, developmental aphasia, etc....

The definition excludes learning problems that are due primarily to other physical causes as well as emotional and environmental factors.

A Bit of History

It is interesting to note that the aforementioned definition includes terminologies having their origins in purported conditions involving reading disabilities. Those who sought explanations for reading failures and could not account for them by citing common physical, psychological, intellectual, and environmental deficits resorted to negative reasoning. If failure cannot be attributed to factors that are measurable, then it must be attributed to hidden ones, however "soft" they might be. Thus, in referring to the problems of children whose poor reading was characterized by an inability to readily recognize or identify words, Hinshelwood (*14*) used the term *congenital wordblindness* to explain the cause of the disability. He was saying that these children could not read because of some neurophysiological disorder. Orton (*19*) suggested that minimal brain damage accounted for serious reading difficulties. Critchley (*3*) used the term *developmental dyslexia* to refer to a constitutional disorder of the nervous system that produces reading failure. Rabinovitch (*21*) attributed some reading failures to "a basic disturbed pattern of neurological organization" and other reading failures to brain damage, in other words "dyslexia." Clements (1) preferred to explain reading failures as products of "minimal brain dysfunction," while Delacato (4) attributed them to neurological immaturity and failure to establish cerebral dominance. This brief summary does not include others who also sought to identify difficulties in learning to read with neurological etiologies.

There is not much hard evidence to support any of these explanations. Proponents rely on the presence of subtle symptoms of possible neurological dysfunction as well as an inability to link reading failures to other conditions as evidence for their beliefs. Some also point to the fact that a tendency toward severe reading problems seems to run in families, a condition which could suggest genetic factors. These findings are more negative than positive and are used in the absence of hard data to infer causality. Until it can be demonstrated that dyslexia, however defined or described, is a reality, reliance upon it to explain poor reading performance is, to say the least, hardly supportable or useful. I should reiterate to what conditions learning disabilities are ascribed: brain damage, minimal brain damage, dyslexia, minimal brain dysfunction." Are they any different from those we have just reviewed?

Theory and Practice

It is apparent that when most authorities speak of learning disabilities they associate them with brain damage or some impairments of the brain. In the overwhelming number of cases involving children identified as learning disabled (estimates vary but it is believed that from one to three percent of the school population experience real learning difficulties), there is no clinical evidence of brain damage. How, then, can they say that the learning disabilities are due to some impairment of the brain or minimal brain dysfunction? Since some of the symptoms of brain damage are found in varying degrees in individuals with learning disabilities, it must mean that such persons are so afflicted, however minimally. Included among the symptoms are hyperactivity, perceptual-motor impairments, coordination deficits, disorders of attention, impulsivity, disorders of memory and thinking. There is no need to point out the fallacy in such reasoning, particularly when there is ample evidence of children who manifest one or more of these symptoms but who are not learning disabled. Some research studies bear on this issue. Routh and Roberts (23) examined 73 boys and 16 girls between the ages of six years, five months and thirteen years, eight months for symptoms cited above. These children had been referred to a university clinic because of their inadequate performances in school. No relationships between symptoms were found except between motor skills deficits and impulsivity and between inattentiveness and failures in memory. Moreover, symptoms were unrelated to scores on achievement tests. Crinella (2) studied 90 children, 19 with known brain damage, 34 diagnosed as suffering from minimal brain damage or dysfunction. The investigator reported that in some ways the children with known brain damage were unlike the children identified as minimally impaired. Moreover, the investigator failed to find a set of symptoms that fitted all the children diagnosed as minimally impaired.

Attempts to identify with psychological tests children who have been medically diagnosed as brain damaged have not been very successful. McIntosh (17) reported that it was not possible on the basis of their performances to identify them as brain damaged. In reviewing these findings, one observer raises the question that if grossly impaired children with known brain damage cannot be differentiated as having or not having brain damage, "how much less likely is it to substantiate something as vague as minimal brain dysfunction?" (22).

Owen and colleagues (20) studied 76 children who were significantly below grade level in reading and spelling. Each received extensive neurological examinations including an electroencephalogram. In only three cases did the children show hard symptoms of organic damage. They concluded that in their sample it was not possible to consider organic damage as a major causative factor of learning problems. The results of these and other related studies must cause us to raise questions or at least withhold firm judgments about the hypothesis that learning disabilities and minimal brain damage or dysfunction are intimately related and that learning disabilities are *caused* by what is referred to as minimal brain damage or dysfunction.

Those who have worked with known cases of grossly damaged brain-injured individuals report impairments in their perceptual-motor processes. Comparable impairments have been noted in children without brain damage but who experience learning difficulties. It appears that because of some similarities of perceptual-motor performances in both groups some theorists and practitioners have concluded that the latter group must have at least minimal brain damage or be suffering from minimal brain dysfunction. Among those are Kephart (*15*), Frostig (*7*), and Cruikshank (*12*). Moreover, many who have made this observation believe that unless children can adequately perform in these areas, they will not be able to succeed in subsequent learning tasks. They also believe that children whose perceptual-motor processes are impaired can overcome these handicaps with appropriate training and that such training will positively influence learning performance.

Without going into the theoretical frameworks involving perceptual-motor models, suffice it to say that they involve dimensions of space and time. It is on these dimensions that Kephart bases his training program of bodily movements such as walking on a balance beam, hopping and jumping, imitation and drawing, copying, and eye following. Getman et al. (*8*) advocate a similar program with emphasis upon eye movements and hand-eye coordination. Frostig concentrates on such activities as feeling and drawing shapes, following directions, recognizing objects through feeling, differentiating between visual and auditory patterns, and recognizing objects in pictures.

How effective are these programs and what impact do they have on academic progress? We can do no more than summarize the results since there are numerous investigations involving the aforementioned programs. Insofar as the Frostig program is concerned, several investigators reported that children who participated in training programs did not do any better on specific tasks than children who did not receive the training. Other investigators noted that the program improved perception. We might conclude that the findings on this question are inconclusive; that is, at times they have been shown to be effective as well as ineffective in improving perceptual skills of children. The findings on the program's effectiveness in improving reading performance are less equivocal. Most investigators report no concomitant improvement in reading as a result of the training program (*13*).

How effective are the Kephart and Getman programs? In the majority of the studies reviewed by Goodman and Hammill (*10*), experimental subjects did not perform better than control subjects on visual-motor tasks. In the same review the authors reported that in ten studies that investigated the impact of the programs on school achievement, there was little evidence to conclude that they produced improved academic performances. I should point out that Getman and others (*8*) have reported significantly better performance in reading for experimental children who participated in a reading program supplemented by perceptual-motor training, but such positive reports are to be judged along with the larger number that report negative results. However generous we are in interpreting the findings, we cannot conclude from the available evidence that perceptual-motor programs are likely to improve reading performance.

One additional observation regarding perceptual-motor programs. If children perform poorly in any of the areas covered by them, there is no reason why efforts to help children overcome these weaknesses should not be made. But it is an entirely different matter to assume that in working to overcome these weaknesses teachers are helping children to improve their reading ability.

A program somewhat related to those described, in that it involves so-called neurological organization and is recommended for disabled readers, is that of Delacato (*5*). He believes that individuals who fail to establish cerebral dominance have nervous systems that have not matured and that learning disabilities arise from this lack of complete organization. In order to facilitate movement to maturity Delacato recommends treatment that includes crawling and creeping, sleeping in designated positions, and activities to establish hand-eye dominance.

How valid are these treatments? Delacato has cited fifteen studies to support them. However, in a critical review of these studies Glass and Robbins (*9*) concluded that "without exception these experiments contained major faults in design and analysis.... Enough doubt has been cast on the results of all the experiments that either replications of them under improved conditions or the publication of adequate research reports will be required before the conclusions drawn from them are admissable." The reviewers cited several whose results indicated lack of association between cerebral dominance and reading.

The use of drugs to treat learning disabled children who display hyperactivity is not uncommon. Since hyperactivity is often associated with learning disabilities, it is an easy step to erroneously conclude that, if drugs like methylphenidate reduce instead of increase hyperactivity in these children, they must be minimally brain damaged or suffering from minimal brain dysfunction (24). There is no doubt that medication can make it possible for some children to become amenable to learning, but medical specialists are aware that there are inherent dangers in administering drugs to some children. Moreover, there doesn't seem to be much evidence that drug therapy is very effective in improving learning. Therefore, this therapy must be used with care, it must be monitored for adverse side effects and must be accompanied by instructional programs.

One final thought about tangential treatments for learning disabled children. Until proponents can demonstrate that a given treatment actually has an impact upon reading performance, we must view the treatment with caution. This does not mean that the underlying rationales are invalid; but until it can be shown that treatments do change behaviors, we must continue to question their validity.

Insofar as teaching reading to learning disabled children with word recognition weaknesses is concerned, there is no agreement as to how they should be treated. One author, in discussing traditional and innovative procedures and materials, suggests that "each ... may be useful for the child with learning disabilities, but the teacher must be aware of the attributes and limitations of the method or material" (16). Another refers to visual dyslexic children for whom isolated phonics instruction is recommended and to auditory dyslexic children for whom the so-called whole word method is suggested. If children are visual-auditory dyslexic, then remediation "must be accomplished through the tactual kinesthetic channel" (6). These latter recommendations sound much like those suggested for modality teaching for which there is little evidence at hand. It would be safe to say that the usual reading treatments for children who are diagnosed as learning disabled follow some form of the alphabetic approach which stresses the learning of letter-sound associations followed by the blending of sounds to form words.

Surely if children with a learning disability are a unique population, they ought to be uniquely treated. But this is not the case. It seems quite clear that learning disability specialists depend in large measure upon procedures found in reading methods textbooks. It would not be difficult to identify methods and materials recommended for children who have no learning problems as being appropriate for learning disabled children. This fact raises more doubts as to the validity of learning disability rationales.

In conclusion, there appear to be many unresolved questions regarding theories of learning disabilities and their translation into practice. It seems only reasonable not to place our trust in procedures which have not been shown to produce results claimed for them. Until demonstrated otherwise, we should place our confidence in procedures based upon sound psychological and linguistic principles. And we ought not entrust our children to anyone who is not firmly grounded in them. Well prepared reading teachers are the ones who are best qualified to work with children who have reading difficulties. We should not be willing to settle for less.

References

1. Clements, Sam D. *Minimal Brain Dysfunction in Children: Terminology and Identification.* Public Health Service Publication No. 1415. Washington, D.C.: U.S. Government Printing Office, 1966.
2. Crinella, F.M. "Identification of Brain Dysfunction Syndromes in Children through Profile Analysis: Patterns Associated with So-Called Minimal Brain Dysfunction," *Journal of Abnormal Psychology*, 82 (1973), 33-45.
3. Critchley, Macdonald. *Developmental Dyslexia.* Springfield, Illinois: Charles C. Thomas, 1964.
4. Delacato, Carl H. *The Diagnosis and Treatment of Speech and Reading Problems.* Springfield, Illinois: Charles C. Thomas, 1963.
5. Delacato, Carl H. *Neurological Organization and Reading.* Springfield, Illinois: Charles C. Thomas, 1966.
6. Fass, Larry A. *Learning Disabilities: A Competency Based Approach.* Boston: Houghton Mifflin, 1976.

7. Frostig, M., and P. Maslow. *Learning Problems in the Classroom.* New York: Grune and Stratton, 1973.
8. Getman, Gerald N., and others. *Developing Learning Readiness: A Visual-Motor Tactile Skills Program.* Manchester, Missouri: Webster, 1968.
9. Glass, Gene V., and Melvyn P. Robbins. "A Critique of Experiments on the Neurological Organization in Reading Performance," *Reading Research Quarterly*, 3 (1967), 5-51.
10. Goodman, L., and D. Hammill. "The Effectiveness of Kephart-Getman Activities in Developing Perceptual Motor and Cognitive Skills," *Focus on Exceptional Children*, 4 (1973), 1-9.
11. Haliwell, D.P., and H.A. Solan. "The Effects of a Supplemental Perceptual Training Program on Reading Achievement," *Exceptional Children*, 38 (1972), 613-621.
12. Hallahan, D.P., and W.M. Cruickshank. *Psychoeducational Foundations of Learning Disabilities.* Englewood Cliffs, New Jersey: Prentice-Hall, 1973.
13. Hammill, Donald, and others. "Visual-Motor Processes: Can We Train Them?" *Reading Teacher*, 27 (1974), 469-478.
14. Hinshelwood, James. *Congenital Wordblindness.* London: H.K. Lewis, 1917.
15. Kephart, N.C. *The Slow Learner in the Classroom*, Second Edition. Columbus, Ohio: Charles E. Merrill, 1971.
16. Lerner, Janet W. *Children with Learning Disabilities*, Second Edition. Boston: Houghton Mifflin, 1976.
17. McIntosh, W.J. "Clinical and Statistical Approaches to the Assessment of Brain Damage in Children," *Journal of Abnormal Child Psychology*, 1 (1973), 181-195.
18. National Advisory Committee on Handicapped Children, *Special Education for Handicapped Children*, First Annual Report. Washington, D.C.: U.S. Department of Health, Education, and Welfare, 1968, 4.
19. Orton, Samuel T. *Reading, Writing, and Speech Problems in Children.* New York: W.W. Norton, 1937.
20. Owen, F.W., and others. *Learning Disorders in Children: Sibling Studies.* Monographs of the Society for Research in Child Development, Serial No. 144, 1971.
21. Rabinovitch, Ralph D. "Dyslexia: Psychiatric Consideration," in John Money (Ed.), *Progress and Research Needs in Dyslexia.* Baltimore: Johns Hopkins Press, 1962, 73-79.
22. Ross, Alan O. *Psychological Aspects of Learning Disabilities and Reading Disorders.* New York: McGraw-Hill, 1976, 69.
23. Routh, D.K., and R.D. Roberts. "Minimal Brain Dysfunction in Children," *Psychological Reports*, 31 (1972), 307-314.
24. Wender, P.H. *Minimum Brain Dysfunction in Children.* New York: Wiley, 1971.

Current Issues in the Diagnosis and Treatment of Reading Disabilities

Albert J. Harris
Emeritus, City University of New York

Current issues in reading diagnosis and remediation may be classified as political issues, diagnostic issues, and remedial issues. Only a few of the most important issues can be discussed in a paper of this length.

Political Issues

The main political issue that has emerged in recent years is the overlapping between the concepts of learning disability and reading disability, and the consequent overlapping of jurisdictions between reading specialists and learning disability specialists.

The Children with Specific Learning Disabilities Act of 1969 defined a learning disability as a "disorder in one or more of the basic psychological processes involved in understanding or using spoken or written language," and listed dyslexia among the conditions included. It did not provide any definite diagnostic criteria. As a result, recent state laws in this area use various terms such as perceptually handicapped, educationally handicapped, and minimally brain damaged, as well as learning disabled, and there is no uniformity in the definitions used or the criteria specified (5).

Federal assistance to the states is covered by Public Law 94-142, Education of the Handicapped Act. Proposed rules to implement the section on specific learning disabilities were published in the *Federal Register* on November 29, 1976, and after months of discussion, final rules were approved and published in the *Federal Register*, Vol. 42, No. 250, December 29, 1977; they went into effect in September 1978.

Evaluation of a child suspected of having a specific learning disability is to be made by a multidisciplinary team including the child's teacher (or other suitable teacher) and at least one person "qualified to conduct individual diagnostic examinations of children, such as a school psychologist, speech-language pathologist, or remedial reading teacher." The criterion set is that a child, having been provided with appropriate learning experiences, has a "severe discrepancy" between achievement and intellectual ability in one or more of the following areas: oral expression, listening comprehension, written expression, basic reading skill, reading comprehension, mathematics calculation, mathematics reasoning. Those whose severe discrepancy is primarily the result of one of the following are not classifiable as having a specific learning disability: visual, hearing, or motor handicap; mental retardation; emotional disturbance; environmental, cultural, or economic disadvantage.

A formula proposed in the preliminary draft for determining whether or not a discrepancy is severe was deleted from the final regulations, leaving it to the multidisciplinary team to make the determination. An upper limit or cap of not more than 2 percent was also deleted. Study of the child must include an individual intelligence examination and observation of the child in the classroom by a team member other than the child's teacher. A written report must be prepared by the team stating the evidence on which the team's conclusion is based.

These regulations allow for considerable local variation in interpretation, and the ambiguity of the term "severe discrepancy" makes it difficult to estimate what percentage of the school population will qualify as having specific learning disabilities. However, the 2 percent cap that was part of the preliminary draft indicates the intention to limit funding, and the inclusion of children with receptive and productive speech and language problems, writing difficulties, and mathematical difficulties in the category of specific learning disabilities suggests that the percent with reading disabilities will probably not be more than 2 or 3 percent of the school population—more in some school districts, less in others.

What will be the effect on jobs for reading specialists when this procedure is adopted? Probably not the catastrophe that some are fearing.

First, the number of disabled readers that might be classified as learning disabilities and assigned to learning disability teachers is probably less than 3 percent of the school population. If we assume that 15 percent of the school population have some degree of reading disability, the remaining 12 or 13 percent are far more than can be cared for by present remedial reading programs and personnel. For example, a recent survey in Delaware showed that 28 percent of schools had no special reading programs and, in the schools that did, only 41 percent had remedial reading teachers who were certified as reading specialists (11). And a recent survey in New York, New Jersey, and Connecticut seems to show no diminution in positions for reading teachers in the near future (13).

Second, the most severe cases of reading disability are the ones hardest to teach, slowest to learn, most likely to have complex combinations of handicapping factors, and most likely to require intensive, highly individualized, and long continued tutoring. Relieved of them, the reading specialist could provide improved service to the remaining reading disabled children.

Third, it is not unlikely that a situation similar to that in psychotherapy will evolve. The bulk of psychotherapy today is carried on by psychologists, social workers, and even some nurses. It is recognized that similar competencies can be achieved through more than one kind of training. If some reading specialists are particularly interested in the most severe cases and are particularly good with them, it is probable that their expertise will be recognized and put to use. However, it is clear that if reading specialists are to function effectively as members of multidisciplinary teams, they will be well advised to include individual intelligence testing and some work in learning disabilities in graduate study. A new and broader type of professional preparation may evolve.

Causation and Diagnosis

The search for the causes of reading disabilities has become more sophisticated. There is growing acceptance of the idea that the reading disability population contains subgroups with different and sometimes contrasting characteristics, so that comparing a group of the reading disabled with a group of normal readers is a useless type of activity. Among the subgroups suggested by recent research are the following: those with auditory and language deficiency, those with visual perceptive deficiency, and those with both auditory and visual deficits; those with an arousal deficiency and those unable to sustain attention; those who are slow but comparatively accurate versus the fast but sloppy readers; those who respond favorably to stimulant drugs and those helped by depressants or tranquilizers; those with demonstrable central nervous system dysfunctions and those without.

There has been renewed interest in brain functioning as related to reading. It seems well established that the left hemisphere is dominant for functions involving language, logical thinking, and sequence, and that the right hemisphere is dominant for Gestalt perception of space and perception of other nonlinguistic patterns such as music—in most left handed people as well as nearly all of the right handed. The dominant hemisphere for language has been studied using the dichotic listening technique, in which different stimuli are fed simultaneously to the two ears, and the side with the more complete recall is thought to represent the dominant hemisphere. The results of these experiments with children are inconsistent, however, and their interpretation is somewhat ambiguous (12).

Another part of the brain to receive current attention is the cerebellum, a large mass below the cerebral hemispheres which controls movement and fine coordination, in close relation with the semicircular canals of the inner ear which provide the sense of balance. A high proportion of children with reading disability are reported to show abnormal cerebellar-vestibular functioning by de Quiros of Argentina (2) and by Frank and Levinson of New York (3).

A diagnostic breakthrough is claimed for a new, computerized method of interpreting the electrical currents of the brain (4, 8). The Quantitative Electrophysiological Battery is said to take only 15 minutes and to provide diagnostic differentiations of superior accuracy. Like all claims for radical innovations, this one requires independent verification.

With regard to diagnostic procedures, there is fairly general agreement that the reading specialist should concentrate on analysis of a child's reading and closely related skills, and refer the minority of nonresponding cases to multidisciplinary centers or clinics for more detailed study. The reading specialist is increasingly called upon to organize for a child a learning plan which can be carried on in whole or part by someone else—classroom teacher, parent, aide, or volunteer. Thus, skill in the translation of diagnostic findings into practical teaching procedures and in selection of appropriate materials should be a major objective of programs that train reading specialists.

It seems probable that reading specialists have been making insufficient use of two readily available diagnostic procedures. One of these is the use of sample lessons, which have been recommended for many years (6). From performance on diagnostic reading tests one can determine what the children have learned and what remains to be mastered. In a sample lesson, one can get a preview of how children are likely to respond to remedial teaching—their motivation and attention, presence or absence of resistance, as well as rate of learning and adequacy of retention. By trying alternative modes of teaching, one can often select the particular one that is most appropriate for a particular child.

The second neglected procedure is getting the child's own point of view. As Meichenbaum (9:439) has written, "...one infrequently, if ever, hears anything from the child. His perception of the task, his description of his strategy, his appraisal of his performance, and his assessment of his own situation (will he go to a separate class; does he think that people feel he's crazy; is he ridiculed as he goes for assessment, etc.) are absent. It is suggested that the children have something to tell us, if we would only ask and then listen."

Remedial Treatment

Reading specialists need to recognize that certain kinds of noneducational treatment can be helpful in specific cases. Findings on the effectiveness of stimulant drugs have been summarized by Conners (1) as follows: "Basically, then, inattentive, distractible, and impulsive children who fail certain academic functions despite adequate general intelligence may have secondary learning disabilities that improve with stimulant drug treatment. Other forms of learning disability, e.g., specific dyslexia, are unlikely to show much change except insofar as the drugs simply increase general alertness in bored or fatigued children." There seems to be no opposition to the notion that when a child has a serious personal maladjustment problem as well as a reading disability, both should be treated, whether or not they are causally related. The recent trend toward family therapy seems a wholesome one.

Behavior modification is an area of special interest to remedial teachers. There is a new name, and a new set of explanatory concepts, for practices which good remedial teachers have been employing for decades: analyzing the global task into learnable bits; identification of key items to be learned first; determining an appropriate sequence; adjusting teaching to the child's rate and style of learning; and, above all, judicious use of many kinds of reward.

A recent development in behavior modification is Meichenbaum's emphasis on the child's way of thinking as a determiner of his behavior in a learning situation. He has shown that by teaching a child to talk to himself differently one can alter his thinking, his self-image, and his feelings about learning (9, 10).

Turning to remedial teaching, probably the main current issue is how best to use the reading specialist's time. As more time becomes needed for diagnostic work and consultations with teachers and parents, less time is left for direct work with children. The reading teacher's domain, in many schools, has been restructured into a reading resource room with many functions. One way to meet this change is to multiply the reading specialist's hands by making maximum use of assistants. These may include paraprofessional aides, students in teacher education programs, adult volunteers including parents (assigned to children other than their own), and older children tutoring younger children. The recruitment, training, scheduling, and supervision of teaching assistants are becoming increasingly important functions of the up-to-date reading specialist.

The other main resource to the remedial teacher in reaching more children is to provide a teaching program and materials to a child's teacher, when that teacher is willing to try. If the reading specialist does the first teaching of new skills and provides the classroom teacher with follow up activities, the children's rates of learning can be enhanced and the length of time they will need the personal attention of a reading specialist can be diminished.

Of course, the plethora of materials for skill building that provide multisensory presentations and self-checking exercises make it easier than it used to be to provide independent reading activity for poor readers. There is the danger, however, that excessive reliance on such materials may diminish the personal relationship between remedial teacher and pupil—that rapport which provides the magic spark in a successful remedial program.

To summarize briefly, the current jurisdictional overlapping between reading personnel and learning disability personnel may be solved when the new criteria for identifying learning disabilities are put into effect. Only the most serious reading disabilities would qualify as learning disabilities, leaving plenty of work for reading specialists. The search for deviant brain functioning as a cause for reading disability continues, with some exciting new developments. The stimulant drugs are of some limited value in some cases of reading disability. Behavior modification, many of the principles of which have been practices by remedial teachers for many years, is becoming more sophisticated and may have some valuable new techniques for our field. Finally, the reading specialist is gradually spending more time as a consultant and supervisor and less time in direct teaching, a new role for which many would welcome additional training.

References

1. Conners, C. Keith. "Learning Disabilities and Stimulant Drugs in Children: Theoretical Implications," in Robert M. Knights and Dirk J. Bakker (Eds.), *The Neuropsychology of Learning Disorders.* Baltimore: University Park Press, 1976, 389-401.
2. de Quiros, Julio B. "Diagnosis of Vestibular Disorders in the Learning Disabled," *Journal of Learning Disabilities,* 9 (January 1976), 39-47.
3. Frank, Jan, and Harold N. Levinson. "Dysmetric Dyslexia and Dyspraxia," *Academic Therapy,* 11 (Winter 1975-1976), 133-143.

4. Goleman, Daniel. "A New Computer Test of the Brain," *Psychology Today*, May 1976, 44-48.
5. Gillespie, Patricia H., Ted L. Miller, and Virginia D. Fielder. "Legislative Definitions of Learning Disabilities: Roadblocks to Effective Service," *Journal of Learning Disabilities*, 8 (December 1975), 660-666.
6. Harris, Albert J., and Florence G. Roswell. "Clinical Diagnosis of Reading Disability," *Journal of Psychology*, 63 (1953), 323-340.
7. Harris, Albert J., and Edward R. Sipay. *How to Increase Reading Ability*, Sixth Edition. New York: David McKay, 1975.
8. John, E. Roy. "How the Brain Works—A New Theory," *Psychology Today*, May 1976, 48-52.
9. Meichenbaum, Donald. "Therapist Manual for Cognitive Behavior Modification," unpublished manuscript. Waterloo, Ontario, Canada: University of Waterloo, 1974.
10. Meichenbaum, Donald. "Cognitive Functional Approach to Cognitive Factors as Determinants of Learning Disabilities," in Robert M. Knights and Dirk J. Bakker (Eds.), *The Neuropsychology of Learning Disorders*. Baltimore: University Park Press, 1976, 423-442.
11. Pugh, K. Theresa, and Aileen W. Tobin. "Survey of Specialized Reading Programs in Delaware," *Journal of Reading*, 20 (November 1976), 132-136.
12. Satz, Paul. "Cerebral Dominance and Reading Disability: An Old Problem Revisited," in Robert M. Knights and Dirk J. Bakker (Eds.), *The Neuropsychology of Learning Disorders*. Baltimore: University Park Press, 1976, 273-294.
13. Wepner, Shelley B. "Are Reading Teachers Obsolete?" *Reading Teacher*, 30 (January 1977), 402-404.

Learning Disabilities versus Reading Disabilities: A Vexing Problem

A. Sterl Artley
University of Missouri at Columbia

Certainly, one of the most vexing problems facing schools today and one that almost defies resolution is the problem surrounding the definitions of two terms—*learning disability* and *reading disability.* In spite of meetings of government agencies, joint committees, and preconference institutes, there is no adequate answer to the question, when is a child who experiences severe difficulty in reading to be labeled and treated as learning disabled and when as reading disabled?

If this issue were one of concern only to professionals in two opposing camps (reading and special education) sparring with each other over federal funds, we could treat it as another academic question the answer to which is of concern only to academia. But the point is that a child with a problem is caught in the middle and becomes an innocent victim of a confusing and meaningless controversy.

The Problem of Applying Labels

Possibly the source of the problem is the unfortunate use of two labels—learning disabled and reading disabled—which in a sense mean the same thing. A child having difficulty in learning to read or with some facet of language learning has a school learning disability—hence, is learning disabled. In the same way, because learning disabilities are manifest chiefly in reading or language areas, the same child could be said to have a reading problem. In other words, one is talking about the same child with the same problem but using two different labels.

This being true, and assuming that there must be predisposing conditions that should differentiate the two types of cases, an attempt was made to define the difference between a learning disability and reading disability child in terms of etiology—to identify causal conditions or symptoms that might characterize learning disabilities and, hence, clearly differentiate the area from reading disabilities.

Accordingly, in an effort to establish a guide for educational planning for children with school learning problems, the National Advisory Committee for the Bureau of Education for the Handicapped, U.S. Office of Education, in 1968 made the recommendation that children "...exhibiting a disorder in one or more of the *basic psychological processes*..." be considered learning disabled. The recommendation clearly excluded problems due to vision, hearing, or motor handicaps as well as mental retardation, emotional disturbances, or environmental deprivation.

But a problem remained for, though by definition the two areas were differentiated, there was confusion over the meaning of the term "disorders of the basic psychological processes." Unless there was a clearly defined medical history, a record of disease or accident that could be indicative of a disorder in the basic psychological processes, there was no way of saying definitively that a child was learning disabled. Certainly there was no test administered in a school setting that could be used. As a result, the diagnostician had to rely on behaviors assumed to be causal factors. But the behaviors assumed to be indicative of psychological disorders were the same ones, in varying degrees, that could be found among children who were excluded by the definition.

The problem of definition has now resurfaced with even greater intensity than before. On November 29, 1975, Congress enacted the Education for All Handicapped Children Act which provides funding to states for the education of handicapped children (1). Among the handicapping conditions specifically referred to is "Children with specific learning disabilities." Moreover, Congress stipulated that the Commissioner of Education should consider whether changes should be made in the 1968 definition, particularly in the way of establishing specific criteria for determining whether a particular disorder or condition should be considered a specific learning disability.

Incidentally, the establishment of such criteria becomes doubly important, for Congress has spelled out the number of children who may be eligible for financial assistance as specific learning disabled. At the most, no more than 2 percent of children between the chronological ages of five and seventeen may be counted in this category (1). Take note, also, that only those children with reading problems who fall within the 2 percent limit are eligible for federal funds under the proposed provision of the Act.

Accordingly, the U.S. Office of Education has formulated a series of proposals regarding specific learning disabilities (note the change in terminology from "basic psychological processes") including definition, criteria for determining the existence of specific learning disabilities, evaluation techniques, medical problems, monitoring responsibilities, etc. In brief, the Department proposes that children be considered as being specific learning disabled if they show "severe discrepancy between achievement and intellectual ability" in one or more areas such as oral expression, written expression, basic reading skill, reading comprehension, spelling, and mathematic reasoning and comprehension. Moreover, according to the proposal, it must be shown that the children have failed to profit from "normal learning experiences." In addition, the same classifications that were to be excluded in the 1968 guidelines (mental retardation, sensory handicaps, environmental deprivation, etc.) are continued as categories for exclusion. In other words, the proposal specifies specific learning disability by a process of elimination. If the individuals are severely handicapped in reading and mathematics, if they have not profited from normal learning experiences, and if the condition is not due to mental retardation, emotional disturbance, or environmental disadvantage, etc. they may be classified as specific learning disabled.

The proposals have been published in the *Federal Register* (1) but, before final approval, the Office of Education held hearings and received recommendations from a variety of agencies, individuals, and committees. One such committee was the Joint Committee on Learning Disabilities made up of representatives of such organizations as the Association for Children with Learning Disabilities, American Speech and Hearing Association, the International Reading Association, and the Orton Society. This group was chaired by Jules Abrams, President of the IRA Disabled Reader Special Interest Group. Dr. Walter MacGinitie, President of IRA, reported the results of this meeting to the Board of Directors of IRA in 1976 (3).

But as necessary as it may be to classify children by concrete and defensible criteria as specific learning disabled for the purpose of receiving government funds, when it comes to the question of the type of educational program to be employed in rehabilitating these children, we will be no better off than we were before. The assumption seems to have been that children with severe reading problems, who have been labeled as learning disabled, required some kind of remedial care apart from reading. This has usually been a heavy program of perceptual or perceptual-motor training, in spite of the fact that studies and reviews of studies are showing very convincingly that this kind of training is ineffective in cases where the children's major learning problems are with reading and language (2, 4, 5). In short, many learning disability teachers are simply not prepared to deal with children's problems as they relate to reading and language.

This may appear to be a very incriminating statement but, as validation, let me point out that in only four states are courses in reading, remedial reading, and practicum experiences required for certification as a learning disability teacher (6). Ten states require one reading course which in most cases is the basic foundations course. Ten states have a "Program Approval Approach" which I take to mean that if the students' advisers deem it important, they will approve reading courses on the students' programs. Otherwise, there will be none. In the other states, according to the IRA summary of State Reading Requirements for Learning Disabilities Certification, no reading requirements are indicated and, in some cases, there is appended "None planned for the future."

Focusing on the Needs of the Child

At our institution we are taking the point of view that the question of the label to be applied to the child is quite academic. What we have is a child with a problem, and the strategy needed to remediate must be selected in relation to the nature of the problem and not in terms of whether the child is in a particular category. Accordingly, our people who are being prepared to work with school learning problems are given precisely the same instruction in reading whether they are in learning disabilities in the department of special education or are in the reading area in the department of curriculum and instruction. The clinic situation to which the child is sent and in which our clinicians receive their practicum experiences is neither a reading clinic nor a learning disability clinic but a place where the child's needs are diagnosed and met whether those needs are perceptual, conceptual, emotional, or educational. We are concerned with the adequacy of a practitioner's preparation—the coursework and the practicum experiences needed for competency—rather than the category into which the child should be placed.

We believe that this is the most satisfactory solution to this vexing problem. I am extremely pleased to find in Dr. MacGinitie's report that the attempt to specify competencies for practitioners is one of the actions that emerged from the meeting of the Joint Committee. He stated that a subcommittee of the Joint Committee has been appointed to try to develop a list of competencies that should be possessed by any specialist who works with learning disabled children. If this is approved, it will have a significant influence on certification requirements and, concomitantly, on training programs.

It is unfortunate for everyone concerned, particularly the child, that the profession has found itself embroiled over this controversy. We have spent an unwarranted amount of time trying to define the characteristics of two or three percent of the school population. We have spent more money and time than can be justified in duplicating training programs and educational services. We have confused parents and school people. It is time now that we give primary consideration to the child, remembering that no one discipline has a monoply on the handicapped learner regardless of cause.

References

1. Department of Health, Education, and Welfare. *Federal Register*, Education of Handicapped Children, Vol. 41, No. 230 (November 29, 1976).
2. Keim, Richard. "Visual-Motor Training Readiness and Intelligence of Kindergarten Children," *Journal of Learning Disabilities*, 3 (May 1970), 19-22.

3. MacGinitie, Walter. "Excerpt Concerning Learning Disabilities," report to the IRA Board, October 28, 1976. Newark, Delaware: International Reading Association.
4. Robinson, Helen. "Perceptual Training: Does It Result in Reading Improvement?" in R.C. Ackerman (Ed.), *Some Persistent Questions on Beginning Reading*. Newark, Delaware: International Reading Association, 1972.
5. Spache, George. *Investigating the Issues of Reading Disabilities*. Boston: Allyn and Bacon, 1976.
6. "State Reading Requirements for Learning Disabilities Certification in the U.S.," *Journal of Reading*, 20 (December 1970), 244-247.

Reverence for Remedial Reading Instruction

Russell G. Stauffer
Emeritus, University of Delaware

If the genesis of this presentation were to be traced to a single influence or inspiration, it would have to be to experiences I had more than forty years ago with two children. One was a twelve year old girl who had repeated first and second grades and finally made it to fourth grade almost a total nonreader. The second was a ten year old boy who, also, had repeated first grade and then been promoted from year to year until he reached fourth grade. In a class of thirty-three children, these two were standout failures, the girl more so than the boy. She was tall for her age and showed early signs of pubescence. The lad, on the other hand, was small for his age and physically blended in with the class.

This was my first year of teaching. In many ways I was quite unprepared to teach reading and to do so in a compartmentalized grades four, five, and six arrangement. I had had a full year of student teaching as my apprenticeship, teaching algebra in a ninth grade. It had been a marvelous year, and I had learned much, but I was ill-prepared to teach reading and language arts at the intermediate grade level and totally unprepared to teach remedial reading. In the midst of the depression of the 1930s, I was fortunate, indeed, to obtain a teaching position of any kind, and I tried to show my appreciation by being as diligent and inspiring as possible.

That year I learned many things about children, about reading programs, about reading instruction, and about success and failure. In each of three classes, I was allotted two different sets of basal readers and was instructed to divide each class into two groups. This was considered an advanced procedure because prior to this year only one set of readers had been available. Then it was the practice to have the top group proceed through the grade level reader at a faster pace than the slow group. As a result the top group would finish the reader by March and with great effort the slow group would "finish" by the end of the school terms.

By ardently pleading the case, I was permitted by midyear to organize a third group but only in the fourth grade. However, I had to teach this third group at the end of the school day because, I was told, my daily schedule did not allow time for three groups. To stay after school was usually considered a punishment, so my remedial instruction had to be done on a voluntary basis and, as I discovered, only with parental permission.

Almost all teachers look back upon their first year of teaching as having been a year of liability. Neophytes in almost any endeavor tend to feel this way about their first year, but when one is influencing the lives of so many people, the awareness seems especially poignant.

My desire to help Pauline and Richard and others like them prompted me to seek help. Graduate school seemed the best starting point. At Duke University I studied with established educators, C.T. Gray, O.B. Douglas, and Donald Adams; and at Penn State and Temple University with Emmett Betts, J. Conrad Seegers, and James Page. Finally, with a doctorate accomplished, I set out on my own.

In my twenty-five years as director of the Reading Study Center at the University of Delaware, during which time I worked closely with innumerable children and young adults in need of specialized and personalized instruction, I found myself most indebted to Grace Fernald (5) and Emmett Betts (3, 4). To the latter I am enormously obligated for his masterpiece, *The Foundations of Reading Instruction*, and for directing my attention to Fernald and demanding that her recommendations be thoroughly studied and mastered.

To Grace Fernald I am inordinately grateful. Not only am I grateful for the remedial techniques she described in detail but also for her unquestionable belief that almost all children of extreme and partial disability could be taught to read at a level almost in keeping with their expectancy.

Lewis M. Terman, a widely known and respected scholar of the early twentieth century, wrote in his foreword to Fernald's text:

> If educational methods were more intelligently adapted to the idiosyncracies of the individual child, all children would achieve up to their mental age level in all the school subjects. It is largely for this reason I believe this book is one of the most significant contributions ever made to experimental pedagogy (5).

This is high praise from a highly respected professional. In his enthusiasm, even Terman was carried away when he said, "*all* children would achieve up to their mental age level in all school subjects." By and large, though, he was right insofar as reading failures are concerned. Most reading disabilities stem from pedagogical undoing.

Terman also refers to the work of Anne Sullivan in training Helen Keller to read and to speak even though she was blind, deaf, and mute from early childhood. This unbelievable success story should be sustaining to all teachers at all times but especially so to remedial reading teachers. All should read *Teacher: Anne Sullivan Macy* (7) and *The Story of My Life* (6) by Helen Keller. Sullivan's untiring effort at coping with the thwarted desire and distemper of Helen Keller is indeed impressive. Equally as impressive is Keller's boundless gratitude to her teacher. By far the most priceless return one can obtain from helping failing children is the immeasurable psychic reward. Undoubtedly this is what Anne Sullivan Macy must have experienced.

Children's Variability

In that first year of teaching I learned that children are different, not only physically but also psychologically. Each year since then has reaffirmed this. Besides their affective and adjustment variabilities, children differ widely in their rates and styles of learning and in maturity and capacity.

That first year I soon found out that Pauline and Richard could read only a few words and did not know how to decode or unlock words they did not recognize at sight. Each year they had been reexposed to the same preprimers and the same intensive phonic efforts. This year, using a different series of preprimers and a slightly different phonic program did not make a bit of difference. Both children hated reading, yet both were willing to try again, largely, I believe, because I was their first male teacher. This, too, did not make a bit of difference. I learned, too, that, as Bettelheim (2) said fifteen years later, "Love is not enough." While it is true that Bettelheim's admonition was aimed primarily at parents, a similar admonition can be directed at teachers in general and particularly at remedial reading teachers filled with patronizing good intentions.

Every school district has in its environs teachers who have retired or who stopped teaching to raise a family or others who may have degrees of various kinds but little or no specialized work in remedial reading techniques, but who still classify themselves as remedial reading teachers. Although these people have good intentions and are perhaps fine classroom teachers, they do not seem to realize (as I didn't) that repeating developmental basal reading programs is not the answer. In addition, they need to learn that "love is not enough." Moreover, they have not learned that even the most thorough reading skills diagnosis and the facts provided thereby are not of as much value in remedial instruction as a thorough understanding of human variability: neurologically, psychologically, and pedagogically. Needed are the attitudes and insights necessary to attend *a particular child's needs at a specific moment.* The thousands of children that have been dealt with at the University of Delaware's Reading Study Center and other similar clinics bear witness to this fact. Well-intentioned teaching is not the answer. All too often, additional difficulties are created for children. Such teachers' circumscribed understanding and limited knowledge of how to deal with children's variabilities malign instruction.

Allport (1) put it well when he said that the outstanding characteristic of a person is his individuality. Each is a unique creation. Most teaching, but particularly remedial teaching, tends to neglect this paramount fact of individuality. The range of generic, structural, and biochemical variability among children requires us to expect temperament and motivation, rate and style of learning, and capacity to vary widely. The remedial teacher, in particular, must think seriously of the implications of wide ranging pupil individuality for pedagogical and therapeutical handling. Rules of thumb will not do because no one child is "normal."

Concepts of Instructional Actions

At almost all levels of teaching and learning within the range of typical learning rates, from remedial rates at one end to the rates of the gifted at the other, instructional activities need to be structured around the concepts of *action, interaction,* and *transaction (8)*. Each of the actions must be viewed as dynamic, an interplay of learning experience. As *purposive behavior* each form of action must be set in motion and unified by the fact that the learner sets out with a problem and seeks a solution.

The power that best commands *action* is the power of self-action motivated by what John Locke called "self-interest," Jean Jacques Rousseau named "grand-motive" and John Dewey described as "felt-need." Before school age, children are constantly acting upon their experiences and learning thereby. In the beginning they do so at a sensorimotor level. This learning is augmented in time at a linguistic-cognitive communication level. It is this dynamic power of motivation through self-action displayed so early in life that must be utilized as fully as possible in any subsequent instructional program structured by a teacher. In teacher structured learning situations children should perform two types of actions: a sensorimotor overt type of acting upon experiences and an intellectual decision making covert type by acting upon options. Cooperative pupil-teacher planning constitutes a major step toward commanding pupil initiative and harnessing the scholarly power of self-action.

The concept of interaction is that of learning in a group. Children not only interact in a sensorimotor way with elements in a situation, but should do so within the social-cultural-personal character of a group. It is in the environs of a group that an individual can see that different children may react differently and do so in fruitful ways that otherwise might have been overlooked. It is this kind of interacting and sharing that eventually helps hone and refine self-regulatory actions.

Transactions, on the other hand, represent the use of language to objectify and obtain quality responses, to communicate and share with others, and to *internalize* the actions and interactions. Internalization is what makes learning productive and durable. Knowledge that has been internalized serves a learner in new situations and often in very creative ways.

It is almost self-evident that if the "actions" defined are to result in maximal development of children, both individualized and group instruction are essential. Since this is true for developmental type instruction, it is unequivocally true for remedial instruction. Interestingly enough, the range of human differences not only makes the wheels of society go around but also can make remedial instruction vital, exciting, and functional. Each remedial student represents a tremendous reservoir of potential. What must be avoided is lockstep, memoriter type instruction, as well as isolated tutor type instruction.

Professionally Sound Remedial Instruction

For "clinical work" purposes, distinction should be made between *nomothetic* and *idiographic* understandings (1). The distinction brings to focus the quandries of instruction, of counseling and of therapy. How to cope with the unique organization of each individual's bodily and mental processes is the question. The "work" is referred to as being clinical because each individual is intensively studied in an effort to bring about better understanding and improved instructional adjustment. Nomothetic discipline, on the one hand, deals with broad, preferably universal laws or norms. Idiographic (not ideographic) discipline, on the other hand, deals with a person as a system of patterned uniqueness.

Clinical Diagnosis. Clinical diagnosis is done with the intention of being idiographic. Tests are given, scores are plotted, evidence is confronted with evidence, and all is synthesized into a final report, in an effort to discover the complex affective manner and achievement patterns of the child being tested. Nomothetic knowledge of group norms or actuarial data does not help very much, if at all. In addition, by virtue of the sacrosanct fact that reading is a process, determining a child's performance in a first hand action "reading situation" is a must. Such an appraisal stands in sharp contrast to the use of standardized tests that measure the products of reading in an incredibly atypical reading situation. Unquestionably the clinician must penetrate beyond the spotting of symptoms of inefficiency. Needed is a precise accounting of the acquired or unacquired capabilities that are essential when one reads for meaning. To manage the reading process requires ability to cope with printed language in much the same manner as is done with oral language on a self-generating basis, so that the process varies in degree and kind according to 1) the purposes of the reader/listener and 2) the nature and difficulty of the material or topic.

In addition, command of the auxilliary aid of unlocking a word not recognized at sight represents an essential skill attainment of an auxilliary nature. Word attack skills, like comprehension, must be measured primarily when the child is reading for meaning. Yet, oddly enough, most tests of word attack skill are done with words in isolation. To round out the picture, depending upon the child's age and degree of reading disability, skills related to language development and concept attainment must also be appraised.

To put all these pieces together to determine what the subject's cognitive and academic skill systems are really like, to see a vitally interrelated mosaic of elements and test scores, requires a clinically trained person. Needed are people who have served at least one year (preferably two years) of clinical apprenticeship in an approved center, undefiled by publisher avarice.

When to all this is added the need to understand children as unique individuals—their particular goals, their values, the directions of their strivings, their abilities and available energy and their ability to make judgments—the complexities of remedial instruction become strikingly evident. Instruction calls for a psychological mindedness that goes well beyond good intentions and intuition. The task is not easy. So many factors influence success or failure. Indeed, one must be very guarded lest the understanding is oversimplified. In addition, all of us are subject to the common sources of error: monopolistic stereotyping, projection, leniency, halo judgments, and undue caution. Even though process and decision making are complex, we must face up to our task.

Teacher Competencies. A first requisite attribute of a successful remedial reading teacher is faith. One must believe sincerely that children can be helped. Faith is not enough, though, just as "love is not enough." Combined with this must be a sound grasp of pedagogical practices, a penetrating appreciation for therapeutics, and an untiring determination. These are the qualities that compass an able teacher.

As a result, the concept of *empathy* (1) provides an essential base. Even though the term has broadened to mean any process of successful understanding, if empathy helps to establish the "thou" of an individual, one can come to know better how a person feels and thinks and acts. In brief, we must locate the children in their worlds, discover their intentions, and adjust.

It is true that in established clinical centers, such as the one at the University of Delaware where both diagnosing and instruction are done only during the regularly scheduled school day, it is generally concluded that to carefully integrate testing and teaching and to immediately start a program of remediation is the most productive. The teaching by skilled teachers, diagnostically, pedagogically and therapeutically trained, causes predictions about achievement to be more substantial. This, combined with frequent staff meetings, helps to prescribe broader and more adequate instructional and therapeutic procedures. The teaching-testing-staffing process permits idiographic interpretations from which can be formed increasingly more insightful instructional concepts about any particular child.

It is true, as Terman says, that in many ways the predicament of the extremely disabled reader is far more tragic than that of the deaf or the blind (5:vii). The handicaps of deafness and blindness are so readily apparent that most folks immediately make some allowance. On the other hand, the plight of nonreaders is quite different. Nonreaders have no readily observable physical defects and as a result people, including teachers, expect achievement similar to that of typical children.

The Home. Parents would not want to return day after working day to a position in which they failed constantly and knew that all of their peers knew they failed. Teachers and principals would not care to do so. In a short time they would be emotional wrecks. Yet the law requires children to attend school every day, even though instruction is far too often not differentiated, and nomothetic norms are made into standards. For these children school takes on the dread and anxieties of concentration camps.

Without question, the failure and knowledge of failure spill over into the home. Siblings either wish to help and try to do so or are embarrassed and annoyed. Parents try and try again and tend to run the gamut from "Chicken Little" to "Pollyanna" emotions. What child could avoid being filled with self-doubt and seek adjustment by devious means?

The marvel of it all is the fact that the nine, ten, and eleven year olds with a four, five, or six year history of failure retain as much poise as they do. The resiliency of children is amazing. If this were not so, society would be forced to act more positively and provide professionally sound, clinically trained help. Usually the need to refer a child to a psychiatrist or a neurologist is more the exception than the rule. When referral is warranted, the typical psychiatric diagnosis is to join forces and provide therapy as well as instruction. What a child needs more than anything else, more than an attentive ear, more than a "label" of some type of dysfunction, is to experience success.

Instructional Circumstances. Success is more likely in a clinical center with clinically trained teachers. Success is also more likely in an open spaced clinical instructional environment, one that avoids small isolated instructional booths. While it may be true that to a large degree remedial instruction is geared to an individual, it must also be true that pupil actions and interactions must occur in groups. In addition, instruction must be based largely upon pupil experience, interests, attitudes, and actions, either those acquired outside of an instructional center or those structured in a center. Pupils do best when instruction is built upon their own interests, their own language, and their own motivations. They must be provided with covert and overt decision making circumstances and required to make judgments. Above all they must learn to act upon their judgments.

In addition, instruction is most fruitful when there are ten or more children present. Then each student realizes readily that he/she is not the only one to have experienced reading failure. There are students of varying sizes and ages who respond and collaborate with each other. The attitude of a helping hand prevails. Each student has the opportunity to work with others, read to and with others, listen to others, and share in their projects. Uniquely enough, in time, each student should take on some teaching responsibility and instruct others, as well as being helped by them. "How would you teach this skill to someone else?" is a marvelous challenge to put to students.

This kind of instructional structuring, based on pupil actions and interactions, must also be premised on the power of conscious and deliberate pupil-teacher planning. Gradually, the increasing pull of children's positive images of themselves asserts a vigorous drive on their conduct. This renewed self-confidence influences the dynamic force of their planning and intentions. Their cognitive and emotive forces become fused into a productive intention for the present but with a marked flavor of future orientation. Gradually the pupils' levels of aspiration go beyond the immediate and they see themselves achieving in future roles. The transition may be gradual but it is, nonetheless, real and impelling.

At every moment, students are conducting their own "ego-world" transactions and in their own ways. Accordingly, the constraints of the instructional situation must be such as to provide environmental and pedagogical support, shaping pupils' self-esteem and self-acceptance and influencing their desire to achieve.

Instruction based on a close teacher-pupil relationship stemming from the semitutor circumstance, whereby a minimum of two students shares one teacher, is most fruitful. This arrangement should be constantly augmented by the interactions of each teacher in a center. In this way, each instructor knows all the children, works with them from time to time, responds to their projects and shares in their creations. Each instructor attends the staff meetings regularly and is quite fully acquainted with each student's etiology and current instructional needs and achievements. In addition, group activities must be deliberately scheduled. Directed Reading-Thinking Activities (8) should be conducted with groups varying in number. In brief, an esprit de corps should pervade a center and embrace all the participants: students, instructors, secretaries, supervisors, and director.

It is impossible to achieve such relationships unless there is some point of focus. From a cognitive-emotive instructional point of view, the answer is identifying students' intentions, that is, their constellation of values and interests. These intentions are the dominating force that bind together a student's life and actions, thought and development. In short, remedial instruction must allow for both nomothetic and idiographic understandings. Test facts alone tell little. Needed is a balance, a method that is seasoned and perceptive.

From the beginning of instruction there must be a "no secrets" understanding between instructors and pupils. A pupil must always know *why* and *how* each activity engaged in is helpful in learning to read. Gradually pupils plan their own activities, selecting from a list that fits their needs. Remedial instruction is a high enterprise activity and requires truth and confidence.

In addition, children should not become school isolates. A school curriculum is designed to provide learning and growth opportunities in each of the knowledge areas: literature, humanities, mathematics, and science. Moreover, the school day provides many other opportunities on the playground, in organized group activities, in the cafeteria's food-for-the-body program, and in the library multimedia center's food-for-the-mind opportunities.

Unquestionably, being an isolate promotes labeling and name calling, invariably of a negative kind. Accordingly, it is essential that all effort be made to offset such damnable practices.

At the end of each six weeks of instruction, the instructor should report to both parents in an interview situation. Without fail, the father should attend. In addition, the instructor should visit the pupil's school and report progress to the teachers involved and the school principal. Not only are reports to be made to the school and the home but, also, further understandings are to be sought. Remedial instruction, to be successful, must represent a joint effort among the remedial reading instructors, the school, and the home (9).

Conclusion

Beyond question the vast majority of children and young people who are in need of remedial help come with the dulling tread of captive beings, reflecting the ugliness of their numerous undistinguished days. The acuteness of their problems, their struggles, anxieties, and defeats, has left them blighted and depressed. School learning-reading was not an inspiring panorama but an overpowering and often treacherous immensity. No thinking, sensitive person can escape these sour realities. Yet, one senses among the afflicted a vitality, a desire to achieve, an almost indescribable independence of spirit that can be harnessed. It is this consciousness, this determination, this will that takes on an influential reality and can give substance to motives and ends posited by pedagogical norms.

How to build a viable psychology and pedagogy upon such contingencies is the imperative. The undeniable rule of cause and effect must be recognized, and we must concede the shaping influences of heredity, environment, indoctrination, and circumstance. All partial or totally disabled readers can think, and this is what gives them identity with their peers and with humankind in general. Their world is just as much a medley of sights, sounds, pressures, temperatures, tastes, smells, and feelings as that of the more successful achievers. They all can and do think of themselves and mold a "for-itself" image. Doubtlessly, it is their past, their environment, and their circumstances that enter into determining their actions. Behind and beneath their actions is a feeling of shame, a sense of guilt, however silent the accusations of others. At the same time there persists a will to achieve, to dignify their lives, to have noble and redeeming goals.

It behooves us, therefore, to use to the fullest those powers and acquisitions that the "disabled" bring with them. It has been said that by the time children are six years old they are graduate students in the world of experience. Experiences provide the most immediate of all instructional realities, obscure at times, but undeniable and real. People are the sum of their past; it is these bountiful "sums" that, when utilized, can yield curriculum potentials for instruction and learner catharsis.

These needy people are not a mess, a nuisance, a mutiny, or a blighted hope. They are a delight. Invariably, they bear their semipoverty with a sense of humor. They are young, strong, and still feel that the world is their own to study, to enjoy, to overcome. A program of instruction that builds upon these assets can be absorbing and gratifyingly successful.

I am convinced that there is hardly a disabled reader so remote that he or she cannot be reached. I have devoted much of my life to the investigation of instructional practices and feel confident that if devotion is given to the study of these children; if remedial reading instruction is truly individualized and based upon the concepts of pupil action, interactions and transaction; and if remedial reading instructors are clinically trained and qualified, we may, by these means, be successful. As Rousseau said so wisely, every experience children engage in is a book that enriches their memories, ripens their judgment, and can benefit them. Hence I can now say, with necessary reservations understood, that what the practices defined here are intended to do is to preserve the talents and ambitions, the courage and open-mindedness of disabled readers, and to inspire them to produce the necessary intellectual energy to achieve. There is a natural aristocracy among these children, and this is our boon.

References

1. Allport, G. *Pattern and Growth in Personality*. New York: Holt, Rinehart and Winston, 1961.
2. Bettelheim, B. *Love Is Not Enough*. New York: Free Press, 1950.
3. Betts, E.A. *Foundations of Reading Instruction*. New York: American Book, 1946.
4. Betts, E.A. *The Prevention and Correction of Reading Difficulties*. New York: Harper and Row, 1936.
5. Fernald, G.M. *Remedial Techniques in Basic School Subjects*. New York: McGraw-Hill, 1943.
6. Keller, H. *The Story of My Life*. New York: Doubleday, 1954.
7. Keller, H. *Teacher: Anne Sullivan Macy*. New York: Doubleday, 1946.
8. Stauffer, R.G. *Directing the Reading-Thinking Process*. New York: Harper and Row, 1975.
9. Stauffer, R.G., J. Abrams, and J. Pikulski. *Diagnosis, Correction, and Prevention of Reading Disabilities*. New York: Harper and Row, 1978.

Section Four
IMPORTANT COMPONENTS IN READING EDUCATION

Teaching Reading and Writing: The Past Ten Years

Margaret Early
Syracuse University

The following article was written in 1975 to review briefly the research and discussion of reading and writing which had influenced teaching in the preceding ten years. It was published in the January 1976 issue of *Phi Delta Kappan*, one of several articles meant to provide background to the persisting debate over how best to emphasize reading, writing, and arithmetic in elementary classrooms. When the editor of the present volume asked for permission to reprint, I was given a chance that every writer welcomes—to say it better a second time—but still within the 2500 words of the first assignment. So here is the revised article, adding information and insights which have become available in the years since its first appearance.

Adapted from "Important Research in Reading and Writing," *Phi Delta Kappan*, January 1976, 298-301.

Since the mid-sixties, the teaching of reading and writing has been influenced by two movements that seem at first at odds with each other. A little more than ten years ago, teachers were being told that to teach reading and writing well they must know the structure of English, its phonology, morphology, and syntax. Then, almost before they could assimilate the first advice, they were told to pay less attention to structure and more attention to how and why children learn to produce langauge and to comprehend its written forms. They were reminded that how children feel is more important than what they know. Good teachers resolved the superficial contrariness of the advice. They knew that the more they learned about the structure of the language the better they could help children to use language to serve their own purposes. When the back-to-the basics movement crested in the mid-seventies, these good teachers knew that both "structure" and "feeling" are basic in classrooms where children learn to read and write.

But many teachers and administrators were confused by advice which appeared to them to be conflicting. They asked for instructional materials that would make their decisions for them, and they got very structured programs that exercised children in the more mechanical skills of reading and writing and left very little time for real reading and writing. Where do good teachers derive support for their middle-of-the-road decisions? Where can confused teachers turn when they wish to avoid the hard sell of either the far right or the far left? In this short article, I shall review some of the studies, both empirical and theoretical, which offer answers to these questions. This quick backward glance over the past ten years may help taxpayers, as well as teachers and administrators, to understand the directions that school programs in reading and writing have taken recently. For a more detailed review that covers the same period I recommend *Reading 1967-1977: A Decade of Change and Promise* (7). This thin pamphlet, number 97 in the Phi Delta Kappa fastback series, is particularly useful for administrators and lay groups.

At first, psychologists and linguists, merging their disciplines in the new field of psycholinguistics, focused attention more on how children learn language than on how parents and teachers can assist them in doing so. Probably because of that early emphasis, psycholinguistics has had minimal influence on school practice so far. In the past ten years there has probably been more talk about psycholinguistic research at reading and language conferences than transfer of principles into the nation's classrooms. Since psycholinguistics is a very new science indeed, it is not surprising that its influence on teaching is still more potential than real. And the situation may be changing.

Language Development

The new research on language learning is becoming more accessible to teachers as it is interpreted for them in books like Smith's *Understanding Reading* (25) and Cazden's *Child Language and Education* (6), synthesizing many studies which describe and systematize language development from infancy to adolescence. In dozens of journal articles and other books in addition to the two just named, teachers can get the message that learning to read is a further extension of learning to speak. Just as children in learning to speak acquire rule governed behavior without any formal knowledge of the rules, so children may learn to read without explicitly knowing the graphophonemic rules. But teachers who are willing to accept this theory of language acquisition still want to know what kind of support and how much of it they should be offering to beginning readers. They want to know whether they must modify their methods to conform with psycholinguistic insights and, if so, how.

Teachers are confused when implications from psycholinguistic studies run counter to what they have been taught or what they have observed among their own students. For example, having learned that children become frustrated and reject reading when they read haltingly, mispronouncing and substituting words, teachers are puzzled by advice from psycholinguists suggesting that children should be allowed to get what they can from texts that are above their level. Nor are they happy to be told now that they may be doing more harm than good by stressing phonics, especially when they were so recently told that code emphasis reading programs tend to produce better overall reading achievement, at least in the beginning, then do meaning-emphasis programs (8).

Most recently, teachers' confusions have been intensified by the failure of the psychologists to agree on whether reading is the same process for beginners and for mature readers. Those who believe that it is insist that children learn to read by bringing to their reading a knowledge of language and of the world which assists them in making predictions about the author's meaning, using the letter-sound code to confirm or correct these predictions (*13, 26*). Those who believe the reading process is qualitatively different for beginners believe that children depend on their knowledge of letter-sound relationships in order to identify words which trigger meanings that exist in the text and in the readers' experiences. Adams, Anderson, and Durkin (*1*) support a view of beginning reading as an essentially interactive process in which beginning readers rely equally on the cues from the text and the information in their heads. While this compromise position between "top down" and "bottom up" processing seems reasonable, it still leaves teachers with many decisions to make about the quality and weight of phonics instruction which will be most helpful to beginning readers in all their variety.

Pearson argues that language based models of the reading process, even if they are not yet in perfect agreement can, nevertheless, help teachers with tasks such as selecting language activities that emphasize different kinds of information (phonic, semantic, syntactic), evaluating instructional materials and activities, understanding children who are experiencing difficulties with reading and writing, and analyzing the errors children make in oral reading (*23*).

I believe that psycholinguistic research and theory will become increasingly significant to elementary teachers as studies accumulate and diversify, examining the process as it occurs in readers of different ages, backgrounds, and purposes, reading many different kinds of discourse. Meanwhile, the growing body of work on language acquisition lends support to ideas which good teachers have long recognized; for example, that talk should be well developed before reading begins, that familiarity with written language should be developed through reading to very young and maturing children, that sounds and letters should not be isolated from words, that words should be studied always in context, that sentences are understood fully only in larger chunks of context, that speaking, listening, reading, writing are related abilities and therefore classroom strategies to improve one must involve all the others. Except as they confirm already established practices, however, psycholinguistic studies have scarcely as yet had any great effect on instruction.

Code Emphasis Programs

On the other hand, there is no doubt that Chall's recommendations favoring code emphasis programs overturned beginning reading instruction. *Learning to Read: The Great Debate* (8) was issued at a time when both society and the schools were ready for it. Since 1955 when Rudolf Flesch's *Why Johnny Can't Read* became a best seller, many critics of the schools had blamed all reading failures on look-say methods, and it was to examine the legitimacy of these attacks that Chall evaluated all available studies of the teaching of reading from 1910 to 1965. Her reading of the research led her to recommend a code emphasis only as a *beginning* reading method and to warn against practice without attention to meaning. Moreover, she recognized that her recommendations came at a time "when excellence in academic work is highly valued, when intellectual precociousness is viewed as promise of later accomplishment...."

The shift to code emphasis methods had already begun by the time *Learning to Read* was published. It accelerated thereafter. But, by the late sixties, even as basal series were becoming code oriented, the mood of the times was changing once again. Academic excellence seemed less important than sensitivity to human beings of different backgrounds and aspirations. In educational circles, opinion makers were beginning to cite the values of open classrooms where children's purposes in learning would be central, unrestricted by traditional curricula and environments (24). At the Anglo-American Seminar in the Teaching of English at Dartmouth in 1966, which was an early signal of the coming change, American educators began to hear from British colleagues criticism of our respect for structure and discipline in the study of the language arts. Americans were reminded that children develop language through using language for affective as well as cognitive purposes, that studying *about* language through pursuing exercises in structural linguistics or traditional grammar was probably detrimental to growth in expressing ideas and feelings, and that answering questions about what they have read is not the best way to encourage children's interest in and response to reading (20). The debates at Dartmouth were just the beginning, of course, and they had little immediate impact on elementary schools, which were becoming stocked with new instructional materials inspired by the earlier demands for structure and academic excellence. While Chall's book was in the making and the Dartmouth papers were emerging, the U.S. Office of Education was conducting and publicizing a spate of studies of first grade reading, some of which continued into second and third grades. These studies reflected the decade's overriding concern with method, pitting one approach against another. Altogether, five different basal series, three phonics programs, two linguistic programs, and two i/t/a programs were tried out in classrooms across the country. The results were evaluated with the same tests. Among classes using the same methods, sharper differences showed up in end-of-the-year testing than appeared between classes using the different methods under comparison. This surprising result led many to infer that teachers, not methods, were responsible for the differences. Beyond this inference, the data offered some support for code-emphasis programs but not enough to be conclusive (2).

With or without support from research, phonics returned to reading instruction not only in new and revised basal series but also on TV's "Sesame Street" and "The Electric Company."

No one suggested that ability to identify words would insure comprehension; so it should have come as no surprise in the early seventies that while primary grade reading scores were rising, means were falling on middle grade tests which measure comprehension. But if stressing phonics in beginning reading doesn't insure successful comprehension, neither can it be blamed for comprehension's falling off in the middle grades. Rather, evidence accumulated in this decade suggests that when comprehension scores decline on a national scale— and they seem to be doing just that—factors outside the school contribute as heavily as in-school practices (29).

Influence of Home and Family

Home and family background are dominant in determining achievement in reading, wrote Thorndike (28), summarizing an extensive international evaluation of reading comprehension. In the United States, the 1974 National Assessment of Educational Progress reported that differences in reading performance were related consistently to level of parents' education, community, region, race, and sex (21). Neither these studies, nor those summarized by Jencks (16), should be construed as absolving schools of influence or responsibility. However, they suggest that more factors are at work than unsuccessful experiments with open education, as some critics have alleged. Failure to teach how to comprehend, using any method or in any kind of classroom setting, must be one of the reasons for low achievement, but there are many reasons why teachers fail to teach. Ignorance is only one of them. In this decade, we must consider also the direct effects on teaching of social and political issues such as busing and integration, unions and strikes.

The Mysteries of Comprehension

Research has not yet been very helpful to teachers in this matter of comprehension. We still know next to nothing about the process, even though we are continually devising new measures of whatever it is. Frederick Davis's 1944 factor analysis of comprehension yielded nine subskills, which Louis Thurstone claimed could be subsumed into one or two: word meaning and "another factor." More than twenty years later, Davis (10) reaffirmed eight of his original nine subskills; but Carroll (5) concluded from the amount of variance residing in the tests of these skills that "perhaps only four or five merit recognition as distinct skills." These are remembering word meanings; following the structure of a passage; finding answers to questions answered explicitly or in paraphrase; recognizing a writer's purpose, attitude, tone, or mood; and drawing inferences from the content.

Accumulated research on comprehension tells teachers that behavioral objectives related to comprehension should be few and that measurement of these objectives should be interpreted warily.

Obviously, the next major goal of reading research lies in unraveling the mysteries of comprehension. Recent work in discourse analysis is a step in that direction, but to date most studies have been limited to readers' inferences from single sentences or from pairs. To be useful to teachers in the middle and upper grades, studies of comprehension must go beyond transformational analyses and examine the role of intention, memory, experience, and knowledge in comprehending not only narrative prose but the whole range of discourse, scientific and philosophical as well as poetic (Olson, 1977). It is undoubtedly too early to look to this research for implications for teaching. Reviewing recent research in comprehension for an audience of teachers at the International Reading Association in Houston in May 1978, the director of the Center for the Study of Reading, sponsored by the National Institute of Education, could only affirm what every teacher knows: Children need to be prepared for reading any materials from which they are expected to learn something new.

Diagnosis and Follow Through

Kenneth Goodman and his students have contributed the concept of miscue analysis to the diagnosis of reading performance (12). Based on psycholinguistic principles, miscue analysis tries to determine the reasons why oral reading may not be a perfect match for the text. For example, listening to a child read, the teacher or researcher seeks answers to questions like these: Which of these miscues results from a mismatch between a nonstandard dialect (e.g., black English) and the dialect of the text? Which reveal that a letter-sound relationship has not yet been assimilated? Goodman's research refines diagnostic techniques that teachers have long been urged to use. In essence, Goodman says to teachers: Meaning is more important than coding. If the reader accurately translates the printed message into his own dialect, he is reading successfully. Restoring importance to "reading for meaning" does not dismiss the need for teaching decoding skills. Sensitive analysis of miscues helps the teacher to know which skills are functioning well and which need further support.

Successful individualizing of instruction depends on diagnosis but also on follow through. The spate of systems approaches or "objective based reading programs" now on the market, seem to offer systematic follow through. In these programs, students' skills are diagnosed and exercises are assigned which purport to correct weaknesses revealed by pretests. Students continue to work on a subskill until it is reinforced to the point of mastery as evaluated by criterion referenced tests (27).

Do systems approaches work? Research usually shows that children learn what they have been taught. But pupil progress toward narrowly defined goals is only one answer to "Does it work?" We must also measure what the system costs, not only for materials and personnel but in teacher morale and efficiency and in student attitudes and overall intellecual curiosity. Systems approaches may be teaching and evaluating only peripheral aspects of what successful readers are really learning as they master the process of comprehension.

One questionable side effect of diagnostic-prescriptive instruction is that it can give numerical scores a spurious significance. Scores from a computer seem somehow more reliable than personal judgment. But nothing is less true. Diagnosing reading performance and choosing instructional materials are not a matter of matching reading scores to readability scores. From Winnetka in the twenties to IPI in the seventies, individualizing instruction has spawned readability formulas as an easy way to select books that children can comprehend. But all readability research—and there have been important additions to it in the decade under review (17)— stresses the extreme limitations of the formulas and begs teachers not to substitute computationally derived ratings for experience and judgment.

Motivation

In introducing the topic of motivation at this point, I don't mean to suggest unfairly a polarity between diagnostic-prescriptive teaching and an approach that is centered less on skills than on children's interests. Although coming from different perspectives (to which I refuse to attach such convenient labels as Skinnerian and Piagetian), both approaches partake ultimately of many of the same practices: diagnosis, materials relevant to children's interests, goal setting, recording of progress. (In England, I visited infant schools stoutly defended as "traditional" and found practices there which were as "open" as many in other schools displayed as showcases of open education.) But, on the surface, IPI and SSR (to use another set of labels) appear to be movements and countermovements, and I cannot mention individually prescribed instruction and omit the impact of, say, *Hooked on Books* (*11*) or Lyman Hunt's sustained silent reading. Though not supported by massive research, the message from both of these quite different sources has come through clearly to teachers: Surround children with books, mostly paperbacks; set aside time for them to read; nudge them into books but let them find their own level; and talk to them about their reading.

Reading has taken the lion's share in this review, just as it usurps more than its share of language arts time in the classroom. Yet the really significant research in this decade is in language as it variously affects school learning. This research springs from Noam Chomsky's analyses of language in terms of transformational grammar, and much of it investigates speech from infancy to age five. As this research moves into the language of older children, more of it has to do with children's writing as well as their speech and with the comprehension of language through listening and reading. As the studies accumulate, it becomes increasingly clear that children acquire language in sequence—moving, for instance, from understanding simpler (to more complex constructions (*9*), from writing shorter to longer sentences (*15, 22*), from using little to much subordination. The point is that such sequences are set, are not skipped, and cannot be force fed.

Analyses of children's writing and speaking have often been limited to single situations: one kind of writing, for example, or an interview in a laboratory setting. Newer research asks whether children's language changes according to its purposes and the situations in which it occurs and suggests, not surprisingly, that the forms change to suit the content (*14*). Much situational research has involved black dialects and has revealed their range and complexity (*18*).

How should these many studies affect the teaching of comprehending and composing in language? Perhaps the best summary answer, and the most influential one in this decade, is the theory developed by Moffett in *Teaching the Universe of*

Discourse (*19*). Drawing upon the language studies of the fifties and sixties, Moffett proposed a curricular structure that moves with the child along two dimensions of increasing abstraction. On the first dimension, the distance between speaker and audience widens (egocentric speech to public statement). On the second dimension, the child moves into participating in what is happening, then to reporting, on to generalizing, and finally to theorizing. Moffett's theories are by no means presented in the abstract, for they undergird not only a handbook on curriculum development but also instructional materials for stimulating the uses of language on the dimensions he has conceptualized.

Moffett says that, aside from art, music, and physical education, the only subject of the schools is language, since all other subjects are learned in and through language. "As content, they are what one discourses about; as process, they are acts of discoursing." This is another way of saying that reading, writing, speaking, and listening should be taught through content.

The idea that staffs and administrators in elementary schools should articulate a language policy which will permeate the teaching of every subject is advanced by strong voices here and abroad. For example, in the late sixties and seventies, Britton and others on the staff of the University of London set up a Writing across the Curriculum project which involved teachers in many junior and secondary schools and resulted in several significant publications aimed at teachers of all subjects (*4*). Research and demonstration projects like this one are encouraging teachers to pool what they know about language and learning, to apply knowledge gained from many of the sources cited in this article, and to shape a total curriculum in which children are encouraged to learn concepts in science, for example, through talking and writing in forms that are natural to them rather than forcing them too quickly into expository patterns that often conceal children's true understandings as well as their misconceptions (*3*). It will be interesting to see whether this revitalized effort to integrate language into all areas of the curriculum will be more successful than was the progressive education movement of the thirties in persuading parents that the quality of children's thinking is a more basic educative goal than the conventions of language and that, in any case, the development of thinking in no way causes deterioration of literacy skills.

Summary

If the research of the sixties and seventies says anything to teachers, it is: "Don't go overboard." In teaching reading, keep an eye on decoding and meaning. Look for psycholinguistic studies to reveal more about the process of comprehension and, in the meantime, teach four or five skills such as recognizing the author's organization and purpose, drawing inferences, and recalling information, and do so consistently and repeatedly in all content areas. Balance skills teaching with reading for personal motives and pleasures.

In teaching writing and speaking, remember that language is learned sequentially and that sequences cannot be reversed or stages skipped. Encouraging children to speak and write for many different purposes, whenever possible, purposes that they themselves define, will cause them to use different forms and to expand their language repertoire.

Good teaching of reading and writing can take place in various school settings, no one of which is best for all children. Thus, for growth in reading and writing, a sound educational system offers alternative programs which match, so far as possible, different learning styles with different instructional styles. Good schools develop their own language policies, consistent with what researchers and teachers are learning about children's uses of language, and they encourage teachers to vary their methods within the framework of this policy.

References

1. Adams, Marilyn J., Richard C. Anderson, and Dolores Durkin. "Beginning Reading: Theory and Practice," *Language Arts,* 55 (January 1978), 19-25.
2. Bond, Guy L., and Robert Dykstra. *Coordinating Center for First Grade Reading Instruction Programs,* Final Report, USOE Project No. X-001. Minneapolis: University of Minnesota, 1967; also in *Reading Research Quarterly,* Spring 1967, 5-142.
3. Britton, James. *Language and Learning.* Baltimore: Penguin Books, 1970.
4. Britton, James, et al. *The Development of Writing Abilities.* Urbana, Illinois: National Council of Teachers of English, 1977.

5. Carroll, John B. "Defining Language Comprehension," *Language Comprehension and the Acquisition of Knowledge*. Washington, D.C.: V.H. Winston and Sons, 1972, 1-29.
6. Cazden, Courtney B. *Child Language and Education*. New York: Holt, Rinehart, and Winston, 1972.
7. Chall, Jeanne. *Reading 1967-1977: A Decade of Change and Promise*. Bloomington, Indiana: Phi Delta Kappa Educational Foundation, 1977.
8. Chall, Jeanne. *Learning to Read: The Great Debate*. New York: McGraw-Hill, 1967.
9. Chomsky, Carol S. *The Acquisition of Syntax in Children from 5 to 10*. Cambridge, Massachusetts: MIT Press, 1969.
10. Davis, Frederick B. "Research in Comprehension in Reading," *Reading Research Quarterly*, Summer 1968, 499-545.
11. Fader, Daniel N., and Elton B. McNeil. *Hooked on Books: Program and Proof*. New York: G.P. Putnam's Sons, 1969; new edition, 1978.
12. Goodman, Kenneth S. *Miscue Analysis: Applications to Reading Instruction*. Urbana, Illinois: Eric Clearinghouse on Reading and Communication Skills, NCTE, 1973.
13. Goodman, Kenneth S., and Yetta Goodman. "Learning about Psycholinguistic Processes by Analyzing Oral Reading," *Harvard Educational Review*, 47 (August 1977), 317-333.
14. Halliday, M.A.K. "Relevant Models of Language," *Educational Review*, 22 (November 1969), 26-37.
15. Hunt, Kellogg W. *Grammatical Structures Written at Three Grade Levels*, NCTE Research Report No. 3. Urbana, Illinois: National Council of Teachers of English, 1965.
16. Jencks, Christopher. *Inequality: A Reassessment of the Effect of Family and Schooling in America*. New York: Harper and Row, 1972.
17. Klare, G.R. "Assessing Readability," *Reading Research Quarterly*, 20, (1974-1975), 62-102.
18. Labov, William. *Language in the Inner City: Studies in the Black English Vernacular*. Philadelphia: University of Pennsylvania Press, 1972.
19. Moffett, James. *Teaching the Universe of Discourse*. Boston: Houghton Mifflin, 1968.
20. Mueller, Herbert J. *The Uses of English*. New York: Holt, Rinehart and Winston, 1967.
21. National Assessment of Educational Progress Report 02-R-30. *Recipes, Wrappers, Reasoning, and Rate: A Digest of the First Reading Assessment*. Washington, D.C.: U.S. Government Printing Office, 1974.
22. O'Donnell, Roy C., William J. Griffen, and Raymond C. Norris. *Syntax of Kindergarten and Elementary School Children: A Transformational Analysis*, NCTE Research Report No. 8. Urbana, Illinois: National Council of Teachers of English, 1967.
23. Pearson, P. David. "A Psycholinguistic Model of Reading," *Language Arts*, 53 (March 1976), 309-314.
24. Silberman, Charles. *Crisis in the Classroom*. New York: Random House, 1970.
25. Smith, Frank. *Understanding Reading*, Second Edition. New York: Holt, Rinehart, and Winston, 1978.
26. Smith, Frank. "Making Sense of Reading—and of Reading Instruction," *Harvard Educational Review*, 47 (August 1977), 386-395.

27. Stallard, Cathy. "Comparing Objective Based Reading Programs," *Journal of Reading,* 21 (October 1977), 36-44.
28. Thorndike, Robert L. *Reading Comprehension Education in Fifteen Countries.* International Studies in Evaluation III. New York: John Wiley and Sons, 1973.
29. Wirtz, Willard. *On Further Examination.* Princeton, New Jersey: College Entrance Board Publications, 1977.

Beginning Reading: Theory and Practice

Marilyn Jager Adams
Richard C. Anderson
Dolores Durkin
University of Illinois at Urbana-Champaign

Anyone who knows the literature on beginning reading is forced to conclude that much still needs to be learned about what it is and how it should be taught. Those who know the literature and are also aware of what goes on in classrooms must face up to another inevitable conclusion, namely, the failure of classroom practices to reflect what *is* known.

What *is* known with certainty is meager. Even descriptions of the very nature of the reading process continue to be characterized by diversity rather than agreement. Within the framework of one conception, for example, reading is "bottom-up" processing. According to this interpretation, readers start with letters and, as they attend to these letters, they begin to have expectations for the words the letters will spell. As readers identify the words, they have further expectations for how these words will be strung together and what they will mean when assembled into phrases and sentences.

Contrasting with this "data driven" interpretation is one that sees reading as being "conceptually driven." Within the latter framework, reading is, to use Goodman's words (*3*), "a psycholinguistic guessing game" in the sense that readers' knowledge of language and of their world suggests certain

From *Language Arts*, Vol. 55, No. 1, January 1978. Copyright 1978 by the National Council of Teachers of English. Reprinted with permission.

hypotheses that are tested—that is, accepted or rejected—against what is printed. According to this interpretation, therefore, reading is "top-down" processing.

Still another interpretation, one that underlies this article, views reading as an essentially interactive process (8). From this perspective, top-down and bottom-up processing are seen to occur simultaneously, at least for a skilled reader. This makes successful reading as dependent upon the information that is in the reader's head as upon the information that is in the text. Comprehension will be obstructed whenever a critical skill or a critical piece of knowledge is lacking. When it is, however, proficient readers find a way to compensate. They might pause and sound out a word; or they might rely on top-down processes to solve the problem. In the latter case, they might deduce the meaning of the troublesome word from contextual information. Both types of solutions are regularly used by skilled readers and both contribute to their success. When either top-down or bottom-up processing is followed to the extreme, however, problems arise.

The danger of relying too heavily and exclusively on top-down processing is obvious. Balance between the information the reader brings to the text and that which the text should provide is lost. To the extent that guesses are piled upon prior guesses, the individual is not really reading in any useful way.

Relying exclusively on what is printed may also create problems. Because the human mind is a limited processor, attention directed to decoding means that attention will be taken away from other things—from what previously identified words said, for example. Limited processing capacity is an especially critical problem for new readers since many of the necessary subskills are not yet well learned and demand conscious attention.

The remaining sections of this article will consider a number of problems that beset beginning readers and will point out what they indicate for reading instruction.

Decoding

For everything to work together in a smoothly coordinated way, readers must identify words automatically. Beginners, however, are still working on that requirement. To

Adams, Anderson and Durkin

assist them, phonics is taught. Ideally, it will be taught in a way that concentrates on patterns of letters since it is patterns, not individual letters, that suggest pronunciations. Although instructional materials now highlight patterns, some teachers continue to teach decoding skills as if decisions about a pronunciation can be made letter by letter. The persistence probably reflects the fact that the use of new materials is often affected by old procedures and habits. Such an explanation seems reasonable since materials of the past commonly assigned unmerited importance to individual letters.

Materials of the past also failed to underscore the need for flexible application of what is taught in phonics. More specifically, they failed to portray decoding as a type of problem solving that does not begin with a ready-made answer but, rather, seeks one out with the help both of a word's spelling and of the context in which that word is embedded. Teachers who keep this in mind will steer away from having children decode words presented in lists and, instead, will move toward practice that concentrates on unfamiliar words placed in sentences. Practice (of the right kind) is important because it is only rapid decoding that assists with comprehension.

Although some might take it for granted that children get sufficient and prolonged practice in decoding, classroom observations reveal something else. Once glossaries appear in books—this occurs at about the third or fourth grade level—"Look it up in the glossary" is the directive children commonly receive when they are having trouble with a new or forgotten word. While nobody would deny the value of their knowing how to use reference materials like glossaries and dictionaries, nobody could deny either that it makes little sense to spend huge amounts of time teaching phonics in the primary grades if what is taught there is put on the shelf in subsequent years.

Anyone teaching phonics also needs to keep in mind a point made earlier, namely, that the human mind is a limited processor. Because it is, the processing capacity of readers can be so taken up with sounding out a word that they may block on previously identified words. The meaning of this for teaching is clear: Have children habitually reread any sentence in which a "worked on" word occurs, once that word has been identified. Only in this way is comprehension of the sentence likely.

Simultaneously, the same habit should discourage word-by-word reading, something that hardly promotes comprehension.

Syntax

Anyone interested in promoting comprehension needs to know about syntax. Syntax refers to the order of words in a phrase or sentence. Such order is significant because English is a positional language. That is, it relies heavily on word order to convey meaning. Consequently, to change order is to change meaning. Expressions like *off day* and *day off* effectively demonstrate this.

The dependence of meaning on word order indicates that even though a child's ability to decode is important for reading, it is not sufficient for success. That decoding might be sufficient is associated with a conception of writing that views it as being no more than ciphered speech. According to this view, if children can learn to translate printed words into their spoken equivalents, the problem of reading is solved. All that's needed is the application of previously acquired language skills to the deciphered text. Why such a view is an overly simple and misleading conception of reading can be explained in a variety of ways.

First of all, there is good reason to question whether beginning readers have as much competence in oral language as is often claimed. The frequent assertion that children entering school have mastered the exceedingly complex structure of our language is based on the finding that, even though young children do not produce sentences having the complexity found in adult speech, their own speech does reflect all of the basic syntactic transformations. Concluding that children have mastered syntax because they can use basic grammatical structures is, however, a little like describing people as grand masters simply because they know the legal moves of the chess pieces. Not to be overlooked, either, is the evidence which indicates that children continue to make substantial gains in their ability to use and understand syntactic structures until they are at least thirteen years old (7).

But, let's suppose that children do have the syntactic competence to interpret a given sentence in spoken discourse. Can it automatically be assumed that they will understand it if it is written? Our answer is "Not necessarily" for the following reasons.

Ordinarily, spoken language occurs in a rich context of external events that provide comprehension aids not found on the printed page. Or, to put this differently, the speaker is far more helpful to the listener than is the author to the reader. Furthermore, when speaking fluently, people tend to restrict pauses and breaths to syntactic boundaries. They neither speak as if every word were followed by a comma nor do they move breathlessly on in an attempt to say everything at once. Instead, they provide listeners with temporal cues that help them comprehend because they indicate meaningful units of words. Apparently the listener depends on these temporal cues for when they are distorted, comprehension suffers (4).

Contrasted with spoken language, written discourse is stingy in the help it offers a reader with syntax. Replacing the obviously helpful pauses of oral language is punctuation, but it is a poor substitute. Readers are pretty much on their own, then, as they attempt to group words into such necessary units as phrases and clauses. And unless they can recover the syntactic structure of a printed sentence, it doesn't matter whether they do or do not have the syntactic competence to understand its oral equivalent.

To the extent that the processes of identifying the syntactic units of a sentence are unique to reading, we might expect them to be troublesome for the beginner. It is not surprising, therefore, that studies of beginning readers' troubles have identified the failure to sample written material in phrasal units and the tendency to indulge in many more fixations per line of the text than do mature readers (5, 6).

The failure of beginners to organize sentences into phrases creates memory problems, hence comprehension problems too. This is the case since it is the meaningfulness of a series of words that allows a listener or a reader to remember them. Recalling *ran, boy, little, to, school, the*, for example, is far more difficult than remembering the very same words presented in a meaningful order like *the little boy ran to school*.

The indisputable importance of getting an author's words organized into meaningful units if they are to be both understood and remembered raises questions about some common classroom activities. For example, word identification practice that is routinely carried on by having children read individual, isolated words (flashcard practice) is hardly likely to foster the type of processing that the comprehension of sentences requires. Raising a question about this type of practice, however, is not to question practice itself. To the contrary, for one of the common problems found among poor readers is the inability to identify words sufficiently quickly. Such a problem is not remedied with less practice but, rather, with different and better practice. Better practice would have children concentrate on connected words (*the girl, on the table*), not on isolated words (*the, girl, on, the, table*).

Another common classroom activity called into question by the importance of segmenting a sentence into meaningful parts is the one called "round robin" reading. This is the procedure in which one child reads aloud while others in the group are expected to follow the same material silently. Anyone who has observed the procedure soon learns that, at the beginning level, oral reading is of the halting, word-by-word kind. As such, it hardly provides an ideal model for anyone who is attempting to put an author's words together in a way that will assist with understanding them.

The great emphasis put on oral reading in the primary grades might be encouraging still more problems related to comprehension, for it portrays reading as a performing art rather than an effort to understand what an author has written. The erroneous portrayal is undesirable because it could inhibit young readers from arriving at the understanding that reading is not saying something *to* another but is, instead, getting something *from* another.

Further Differences between Spoken and Written Language

Still more differences between spoken and written language need to be kept in mind because they also help to pinpoint the special requirements of success with reading.

One very significant difference has to do with the setting in which children acquire, use, and respond to oral language. Setting, in this case, refers to such nonlanguage "extras" as shared experiences, gestures, facial expressions, and pointing—

all of which offer considerable assistance with oral language comprehension. In the face of written language, on the other hand, readers have no extralinguistic contexts. Instead, they must construct *mental* contexts from clues that come from the printed page and from their knowledge of the world.

For beginners, constructing the necessary contexts can be difficult. Since writers cannot do such things as point, referring expressions (words like *this, that, here,* and *there*) may be incomprehensible and so, too, may the intended referents of certain words. To illustrate this, consider a "simple" sentence like, *John said to Peter, "Come over to my house tomorrow."* If a child heard this sentence, he or she would understand that *my* referred to the speaker and that *tomorrow* referred to the day after the utterance. To read the same sentence, however, *my* has to be interpreted as meaning John's while *tomorrow* has to be interpreted as meaning the day after John spoke to Peter. For a child, these necessary changes in perspective may not be easy—at least not so easy as we commonly assume them to be.

Since fiction characteristically requires a reader both to establish and shift perspective, the traditional practice of using stories to teach beginning reading may be a faulty one. Admittedly, authors of beginning readers make generous use of pictures, which should aid children in constructing the mental contexts that comprehension requires. However, pictures can lead to other problems; namely, a reliance on pictures instead of on words and reduced motivation to read a story since the pictures tell it.

Semantics

Still more problems that face children when they are trying to learn to read have to do with the need to understand the meanings of words. Such a need is verified not only by the application of common sense but also by test data. Over the years, for example, a persistent research finding has pointed to the close association that exists between scores on vocabulary tests and scores on measures of reading achievement.

Research data on vocabulary itself agree with what is found when classrooms are visited; for, when they are, generous amounts of confusion about meanings are revealed

(*1*). Children as advanced as fourth graders have been heard to define *border* (in the context of "South of the Border") as "somebody who lives with you but he's not your family." In earlier grades, *bold* has been explained as meaning "not having any hair on the top of your head" while *canyon* was described as "a big gun that you use in a war."

Research data uncover vocabulary problems that are more subtle and hidden. One study, for instance, revealed unexpected complications in acquiring correct meanings for words like *give, take, buy*, and *sell* (*2*). At first, it was learned, children assign equivalent meanings to *give* and *sell* and to *take* and *buy*. Only later are they able to deal with a second dimension of meaning for *sell* and *buy* (the transfer of money), which allows for distinctions between *give* and *sell* and between *take* and *buy*. Other studies report well-known findings; for instance, children's tendency to overgeneralize and undergeneralize meanings. Initially, for example, a word like *brother* includes all male children but no male adults. Only with the accumulation of experiences does the true meaning come through.

Meanings for words that are in a context can create even greater problems; for, now, children must move from a wide range of possible meanings to one that fits the context. Often, knowing what does fit requires not only a knowledge of that range but also the ability to infer what is only implied in the context. At times, background knowledge is an additional prerequisite for success.

What all this says to teachers is clear: If each child's potential for reading is to be realized, attention to listening-speaking vocabularies must be viewed both as a serious and a never-ending responsibility.

Text Organization

Just as word-by-word reading thwarts comprehension, so does sentence-by-sentence reading, since relationships also exist among sentences. Generally, classroom instruction first deals with sentence relationships through the avenue of sequence. What happened first? What happened next? And then what happened? These are frequent queries when a selection that was read is being discussed. Relationships other than sequence, however, are common in written discourse and cover such things as cause-effect relationships, explanations, elaborations, examples, exceptions, contradictions, and conclusions.

Even though comprehension depends upon success in integrating information across sentences, research on this topic with primary grade children is practically nonexistent. Nonetheless, based on the best evidence available, it appears that children have a great deal to learn about intersentence relationships.

Authors offer help with interrelationships through the way they organize what they write. Highly visible signs of organization, for instance, characterize most expository material. An introduction (often labeled as such) indicates what is to come, whereas a summary sketches what has been said. In between, headings and subheadings suggest what is major, what is minor, and what relates to what. Exactly how primary grade readers use such organizational aids is unknown; for, again, research is lacking. In this case, the excessively generous use of narrative material in the early grades may be one explanation for the omission.

The structure built into written material, of course, is not the only kind that affects what is comprehended and retained. Another important kind of structure is what is built into the readers themselves in the form of experiences and information. What is used from this knowledge structure is affected by the material; but what is in the written message is also affected by what is in the reader's head. Thus, as was underscored in the initial part of this article, successful reading emerges as a highly complex, interactive process in which what the reader brings to the page is as important as what is written. That is why comprehension always is a highly personal experience.

References

1. Durkin, Dolores. *Teaching Young Children to Read*, Second Edition. Boston: Allyn and Bacon, 1976.
2. Gentner, D. "Evidence for the Psychological Reality of Semantic Components: The Verbs of Possession," in D.A. Norman, D.E. Rumelhart, and the LNR Research Group (Eds.), *Explorations in Cognition*. San Francisco: Freeman, 1975.
3. Goodman, K.S. "Reading: A Psycholinguistic Guessing Game," *Journal of the Reading Specialist*, 4 (1967), 123-135.

4. Huggins, A.W.F. "Timing and Speech Intelligibility," in J. Requin (Ed.), *Attention and Performance*. New York: Academic Press, in press.
5. Kolers, P.A. "Pattern Analyzing Disability in Poor Readers," *Developmental Psychology*, 11 (1975), 282-290.
6. Levin, H., and E. L. Kaplan. "Grammatical Structure and Reading," in H. Levin and J.P. Williams (Eds.), *Basic Studies on Reading*. New York: Basic Books, 1970.
7. Palermo, D., and D.L. Malfese. "Language Acquisition from Age Five Onward," *Psychological Bulletin*, 78 (1972), 409-427.
8. Rumelhart, D.E. "Toward an Interactive Model of Reading," CHIP Report No. 56, Center for Human Information Processing, University of California at San Diego, 1976.

Adams, Anderson and Durkin

Learning to Read with Understanding

John Downing
University of Victoria

Every reading teacher has a theory of how children learn to read. Every reading instruction program is based on some model of the learning-to-read process, whether it is made explicit or not. The way we teach reading depends on our beliefs about how children naturally develop reading skill. The great theoretical rift between teachers has been over "look-say" versus "phonic" methods. Chall (4) reclassified teaching methods into "meaning emphasis" and "code emphasis" approaches because she found that teachers and authors of reading textbooks placed more importance either on teaching children the meaningful functions of written language or on the technical features of the printed code for the spoken language. A similar dichotomy of methods seems to exist in every language (11). Even in Chinese, where most people would believe that phonics is impossible because of the logographic writing system for Chinese morphemes, the printed characters can be analyzed into their parts just as printed words can be in English. Thus teachers everywhere discuss the relative merits of meaning emphasis versus code emphasis approaches.

Currently in the United States the code emphasis is in fashion, but there are signs that meaning emphasis is about to make a comeback in the next swing of the pendulum. The two reading theories most likely to ride the crest of this new wave of meaning emphasis teaching methods in American schools are those of Goodman and Smith.

Smith and Goodman

Smith and Goodman both believe that listening and reading are parallel active processes. Thus Smith (*39*) claims that "reading is an aspect of language, only superficially different from the comprehension of speech...," and Goodman (*19*) states, "...*reading is language*. It's one of two receptive language processes. Speaking and writing are the generative, productive language processes. The other receptive language process is listening. Reading and listening, at least for the literate, are parallel processes." According to Goodman, readers "construct the meaning" on the basis of their past experience of language. School beginners, he asserts, "are already possessed of a language competence and an ability to learn language which are powerful resources." Smith's view is that "speech and writing are both aspects of the same language..., and it is generally quite an unfounded assumption that reading instruction must involve teaching children about language." On the contrary, "the vast majority of children have a firm grasp of language by the time they get to school...."

The essence of the reading process, according to Smith and Goodman, is the construction of meaning. They strongly reject the code emphasis approach. Phonics for Smith is a "vague but laudible concept," "a hope underlying a teaching technique," and a "Spartan deprivation of outside help in word identification." Smith argues that, "'Converting' a written message into verbal form does not itself provide the meaning, it merely interposes an additional stage in the process of comprehension." Goodman also attacks "instructional reading programs that begin with bits and pieces abstracted from language, like words or letters, on the theory that they're making learning simpler," but "in fact make learning to read harder," because it "isn't language any more."

According to the Smith/Goodman theory, children do not need to be aware of the parts of language. For example, Goodman and Burke (*20*) comment: "The language and thought processes which the child is using are abstract and complex. But as a language user he is not called upon to understand them, only to make use of them." More generally, "In order to communicate, speakers, listeners, readers, and writers must follow a similar set of rules. These are not rules of which the language user is consciously aware. In fact, in most cases, people cannot state or explain the language rules they use."

Linguistic Awareness

Psycholinguistics studies lend support to Goodman's and Smith's description of the reading process as a search for meaning. But two of the chief contentions in the Smith/Goodman theory do not accord with some recent developments in linguistics.

First, Mattingly (29) has listed a number of important ways in which listening and reading are different processes—not parallel as Goodman and Smith believe. Mattingly concludes:

> Reading is seen not as a parallel activity in the visual mode to speech perception in the auditory mode; there are differences between the two activities that cannot be explained in terms of the difference of modality. They can be explained only if we regard reading as a deliberately acquired, language-based skill, dependent upon the speaker-hearer's awareness of certain aspects of primary linguistic activity. By virtue of this linguistic awareness, written text initiates the synthetic linguistic process common to both reading and speech, enabling the reader to get the writer's message and so to recognize what has been written.

The second difficulty for the Smith/Goodman theory is provided by Mattingly's description of the role of "linguistic awareness" in learning literacy skills. He states that "the relationship of the process of reading a language to the processes of speaking and listening to it...is much more devious than it is generally assumed to be. Speaking and listening are primary linguistic activities; reading is a secondary and rather special sort of activity that relies critically upon the reader's awareness of these primary activities." Mattingly accepts that much primary linguistic behavior is not accessible to immediate awareness. However, people are aware of certain aspects of their own language behavior, and some of these are related to the writing system of their language. Mattingly states that the reader "must be thoroughly familiar with the rules of the writing system." These may include the rules that relate written language to the elements of speech that are accessible to awareness. We may add that doubtless the creators of writing systems based their rules on this same linguistic awareness that exists in the teachers and students of reading today. Thus learning to read for individual students is in a way rather like reinventing the alphabet and spelling with their natural endowment of linguistic awareness.

The Soviet psychologist, Luria, has arrived at a similar conclusion based on a series of experimental investigations in Russia. His view is known in the U.S.S.R. as the "glass theory." For instance, Luria is cited by Elkonin (15) as stating:

> While actively utilizing grammatical language and while defining with words the corresponding objects and actions, the child cannot make a word and verbal relationship the object of his awareness. During this period, the word may be used but not noticed by the child, and frequently it presents things seemingly *like a glass, through which the child looks at the surrounding world, not making the word itself the object of awareness*, and not suspecting that it has its own existence, its own aspects of construction [italics added].

Elkonin has developed a method for developing children's awareness of the elements of language because he believes that: "The development of awareness of the language's phonological aspect...represents one of the most essential preconditions for...learning literacy."

Elkonin (16) has reported his experiments with various teaching methods that make it easier for children to conceptualize the elements of language. For example, plain counters can be used to represent phonemes in finding out how many phonemes exist in a word. Or counters of different colors can represent different kinds of phonemes. He has shown that Russian kindergartners can be trained to discriminate between vowels, hard consonants, and soft consonants in Russian speech. Awareness of these differences in spoken Russian is essential if the child is to understand the logical rules of the Russian writing system. All this is done *before* the teacher introduces written letters. The advantage seems to be that the child then only has to make one step into the unknown when introduced to the written form of language. When letters and printed words are introduced, the child already understands what "a word" is and what "a phoneme" is. The child already understands the idea of the continuity of speech and how it is related to its parts. The main technical linguistic concepts which the teacher needs to use to explain how writing is related to language are already known to the child. Some of Elkonin's techniques have been adapted for the English language in Canadian kindergartens and found feasible and successful (31).

Cazden (3), in the United States, has commented: "Our concern as educators with this particular kind of language performance comes from increasing arguments that it is at least very helpful—and maybe critically important—not so much in the primary processes of speaking and hearing as in what may be considered the derived or secondary processes of reading and writing."

Cazden proposes that linguistic awareness develops naturally through play. The "glass" of language becomes opaque through children's playful manipulation of the sounds of language outside their use in meaningful communication. For example, Johnson (24) describes a two year old saying as he was being undressed, "Nolly lolly, nolly lolly, nilly lolly, sillie Billie, nolly lolly." Piaget's type of egocentric language that he terms "repetition" seems to have a similar function in play (32). Thus, linguistic awareness is a natural phenomenon, although its development in children can also be fostered deliberately by adults, as in the experiments of Elkonin. In denying the possiblity that linguistic awareness may be a factor in learning to read, Goodman and Smith seem to overlook the human tendency to reflect upon and speculate about one's own behavior and other people's acts. There is no reason to suppose that language behavior must be excluded from such natural introspections and observations. Indeed, as will be shown later in this article, there is growing evidence that children develop linguistic awareness in learning to read and that this awareness is associated with literacy achievements.

Reasoning about Reading

When an individual is required to learn a new skill, his first reaction is to try to understand what he must do to become a skilled performer. In their review of psychological research,

Fitts and Posner (*17*) found that this effort to comprehend the learning task is characteristic of all skill development. They describe this initial approach to the task as the "cognitive phase." In it the beginner tries to find out the functions of the skilled act and its component subskills and the technical concepts needed for talking and thinking about the tasks involved in mastering the skill. This suggests that reasoning may play a part in skill learning and that this reasoning may be especially important in verbal skills such as reading. Indeed, there is considerable evidence from research that this is so.

In her more recent survey of research on reading disability, Vernon (*43*) concludes:

> It would seem that in learning to read it is essential for the child to realize and understand the fundamental generalization that in alphabetic writing all words are represented by combinations of a limited number of visual symbols. Thus it is possible to present a very large vocabulary of spoken words in an economical manner which requires the memorizing of a comparatively small number of printed symbols and their associated sounds. But a thorough grasp of this principle necessitates a fairly advanced stage of conceptual reasoning, since this type of organization differs fundamentally from any previously encountered by children in their normal environment.

Earlier, Vernon's review (*42*) of research on the causes of reading disability led to her conclusion that "the fundamental and basic characteristic of reading disability appears to be cognitive confusion and lack of system.... It must be attributed to a failure in analyzing, abstraction, and generalization, but one which, typically, is confined to linguistics." Vernon said that "the fundamental trouble appears to be a failure in development of this reasoning process." She described the cognitively confused child as being "hopelessly uncertain and confused as to why certain successions of printed letters should correspond to certain phonetic sounds in words."

Several investigations have shown that an important difference between normal readers and disabled readers lies in the inferior conceptual and integrative abilities of the latter (*28, 36, 38*). Vernon (*43*) believes that reasoning and understanding are characteristic of the normal development of reading skill. She states: "The employment of reasoning is almost certainly involved in understanding the variable associations between printed and sounded letters. It might appear that certain writers suppose that these associations may be acquired through rote learning. But even if this is possible with very simple letter-phoneme associations, the more complex associations and the correct application of the rules of spelling necessitate intelligent comprehension." Vernon (42) indicates that "cognitive confusion" is the normal state of the young beginner. Therefore, it would seem that an important part of learning to read consists in reasoning about the reading task in an effort to achieve cognitive clarity. If cognitive confusion is the chief characteristic of reading disability then cognitive clarity would seem to be the mark of success in learning to read.

The Cognitive Clarity Theory

The cognitive clarity theory of learning to read emphasizes the learner's striving to understand the tasks he is required to undertake in reading instruction. It may be expressed by eight postulates: 1) Writing or print in any language was a visible code for those aspects of speech that were accessible to the linguistic awareness of the creators of that code or writing system; 2) this linguistic awareness of the creators of a writing system included simultaneous awareness of the communicative function of language and certain features of spoken language accessible to the speaker-hearer for logical analysis; 3) the learning-to-read process consists in the rediscovery of the functions and the coding rules of the writing system; 4) their rediscovery depends on the learner's linguistic awareness of the same features of communication and language as were accessible to the creators of the writing system; 5) children approach the tasks of reading instruction in a normal state of cognitive confusion about the purposes and techniques of literacy; 6) under reasonably good conditions, children work themselves out of the initial state of cognitive confusion into increasing cognitive clarity about the functions and technical characteristics of written language; 7) although the initial stage of literacy acquisition is the most vital one, cognitive confusion continues to arise and then, in turn, give way to cognitive clarity throughout the later stages of education as new subskills are added to the student's repertory;

and 8) the cognitive clarity theory applied to all languages and writing systems. The communication aspect is universal, but the technical coding rules differ from one language to another. For instance, in languages that have an alphabetic writing system, linguistic awareness of the phoneme is more important than awareness of the syllable, whereas in languages with a syllabary (such as Japanese) awareness of the syllable is more important than awareness of the phoneme.

This listing of the postulates of the cognitive clarity theory has been kept simple deliberately, but it may suggest an oversimplified view of speech and writing. For example, in English there have been many creators of the writing system in its thousand years and more of history. Nevertheless, the learner's task is still to try to understand the intentions of those who created and modified the orthography of the language of instruction.

This cognitive clarity theory of reading does not entirely conflict with the theories of Goodman and Smith. What is suggested rather is that the important truth they have uncovered is only one part of the learning to read process. Their emphasis on the reader's search for meaning by predictions based on past experiences of language is a focus on the communication function of the reading act. But there are two parts to the child's rediscovery of written language: 1) understanding its communicative functions and 2) understanding its technical features. A complete explanation of learning to read must take account of how the child understands the features as well as the function of writing and print.

Functional Concepts

Piaget showed that children of the typical school beginning age have relatively little awareness of the communication function of language. Vygotsky (44) reported that young beginners have "only a vague idea" of the "usefulness" of writing. More recently Reid's research (34) in Scotland found that five year olds begin school with a general lack of any idea "of the purpose and use" of writing or print. A replication of her study led to the conclusion that "young beginners have difficulty in understanding the *purpose* of written language" (9).

Two investigations have shown how environmental experiences may influence the growth of children's concepts of the purpose of writing. In the first (*13*), two groups of Canadian Indian beginners were found to be significantly less aware of the purposes of reading and writing than were non-Indian beginners attending the kindergarten classes in the same school districts. This supported the hypothesis that Indian children's concepts of the functions of writing are less well developed because they come from a home background with no cultural tradition of literacy. In a second study (*14*), it was found that children from the economically poorest third of the population in a Canadian city began kindergarten with significantly less understanding of the functions of writing than children from the better off two-thirds of the population in the same city. Thus children develop understanding of the functions of literacy through observing and sharing communication activities in written language.

Probably the most important single fact about the process of reading is that the purpose of the reading act is inextricably interwoven in its technique. In other words, the ends are an integral part of the means. Many researchers on the psychology of the reading process have recognized this fact (*1, 21, 25, 33, 35, 37, 40*). Different purposes require different reading techniques, and these have been revealed by scientific observations of readers' behavior.

The Bullock Report in England (*7*) strongly recommends that purpose be integrated with skill development:

> Competence in language comes above all through its purposeful use, not through the working of exercises divorced from context.
>
> Language development...involves creating situations in which, to satisfy his own purposes, a child encounters the need to use more elaborate forms and is thus motivated to extend the complexity of language available to him.

These recommendations from this official government report are cognizant of the principle that concepts are learned from experience with their exemplars. Therefore, teaching an understanding of the functions of written language requires the provision of experiences with reading and writing activities that are purposeful for the individual student.

One successful application of this principle has been seen in many American schools using the language-experience approach to reading. Particularly effective have been the programs developed under the leadership of Professor Harry Hahn at Oakland University in Michigan. Several years ago he introducted the idea of "young authors' conferences." At these meetings, children from schools in an area meet with each other and with adult authors of published children's books to confer about the techniques and purposes of creative writing. The Bullock Commission notes that "The novel features in the task and the language it demands can be explored in discussion with the individual or the group, and supporting examples collected and worked upon. The child should thus be led to greater control over his writing, with a growing knowledge of how to vary its effects."

A different approach to developing awareness of the process and functions of communication is being developed in an experimental school in Moscow by Professor Elkonin of the Academy of Pedagogical Sciences of the U.S.S.R. In the primary grades a new system of symbols is being created that provides a code for a functional description of the relations between thought, speech, and writing. Children use this code for analyzing problems of communication individually and in class discussion.

Thus, both Hahn in America and Elkonin in Russia are using discussion procedures to develop children's awareness and understanding of the communications functions of written language.

Featural Concepts

The second major category of problem solving tasks involved in learning to read is understanding the technical linguistic concepts needed for reasoning about the relationships between speech and writing. A number of researchers (5, 22, 23, 26), using a variety of research methods, have found that the speech segments of children's perception do not coincide with the unit "word" or "phoneme" as usually understood by adults. A second approach to the same problem has been to study how children interpret and use such technical terms as "word," "sound," "letter," "number," "reading," "writing," and so on. Reid's study of Scottish five year olds found that these children exhibited considerable confusion about the meaning of such linguistic terms, and they did not know how adults read. Reid concluded that they had "a great poverty of linguistic equipment to deal with the new experiences" in reading instruction.

A replication of Reid's study confirmed her findings (9). This replication was extended to test children's interpretation of two technical terms that are used in reading instruction to refer to features of speech. Following appropriate pretraining in the experimental procedure, five year olds were asked to say whether each of a series of auditory stimuli was "a word." Five types of stimuli were used: a nonverbal sound, a meaningless vowel phoneme, a single word, a phrase, and a sentence. No child's category for "a word" coincided with the usual concept of a spoken word held by teachers. Some children made only random guesses; some excluded nonverbal sounds; and some thought that only the word, the phrase, and the sentence were each "a word." The experiment was repeated at three intervals during the first school year, but although responses were progressively in the direction of interpreting "a word" as a chunk of meaningful speech, no child achieved by the end of the year what teachers would usually consider to be the concept of "a spoken word." Similar results were found for the term "sound," although some pupils understood it as meaning a phoneme by the final testing session (9, 10). Canadian children exhibit the same confusion (12).

Nor are beginners less cognitively confused about the terms used for units of written language such as "word," "letter," or "number." For example, Meltzer and Herse (30) asked American kindergartners and first graders to cut off with scissors a word from a sentence printed on a card. Occasionally a word was cut off, but often it was two words and sometimes a part of a word. A variety of different testing procedures have demonstrated the same confusion in children's understanding of the technical features of written language: Clay (6) in New Zealand; Kingston, Weaver and Figa (27) in the United States; Turnbull (41) in Australia.

How the development of a clear understanding of these technical features is related to learning to read is indicated by four investigations.

Francis (*18*), in her study of English primary school boys and girls, found that her highest correlation was between reading achievement and knowledge of a technical linguistic vocabulary, even with general vocabulary knowledge controlled. She concluded that "factors independent of a general ability to deal with abstract concepts were involved in learning technical vocabulary, and that these were closely related to the reading process." She believes that, under current methods of instruction, children learn these technical concepts by groping their way through mostly unplanned experiences of hearing the technical jargon used by their teachers. Francis writes:

> It was as though the children had never thought to analyze speech, but in learning to read had been forced to recognize units and subdivisions. The use of words like *letter, word* and *sentence* in teaching was not so much a direct aid to instruction but a challenge to find their meaning.

This technical language of reading instruction is part of what DeStefano (*8*) has called the "language instruction register"—the specialized language used in talking and thinking about teaching and learning language skills. Some idea of the confusion in the mind of an individual who is not yet fully initiated into the mysteries of the language instruction register may be gathered from the following passage:

> I'm going to sove some mivvirs. See these mivvirs. Their names are snow and orsh. They say "haagh." Who knows a zasp with the tauf "haagh" in it?

Translated into the actual register it is still nonsense to the beginner: "I'm going to *write* some *letters*. See these letters. Their names are *sea* and *aitch*. They say 'haagh' (as in Scottish Loch Ness). Who knows a *word* with the *sound* 'haagh' in it?" The young beginner, of course, cannot translate but must puzzle out the meanings of these technical terms by observing exemplars and nonexemplars. Moreover, the terms used in the above passage are merely the simplest examples of the many phonological and syntactical concepts needed for talking and thinking about features of spoken and written language.

Two of the studies referred to earlier in this article also provide evidence on the effects of the child's environmental experiences on the development of featural concepts. In the comparison of Indian and non-Indian kindergartners, the former were found to be significantly more immature in their understanding of featural concepts than were the latter (13). In a survey of kindergarten children in a Canadian city, this test also found a significant difference favoring the upper two-thirds socioeconomically in comparison with the lowest third in respect to the development of featural concepts. This difference remained significant even after a year of kindergarten education. Furthermore, these results were quite highly correlated with more traditional tests of reading readiness, notably those of letter-name knowledge and auditory discrimination that are well-known to be the best predictors of later attainments in reading (14). This correlation suggests that the test of featural concepts and the more traditional reading readiness tests probe the same underlying basic factor—the child's cognitive clarity or confusion about the featural concepts used in reading instruction.

A fourth study that shows a significant relationship between reading ability and the development of featural concepts is that by Calfee, Lindamood, and Lindamood (2). Children from grades ranging from kindergarten to grade twelve were tested to determine their ability to match phonetic segments by use of a sequence of colored blocks to represent auditory stimuli. They were tested also for reading and spelling achievements. The results showed that more than 50 percent of the total variance in reading ability could be predicted from the student's ability to perform this extremely simple acoustic segmentation task. Calfee et al. added: "The major implication of these findings was that relatively simple phonological skills are significantly and substantially related to reading and spelling performance through high school."

The research findings reviewed in this section of this article indicate that the child's understanding of the features of speech and writing as well as linguistic awareness are important in the development of reading skill. This is the other component of cognitive clarity that the child must develop in understanding the tasks of reading and writing.

Comprehensive Methods

In this article I have attempted to show that learning literacy skills consists mainly in the child's rediscovery of the greatest invention of civilisation—writing. That invention involved two creative ideas. The first was that meaning could be communicated graphically instead of vocally. The second was in the specific system of written symbols devised for the new visible language. In every language this writing system has been subject to many modifications by its more creative users in the history of its development. These developers of written language employed their own natural linguistic awareness in their creative work. The same natural linguistic awareness is used by children in rediscovering the features of the writing system of their language. They also need experiences that will lead them to discover the functions of written language in communicating meaning. The successful reader has developed cognitive clarity through understanding *both* aspects of the task: its functions and its technical features. Therefore, what may be needed at this time, rather than a simple rebirth of meaning emphasis methods in reading instruction, is a more comprehensive theory that takes account of both aspects of learning to read. This should be a theory of instruction in reading that should give equal weight to both meaning and code, deliberately not overemphasizing one aspect or the other because that may mislead the child's understanding of the total task which does, in truth, integrate both aspects.

References

1. Bond, G.L., and M.A. Tinker. *Reading Difficulties: Their Diagnosis and Correction.* New York: Appleton-Century-Crofts, 1973.
2. Calfee, R.C., P. Lindamood, and C. Lindamood. "Acoustic-Phonetic Skills and Reading—Kindergarten through Twelfth Grade," *Journal of Educational Psychology,* 64 (1973), 293-298.
3. Cazden, C.B. "Play with Language and Metalinguistic Awareness: One Dimension of Language Experience," *Organization Mondiale pour l'Education Préscolaire,* 6 (1974), 12-24.
4. Chall, J. *Learning to Read: The Great Debate.* New York: McGraw-Hill, 1967.
5. Chappell, P.R. "Early Development of Awareness of Lexical Units," paper presented at the annual meeting of the American Educational Research Association, Chicago, 1968.

6. Clay, M.M. *Reading: The Patterning of Complex Behaviour*. Auckland, New Zealand: Heinemann, 1972.

7. Department of Education and Science. *A Language for Life* (the Bullock Report). London: Her Majesty's Stationery Office, 1975.

8. DeStefano, J.S. *Some Parameters of Register in Adult and Child Speech*. Louvain, Belgium: Institute of Applied Linguistics, 1972.

9. Downing, J. "Children's Concepts of Language in Learning to Read," *Educational Research*, 12 (1970), 106-112.

10. Downing, J. "Children's Developing Concepts of Spoken and Written Language," *Journal of Reading Behavior*, 4 (1972), 1-19.

11. Downing, J. (Ed.). *Comparative Reading*. New York: Macmillan, 1973.

12. Downing, J., and P. Oliver. "The Child's Conception of 'a Word'," *Reading Research Quarterly*, 9 (1974), 568-581.

13. Downing, J., L. Ollila, and P. Oliver. "Cultural Differences in Children's Concepts of Reading and Writing," *British Journal of Educational Psychology*, 45 (1975), 312-316.

14. Downing, J., L. Ollila, and P. Oliver. "Concepts of Language in Children from Differing Socioeconomic Backgrounds," *Journal of Educational Research*, 70 (1977), 277-281.

15. Elkonin, D.B. "Development of Speech," in A.V. Zaporozhets and D.B. Elkonin (Eds.), *The Psychology of Preschool Children*. Cambridge, Massachusetts: MIT Press, 1971.

16. Elkonin, D.B. "U.S.S.R." in J. Downing (Ed.), *Comparative Reading*. New York: Macmillan, 1973.

17. Fitts, P.M., and M.I. Posner. *Human Performance*. Belmont, California: Brooks-Cole, 1967.

18. Francis, H. "Children's Experience of Reading and Notions of Units in Language," *British Journal of Educational Psychology*, 43 (1973), 17-23.

19. Goodman, K.S. "What We Know about Reading," in P.D. Allen and D.J. Watson (Eds.), *Findings of Research in Miscue Analysis: Classroom Implications*. Urbana, Illinois: National Council of Teachers of English, 1976.

20. Goodman, Y., and C. Burke. "Reading: Language and Psycholinguistic Bases," in P. Lamb and R. Arnold (Eds.), *Reading: Foundations and Instructional Strategies*. Belmont, California: Wadsworth, 1976.

21. Gray, C.T. "Types of Reading Ability as Exhibited through Tests and Laboratory Experiments," *Supplementary Educational Monographs*, No. 5. Chicago: Department of Education, University of Chicago, 1917.

22. Holden, M.H., and W.H. MacGinitie. "Children's Conceptions of Word Boundaries in Speech and Print," *Journal of Educational Psychology*, 63 (1972), 551-557.

23. Huttenlocher, J. "Children's Language: Word-Phrase Relationship," *Science*, 143 (1964), 264-265.

24. Johnson, H.M. *Children in "the Nursery School."* New York: Agathon Press, 1972.

25. Judd, C.H., and G. Buswell. "Silent Reading: A Study of the Various Types," *Supplementary Educational Monographs*, No. 23. Chicago: University of Chicago Press, 1922.

26. Karpova, S.N. "Osoznaniye Slovesnogo Sostava Rechi Rebeyonkom Doshkolnogo Vozrasta" (Realization of the Verbal Composition of Speech by a Preschool Child), *Voprosy Psikhologii* (Questions of Psychology), 4 (1955), 43-55.

Learning to Read with Understanding   177

27. Kingston, A.J., W.W. Weaver, and L.E. Figa. "Experiments in Children's Perception of Words and Word Boundaries," in F.P. Greene (Ed.), *Investigations Relating to Mature Reading*. Milwaukee, Wisconsin: National Reading Conference, 1972.

28. Klapper, Z.S. "Psychoeducational Aspects of Reading Disabilities," in G. Natchez (Ed.), *Children With Reading Problems*. New York: Basic Books, 1968.

29. Mattingly, I.G. "Reading, the Linguistic Process, and Linguistic Awareness," in J.F. Kavanagh and I.G. Mattingly (Eds.), *Language by Ear and by Eye*. Cambridge, Massachusetts: MIT Press, 1972.

30. Meltzer, N.S., and R. Herse. "The Boundaries of Written Words as Seen by First Graders," *Journal of Reading Behavior*, 1 (1969), 3-14.

31. Ollila, L., T. Johnson, and J. Downing. "Adapting Russian Methods of Auditory Discrimination Training for English," *Elementary English*, 51 (1974), 1138-1141, 1145.

32. Piaget, J. *The Language and Thought of the Child*. London: Routledge and Kegan Paul, 1959.

33. Postman, L., and V. Senders. "Incidental Learning and Generality of Set," *Journal of Experimental Psychology*, 36 (1946), 153-165.

34. Reid, J.F. "Learning to Think about Reading," *Educational Research*, 9 (1966), 56-62.

35. Rickards, J.P., and G.J. August. "Generative Underlining Strategies in Prose Recall," *Journal of Educational Psychology*, 67 (1975), 860-865.

36. Robinson, H.M. "Diagnosis and Treatment of Poor Readers with Vision Problems, Clinical Studies in Reading II," *Supplementary Educational Monographs*, No. 77. Chicago: University of Chicago Press, 1953.

37. Russell, D.H. *The Dynamics of Reading*. Waltham, Massachusetts: Ginn-Blaisdell, 1970.

38. Serafica, F.C., and I.E. Sigel. "Styles of Categorization and Reading Disability," *Journal of Reading Behavior*, 2 (1970), 105-115.

39. Smith, F. *Understanding Reading*. New York: Holt, Rinehart and Winston, 1971.

40. Thorndike, E.L. "Reading as Reasoning: A Study of Mistakes in Paragraph Reading," *Journal of Educational Psychology*, 8 (1917), 323-332.

41. Turnbull, K. "Children's Thinking: When Is a Letter a Number?" *Curriculum and Research Bulletin* (Victoria, Australia), 1970, 126-131.

42. Vernon, M.D. *Backwardness in Reading*. London: Cambridge University Press, 1957.

43. Vernon, M.D. *Reading and Its Difficulties*. London: Cambridge University Press, 1971.

44. Vygotsky, L.S. *Thought and Language*. Cambridge, Massachusetts: MIT Press, 1962.

Learning about Psycholinguistic Processes
by Analyzing Oral Reading

Kenneth S. Goodman
Yetta M. Goodman
University of Arizona

Over the past dozen years we have studied the reading process by analyzing the miscues (or unexpected responses) of subjects reading written texts. We prefer to use the word *miscue* because the term *error* has a negative connotation and history in education. Our analysis of oral reading miscues began with the foundational assumption that reading is a language process. Everything we have observed among readers from beginners to those with great proficiency supports the validity of this assumption. This analysis of miscues has been in turn the base for our development of a theory and model of the reading process.

In this paper we will argue that the analysis of oral reading offers unique opportunities for the study of linguistic and psycholinguistic processes and phenomena. We will support this contention by citing some concepts and principles that have grown out of our research.

We believe that reading is as much a language process as listening is. In a literate society there are four language processes: two are oral (speaking and listening), and two are written (writing and reading). Two are productive and two receptive. In the study and observation of productive language,

Reprinted from *Harvard Educational Review*, 47, 3 (August 1977), 317-333.
Copyright © 1977 by President and Fellows of Harvard College.

we may analyze what subjects say or write; however, except for an occasional slip of the tongue, typographical error, or regression to rephrase, speech and writing offer no direct insight into the underlying process of what the speaker or writer intended to say. The study of receptive language—listening and reading—is even more difficult. Either we analyze postlistening or postreading performance, or we contrive controlled-language tasks to elicit reactions for analysis.

Reading aloud, on the other hand, involves the oral response of the reader, which can be compared to the written text. Oral readers are engaged in comprehending written language while they produce oral responses. Because an oral response is generated while meaning is being constructed, it not only is a form of linguistic performance but also provides a powerful means of examining process and underlying competence.

Consider how Peggy, a nine year old from Toronto, reads aloud. Peggy was chosen by her teacher as an example of a pupil reading substantially below grade level. The story she read was considered to be beyond her current instructional level. Peggy read the story hesitantly, although in places she read with appropriate expression. Below are the first fourteen sentences (S1-S14) from "The Man Who Kept House" (*11*). In this and other excerpts from the story, the printed text is on the left; on the right is the transcript of Peggy's oral reading.

text	*transcript*
(S1a) Once upon a time there was a woodman who thought that no one worked as hard as he did.	*(S1b) Once upon a time there was a woodman. He threw...who thought that no one worked as hard as he did.*
(S2a) One evening when he came home from work, he said to his wife, "What do you do all day while I am away cutting wood?"	*(S2b) One eveneing when he... when he came home from work, he said to his wife, "I want you do all day...what do you do all day when I am always cutting wood?"*
(S3a) "I keep house," replied the wife, "and keeping house is hard work."	*(S3b) "I keep...I keep house," replied the wife, "and keeping... and keeping...and keeping house is and work."*

(S4a) "Hard work!" said the husband.

(S5a) "You don't know what hard work is!

(S6a) You should try cutting wood!"

(S7a) "I'd be glad to," said the wife.

(S8a) "Why don't you do my work some day?

(S9a) I'll stay home and keep house," said the woodman.

(S10a) "If you stay home to do my work, you'll have to make butter, carry water from the well, wash the clothes, clean the house, and look after the baby," said the wife.

(S11a) "I can do all that," replied the husband.

(S12a) "We'll do it tomorrow!"

(S13a) So the next morning the wife went off to the forest.

(S14a) The husband stayed home and began to do his wife's work.

(S4b) "Hard work!" said the husband.

(S5b) "You don't know what hard work is!

(S6b) "You should try cutting wood!"

(S7b) "I'll be glad to," said the wife.

(S8b) "Why don't you... Why don't you do my work so... some day?

(S9b) I'll start house and keeping house," said the woodman.

(S10b) "If you start house... If you start home to do my work, well you'll have to make bread, carry... carry water from the well, wash the clothes, clean the house, and look after the baby," said the wife.

(S11b) "I can do that... I can do all that," replied the husband.

(S12b) "Well you do it tomorrow!"

(S13b) So the next day the wife went off to the forest.

(S14b) The husband stayed home and began to do his wife's job.

Peggy's performance allows us to see a language user as a functional psycholinguist. Peggy's example is not unusual; what she does is also done by other readers. She processes graphic information: many of her miscues show a graphic relationship between the expected and observed response. She processes syntactic information: she substitutes noun for noun, verb for verb, noun phrase for noun phrase, verb phrase for verb phrase. She transforms: she omits an intensifier, changes a dependent clause to an independent clause, shifts a "wh-" question sentence to a declarative sentence. She draws on her conceptual background and struggles toward meaning, repeating, correcting, and reprocessing as necessary. She predicts grammar and meaning and monitors her own success.

She builds and uses psycholinguistic strategies as she reads. In short, her miscues are far from random.

From such data one can build and test theories of syntax, semantics, cognition, comprehension, memory, language development, linguistic competence, and linguistic perform- ance. In oral reading all the phenomena of other language processes are present or have their counterparts, but in oral reading they are accessible. The data are not controlled and clean in the experimental sense. Even young readers are not always very considerate. They do complex things for which we may be unprepared; and, not having studied the latest theories, they do not always produce confirming evidence. But they are language users in action.

Miscues and Comprehension

If we understand that the brain is the organ of human information processing, that the brain is not a prisoner of the senses but that it controls the sensory organs and selectively uses their input, then we should not be surprised that what the mouth reports in oral reading is not what the eye has seen but what the brain has generated for the mouth to report. The text is what the brain responds to; the oral output reflects the underlying competence and the psycholinguistic processes that have generated it. When expected and observed responses match, we get little insight into this process. When they do not match and a miscue results, the researcher has a window on the reading process.

Just as psycholinguists have been able to learn about the development of oral-language competence by observing the errors of young children, so we can gain insights into the development of reading competence and the control of the underlying psycholinguistic processes by studying reading miscues. We assume that both expected and unexpected oral responses to printed texts are produced through the same process. Thus, just as a three-year-old reveals the use of a rule for generating past tense by producing "throwed" for "threw" (Brown, 1973), so Peggy reveals her control of the reading process through her miscues.

We use two measures of readers' proficiency: *compre- hending*, which shows the readers' concern for meaning as expressed through their miscues, and *retelling*, which shows the readers' retention of meaning. Proficient readers can usually retell a great deal of a story and they produce miscues that do not interfere with gaining meaning. Except for S3, S8, and S9, all of Peggy's miscues produced fully acceptable sentences or were self-corrected. This suggests that Peggy's usual concern was to make sense as she read. In contrast, many nonproficient readers produce miscues that interfere with getting meaning from the story. In a real sense, then, a goal of reading instruction is not to eliminate miscues but to help readers produce the kind of miscues that characterize proficient reading.

Miscues reflect the degree to which a reader is understanding and seeking meaning. Insight can be gained into the reader's development of meaning and the reading process as a whole if miscues are examined and researchers ask: "Why did the reader make this miscue and to what extent is it like the language of the author?"

Miscue analysis requires several conditions. The written material must be new to the readers and complete with a beginning, middle, and end. The text needs to be long and difficult enough to produce a sufficient number of miscues. In addition, readers must receive no help, probe, or intrusion from the researcher. At most, if readers hesitate for more than thirty seconds, they are urged to guess, and only if hesitation continues are they told to keep reading even if it means skipping a word or phrase. Miscue analysis, in short, requires as natural a reading situation as possible.

Depending on the purpose of the research, subjects often have been provided with more than one reading task. Various fiction and nonfiction reading materials have been used, including stories and articles from basal readers, textbooks, trade books, and magazines. Subjects have been drawn from various levels in elementary, secondary, and adult populations and from a wide range of racial, linguistic, and national backgrounds. Studies have been concluded in languages other than English: Yiddish (*6*), Polish (*14*), and American Sign Language (*2*). Studies in German and Spanish are in progress.

The open-ended retellings used in miscue analysis are an index of comprehension. They also provide an opportunity for the researcher or teacher to gain insight into how concepts and language are actively used and developed in reading. Rather than asking direct questions that would give cues to the reader about what is significant in the story, we ask for unaided retelling. Information on the readers' understanding of the text emerges from the organization they use in retelling the story, from whether they use the author's language or their own, and from the conceptions or misconceptions they reveal. Here is the first segment of Peggy's retelling:

> um...it was about this woodman and um...when he...he thought that he um...he had harder work to do than his wife. So he went home and he told his wife, "What have you been doing all day." And then his wife told him. And then, um...and then, he thought that it was easy work. And so...so...so his wife, so his wife, so she um...so the wife said, "well so you have to keep," no...the husband says that you have to go to the woods and cut...and have to go out in the forest and cut wood and I'll stay home. And the next day they did that.

By comparing the story with Peggy's retelling and her miscues, researchers may interpret how much learning occurs as Peggy and the author interact. For example, although the story frequently uses "woodman" and "to cut wood," the noun used to refer to setting, "forest," is used just twice. Not only did Peggy provide evidence in her retelling that she knew that "woods" and "forest" are synonymous, but she also indicated that she knew the author's choice was "forest." The maze she worked through until she came to the author's term suggests that she was searching for the author's language. Although in much of the work on oral-language analysis mazes are not analyzed, their careful study may provide insight into oral self-correction and the speaker's intention.

There is more evidence of Peggy's awareness of the author's language. In the story the woodman is referred to as "woodman" and "husband" eight times each and as "man" four times; the wife is referred to only as "wife." Otherwise pronouns are used to refer to the husband and wife. In the retelling, Peggy used "husband" and "woodman" six times and "man" only once; she called the wife only "wife." Peggy always used appropriate pronouns in referring to the husband and wife. However, when cow was the antecedent, she substituted "he" for "she" twice. (What does Peggy know about the sex of cattle?)

Comparing Peggy's miscues with her retelling gives us more information about her language processes. In reading, Peggy indicated twice that "said" suggested to her that a declarative statement should follow: One such miscue was presented above (see S2); the other occurred at the end of the story and is recorded below.

text	transcript
(S66a) Never again did the wood-man say to his wife, "What did you do all day?"	(S66b) Never again did the wood-man say to his wife, "That he ... what did you do all day?"

In both instances she corrected the miscues. In the retelling she indicated that after "said" she could produce a question: "And then, from then on, the husband did ... did the cutting and he never said, 'What have you been doing all day?'" Even though she had difficulty with the "wh-" question structure in her reading, she was able to develop the language knowledge necessary to produce such a structure in her retelling.

It has puzzled teachers for a long time how a reader can know something in one context but not know it in another context. Such confusion comes from the belief that reading is word recognition: on the contrary, words in different syntactic and semantic contexts become different entities for readers, and Peggy's response to "keep house" suggests this. In S3, where the clauses "I keep house" and later "and keeping house" occur for the first time, Peggy produced the appropriate responses but repeated each several times. In S9 she produced "stay home and keep house" as "start house and keeping house," and she read the first phrase in S10 as "If you start home to do my work." The phrase "keep house" is a complex one. First, to a nine-year-old "keep" is a verb that means being able to hold on to or take care of something small. Although "keeping pets" is still used to mean taking care of, "keeping house" is no longer a common idiom in American or Canadian English. When "stay home" is added to the phrase "keep house," additional complexities arise. Used with different verbs and different function words, "home" and "house" are sometimes synonyms and sometimes not. The transitive and intransitive nature of the verbs as well as the infinitive structure, which is not in the surface of a sentence, add to the complexities of the verb phrase.

Peggy, in her search for meaning and her interaction with the print, continued to develop strategies to handle these complex problems. In S14 she produced "stayed home"; however, in S35 she encountered difficulty with "keeping house" once again and read: "perhaps keeping house...home and...is...hard work." She was still not happy with "keeping house." She read the phrase as written and then abandoned her correct response. Throughout the story "home" appears seven times and "house" appears ten times. Peggy read them correctly in every context except in the patterns "staying home" and "keeping house." Yet she continued to work on these phrases through her interaction with the text until she could finally handle the structure and could either self-correct successfully or produce a semantically acceptable sentence. Thus Peggy's miscues and retelling reveal the dynamic interaction between a reader and written language.

Oral and Written Language

The differences between oral and written language result from differences of function rather than from any differences in intrinsic characteristics. While any meaning that can be expressed in speech can also be expressed in writing and vice versa, we tend to use oral language for face-to-face communication and written language to communicate over time and space. Oral language is likely to be strongly supported by the context in which it is used; written language is more likely to be abstracted from the situations with which it deals. Written language must include more referents and create its own context minimally supplemented by illustrations. Written language can be polished and perfected before it is read; therefore, it tends to be more formal, deliberate, and constrained than oral language.

For most people, oral-language competence develops earlier than written-language competence because it is needed sooner. But children growing up in literate societies begin to respond to print as language almost as early as they begin to talk. Traffic signs and commercial logos, the most functional and situationally embedded written language in the environment, are learned easily and early (5). Despite their differences and history of acquisition, oral- and written-language processes become parallel for those who become literate; language users can choose the process that better suits their purposes. Readers may go from print to meaning in a manner parallel to the way they go from speech to meaning.

Since the deep structure and rules for generating the surface structure are the same for both language modes, people learning to read may draw on their control of the rules and syntax of oral language to facilitate developing proficiency in written language. This is not a matter of translating or recoding print to sound and then treating it as a listening task. Rather, it is a matter of readers using their knowledge of language and their conceptualizations to get meaning from print, to develop the sampling, predicting, confirming, and correcting strategies parallel to those they use in listening. Gibson and Levin (3) seem to agree with us that recoding print to sound is not necessary for adults, and Rader (13) finds that it is not even necessary for children.

We are convinced that oral and written language differ much more in how they are taught than in how they are learned. Although most oral-language development is expected to take place outside of school, the expectation is that literacy development will take place in school programs under teachers' control. Attempts to teach oral language in school are not noted for being as successful as what children achieve outside school. Similarly, literacy instruction is not totally successful. Furthermore, capable readers and writers demonstrate the use and integration of strategies not included in the structured literacy curriculum. Although this paper is primarily concerned with the study of the reading process and not with reading instruction, we are convinced that a major error in many instructional programs has been to ignore or underestimate the linguistic competence and language-learning capabilities of children learning to read.

Reading and Listening: Active Receptive Processes

A producer of language can influence the success of communication by making it as complete and unambiguous as possible. The productive process must carry through from thought to underlying structures to graphic or oral production. Written production, particularly, is often revised and edited to correct significant miscues and even to modify the meaning. The receptive process, however, has a very different set of constraints. Listeners and readers must go through the reverse sequence from aural or graphic representation to underlying structure to meaning. Receptive language users are, above all, intent on comprehending—constructing meaning.

Readers and listeners are *effective* when they succeed in constructing meaning and are *efficient* when they use the minimal effort necessary. Thus, through strategies of predicting, sampling, and confirming, receptive language users can leap toward meaning with partial processing of input, partial creation of surface and deep structures, and continuous monitoring of subsequent input and meaning for confirmation and consistency. Many miscues reflect readers' abilities to liberate themselves from detailed attention to print as they leap toward meaning. Consequently, they reverse, substitute, insert, omit, rearrange, paraphrase, and transform. They do this not just with letters and single words, but with two-word sequences, phrases, clauses, and sentences. Their own experiences, values, conceptual structures, expectations, dialects, and life styles are integral to the process. The meanings they construct can never simply reconstruct the author's conceptual structures. That every written text contains a precise meaning, which readers passively receive, is a common misconception deterimental to research on comprehension.

We have argued above that reading is an active, receptive process parallel to listening. Oral-reading miscues are less accessible, since listeners can only report those they are aware of; still these must be quite similar to reading miscues. Anyone who has ever tried to leave an oral message knows that listening miscues are surely not uncommon. In both reading and listening, prediction is at least as important as perception. What we think we have heard or read is only partly the result of sensory data; it is more the result of our expectations.

A major difference between reading and listening is that the reader normally can regress visually and reprocess when a miscue has led to a loss of meaning or structure. The listener, on the other hand, must reprocess mentally, await clarification, or ask a speaker to explain. Furthermore, the speaker may continue speaking, unaware of the listener's problem. Readers are in control of the text they process; listeners are dependent upon the speaker.

The receptive activity during the reading process is especially evident in two different types of miscues—those that are semantically acceptable with regard to the whole text and those that are semantically acceptable only with the prior portion of the text. A miscue may change the author's meaning; but, if it fits the story line, it can be considered semantically acceptable. For example, in S2 of the story Peggy read "when I am always cutting wood?" for "while I am away cutting wood?" These two miscues produced a sentence that fitted in with the meaning of the rest of the story. The more proficient a reader is, the greater the proportion of semantically acceptable miscues. The proportion and variety of high-quality miscues suggest that good readers constantly integrate their backgrounds with that of the author as if they are putting the author's ideas into their own language. This ability is often seen in oral language as a mark of understanding. "Tell me in your own words" is a common request from teachers to discover whether a student has understood something.

Semantically acceptable miscues may be more complex than word-for-word substitutions. Many readers produce reversals in phrase structures such as "said Mother" for "Mother said" or other types of restructuring like the one Peggy produced in S12: "Well, you do it tomorrow" instead of "We'll do it tomorrow." Although it seems that Peggy merely substituted "well" for "we'll" and inserted "you," the miscue is more complex at phrase and clause levels. Peggy inserted an interjection prior to the subject "you" to substitute for the noun phrase. There was also a substitution of the verb phrase because the verb marker "will," indicated by the contraction of "we'll," was omitted, and the verb "do" has been substituted for "will do." In addition, Peggy shifted intonation so that the wife rather than the husband says the sentence. Apparently Peggy thought the wife was going to speak, and her shifted intonation reflected changes in the grammatical pattern and meaning, although the sentence retained its acceptability within the story.

A reader's predicting strategies are also evident in those miscues that are acceptable with the prior portion of the text but that do not produce fully acceptable sentences. Such miscues often occur at pivotal points in sentences such as junctures between clauses or phrases. At such points the author may select from a variety of linguistic structures; the reader may have the same options but choose a different structure. Consider these examples from Peggy's reading:

text	transcript
(S38a) "I'll light a fire in the fire-place and the porridge will be ready in a few minutes."	*(S38b) "I'll light a fire in the fire-and I'll...and the porridge will be ready in a flash...a few minutes."*
(S48a) Then he was afraid that she would fall off.	*(S48b) Then he was afraid that the...that she would fall off.*

Peggy's use of "I'll" for "the" in the second clause of the first example is highly predictable. Since "and" generally connects two parallel items, it is logical that the second clause would begin with the subject of the first clause. The substitution of "the" for "she" in the second example occurs frequently in young readers' miscues. Whenever an author uses a pronoun to refer to a previously stated noun phrase, a reader may revert to the original noun phrase. The reverse phenomenon also occurs. When the author chooses a noun phrase for which the referent has been established earlier, the reader may use that pronoun. In the second example, Peggy was probably predicting "the cow" which "she" refers to. These miscues clearly show that Peggy is an active language user as she reads.

Readers' monitoring of their predictions is observed through their self-correction strategies. Clay's research (1) and our own (4) support the idea that a miscue semantically acceptable to the story line is less likely to be corrected than one that is not acceptable or is acceptable only with the immediately preceding text. For example, of the ten semantically acceptable miscues that Peggy produced in the first excerpt, she only corrected one ("all" in S11). However, of the six miscues that were acceptable only with the prior portion of the text, she corrected four. Such correction strategies tend to occur when the readers believe they are most needed: when a prediction has been disconfirmed by subsequent language cues.

Sentences that are fully unacceptable are corrected less than sentences with miscues acceptable with the prior portion of the sentence. Perhaps it is harder for readers to assign underlying structure to sentences in which fully unacceptable miscues occur. Without such a structure, they have difficulty unpacking the grammatical or conceptual complexity of a sentence and so are less able to self-correct. We believe that the two most important factors that make reading difficult are hard-to-predict grammatical structures and high conceptual load (16). What any particular reader finds hard to predict and difficult depends on the reader's background and experience.

The linguistic and conceptual background a reader brings to reading not only shows in miscues but is implicit in the developing concepts or misconceptions revealed through the reader's retelling. Peggy added to her conceptual base and built her control of language as she read this story, but her ability to do both was limited by what she brought to the task. In the story, the husband has to make butter in a churn. Peggy made miscues whenever buttermaking was mentioned. For example, in S10 she substituted "bread" for "butter." The next time "butter" appears, in S15, she read it as expected. However, in S18, "Soon the cream will turn into butter," Peggy read "buttermilk" for "butter." Other references to buttermaking include the words "churn" or "cream." Peggy read "cream" correctly each time it appears in the text but had trouble reading "churn." She paused about ten seconds before the first appearance of "churn" and finally said it. However, the next two times churn appears, Peggy read "cream."

text	transcript
(S25a)...he saw a big pig inside, with its nose in the churn.	*(S25b)...he saw a big pig inside, with its nose in the cream.*
(S28a) It bumped into the churn, knocking it over.	*(S28b) It jumped...it bumped into the cream, knocking it over.*
(S29a) The cream splashed all over the room.	*(S29b) The cream shado... splashed all over the room.*

In the retelling Peggy provided evidence that her miscues were conceptually based and not mere confusions:

And the husband was sitting down and he poured some buttermilk and um...in a jar. And, and, he was making buttermilk, and then, he um...heard the baby crying. So, he looked all around in the room and um,...And then he saw a big, a big, um...pig. Um...He saw a big pig inside the house. So, he told him to get out and he, the pig, started racing around and um...he di...he um...bumped into the buttermilk and then the buttermilk fell down and the pig, um...went out.

Peggy, who is growing up in a metropolis, knows little about how butter is made in churns. Although she knows that there is a relationship between cream and butter, she does not know the details of that relationship. According to her teacher, she has also taken part in a traditional primary-school activity in which sweet cream is poured into a jar, closed up tightly, and shaken until butter and buttermilk are produced. Although Peggy's miscues and retelling suggest that she had little knowledge about buttermaking, the concept is peripheral to comprehending the story. All that she needed to know was that buttermaking is one of the wife's many chores that can cause the woodman trouble.

Reading is not simply knowing sounds, words, sentences, and the abstract parts of language that can be studied by linguists. Reading, like listening, consists of processing language and constructing meanings. The reader brings a great deal of information to this complex and active process. Whenever readers are asked to read something for which they do not have enough relevant experience they have difficulty. That is why even proficient adult readers use such excuses as "It's too technical" and "He just writes for those inside the group." For this reason, proficient readers go to pharmacists or lawyers, for example, to read certain texts for them.

Oral and Silent Reading

The basic mode of reading is silent. Oral reading is special since it requires production of an oral representation concurrently with comprehending. The functions of oral reading are limited. It has become a kind of performing art used chiefly by teachers and television and radio announcers. We have already explained why we use oral reading in miscue analysis. But a basic question remains: are oral and silent reading similar enough to justify generalizing from studies of oral-reading miscues to theories and models of silent reading?

In our view a single process underlies all reading. The cycles, phases, and strategies of oral and silent reading are essentially the same. The miscues we find in oral reading occur in silent reading as well. Current unpublished studies of nonidentical fillers of cloze blanks (responses that do not match the deleted words) show remarkable correspondence to oral-reading miscues and indicate that the processes of oral and silent reading are much the same (*10, 15*).

Still, there are some dissimilarities between oral and silent reading that produce at least superficial differences in process. First, oral reading is limited to the speed at which speech can be produced. It need not, therefore, be as efficient as rapid silent reading. Next, superficial misarticulations such as "cimmanon" for "cinnamon" occur in oral reading but are not part of silent reading. Also, oral readers, conscious of their audience, may read passages differently than if they read them silently. Examples are production of nonword substitutions, persistence with several attempts at problem spots, overt regression to correct miscues already mentally corrected, and deliberate adjustments in ensuing text to cover miscues so that listeners will not notice them. Furthermore, oral readers may take fewer risks than silent readers. This can be seen in the deliberate omission of unfamiliar words, reluctance to attempt correction even though meaning is disrupted, and avoidance of overtly making corrections that have taken place silently to avoid calling attention to miscues. Finally, relatively proficient readers, particularly adults, may become so concerned with superficial fluency that they short-circuit the basic concern for meaning. Professional oral readers, newscasters for example, seem to suffer from this malady.

The Reader: An Intuitive Grammarian

Recently, linguists have equated or blurred the distinction between deep structure and meaning. We, however, find this distinction useful to explain a common phenomenon in our subjects' reading. Moderately proficient readers are able to cope with texts that they do not understand by manipulating language down to a deep structure level. Their miscues demonstrate this. Readers may also correctly answer a question they do not understand by transforming it into a statement and then finding the sentence in the text with the appropriate structure. Thus, when confronted by an article entitled "Downhole Heave Compensator" (9:88), most readers claim little comprehension. But they can answer the question, "What were the two things destroying the underreamers?" by finding the statement in the text that reads, "We were trying to keep drillships and semisubmersibles from wiping out our underreamers." Thus it is dangerous for researchers and teachers to equate comprehension with correct answers obtained by manipulating and transforming grammatical structures. Our research may not prove the psycholinguistic reality of the deep structure construct as distinct from meaning, but it demonstrates its utility. In our research we judge syntactic acceptability of sentences separately from semantic acceptability, since readers often produce sentences that are syntactically, but not semantically, acceptable. In S10 Peggy read "If you stay home to do my work" as a sentence which she finally resolved as "If you start home to do my work." This is syntactically acceptable in the story but unacceptable semantically since it is important to the story line that the woodman "stay home."

The first evidence used to separate syntactic from semantic acceptability came from research on the phenomenon of nonwords. Such nonsense words help give us insight into readers' grammatical awareness because sentences with nonwords often retain the grammatical features of English although they lose English meaning. Use of appropriate intonation frequently provides evidence for the grammatical similarity between the nonword and the text word. Nonwords most often retain similarities not only in number of syllables, word length, and spelling but also in bound morphemes—the smallest units that carry meaning or grammatical information within a word but cannot stand alone, for example, the *ed* in carri*ed*. The following responses by second, fourth, and sixth graders represent nonwords that retain the grammatical function of the text (4). A different subject produced each response. Notice that "surprise" and "circus" are singular nouns and that, in producing the nonwords, the subjects did not produce *s* or *z* sounds at the ends of the words as they would with plural nouns.

expected response	*nonword substitutions*
Second graders:	
The *surprise* is in my box.	*supra, suppa*
Then they will know the *circus* is coming.	*ception, chavit*
"Penny, why are you so *excited?*" she asked.	*excedled, encited*
Fourth graders:	
He saw a little *fawn.*	*frawn, foon, faunt*
What queer *experiment* was it?	*espressment, explerm, explainment*
Sixth graders:	
Clearly and *distinctly* Andrew said "philosophical."	*distikily, distinctly, definely*
A *distinct* quiver in his voice.	*dristic, distinc, distet*

There is other evidence in miscues of readers' strong awareness of bound morphemic rules. Our data on readers' word-for-word substitutions, whether nonwords or real words, show that, on the average, 80 percent of the observed responses retain the morphemic markings of the text. For example, if the text word is a noninflected form of a verb, the reader will tend to substitute that form. If the word has a prefix, the reader's substitution will tend to include a prefix. Derivational suffixes will be replaced by derivational suffixes, contractional suffixes by contractional suffixes.

Miscue analysis provides additional data regarding the phenomenon of grammatical-function similarity. Every one of Peggy's substitution miscues in the portion of the text provided earlier had the same grammatical function as the text word. Table 1 (4) indicates the percentage of miscues made by a sample of fourth and sixth graders that had the same grammatical function. These substitutions were coded prior to any attempt to correct the miscues.

Our research suggests that nouns, noun modifiers, and function words are substituted for each other to a much greater degree than they are for verbs. Out of 501 substitution miscues produced by fourth graders, only three times was a noun substituted for a verb modifier, and sixth graders made such a substitution only once out of 424 miscues.

Evidence from miscues occurring at the beginning of sentences also adds insight into readers' awareness of the grammatical constraints of language. Generally, in prose for children, few sentences begin with prepositions, intensifiers, adjectives, or singular common nouns without a preceding determiner. When readers produced miscues on the beginning words of sentences that did not retain the grammatical function of the text, we could not find one miscue that represented any of these unexpected grammatical forms. (One day we will do an article called "Miscues Readers Don't Make." Some of the strongest evidence comes from all the things readers could do that they do not.)

TABLE 1

Percent of Miscues with Grammatical Function Similarity

Identical Grammatical Function	4th Graders	6th Graders
Nouns	76%	74%
Verbs	76%	73%
Noun Modifiers	61%	57%
Function Words	67%	67%

Readers' miscues that cross sentence boundaries also provide insight into the readers' grammatical sophistication. It is not uncommon to hear teachers complain that readers often read past periods. Closer examination of this phenomenon suggests that when readers do this they are usually making a logical prediction that is based on a linguistic alternative. Peggy did this with the sentence (S35): "Perhaps keeping house is harder than I thought." As previously noted, Peggy had problems with the "keeping house" structure. She resolved the beginning of this sentence after a number of different attempts by finally reading "perhaps keeping home is hard work." Since she has rendered that clause as an independent unit, she has nothing to which she can attach "than I thought." She transformed this phrase into an independent clause and read it as "Then I thought."

Another example of crossing sentence boundaries occurs frequently in part of a story we have used with fourth graders: "He still thought it more fun to pretend to be a great scientist, mixing the strange and the unknown" (*12*:62). Many readers predict that "strange" and "unknown" are adjectives and intone the sentence accordingly. This means that when they

Goodman and Goodman

come to "unknown" their voice is left anticipating a noun. More proficient readers tend to regress at this point and correct the stress patterns.

Parts and Wholes

We believe that too much research on language and language learning has dealt with isolated sounds, letters, word parts, words, and even sentences. Such fragmentation, although it simplifies research design and the complexity of the phenomena under study, seriously distorts processes, tasks, cue values, interactions, and realities. Fortunately, there is now a strong trend toward use of full, natural linguistic text in psycholinguistic research. Kintsch (8:2) notes:

> Psycholinguistics is changing its character.... The 1950s were still dominated by the nonsense syllables... the 1960s were characterized by the use of word lists, while the present decade is witnessing a shift to even more complex learning materials. At present, we have reached the point where lists of sentences are being substituted for word lists in studies of recall recognition. Hopefully, this will not be the end-point of this development, and we shall soon see psychologists handle effectively the problems posed by the analysis of connected texts.

Through miscue analysis we have learned an important lesson: other things being equal, short language sequences are harder to comprehend than long ones. Sentences are easier than words, paragraphs easier than sentences, pages easier than paragraphs, and stories easier than pages. We see two reasons for this. First, it takes some familiarity with the style and general semantic thrust of a text's language for the reader to make successful predictions. Style is largely a matter of an author's syntactic preferences; the semantic context develops over the entire text. Short texts provide limited cues for readers to build a sense of either style or meaning. Second, the disruptive effect of particular miscues on meaning is much greater in short texts. Longer texts offer redundant opportunities to recover and self-correct. This suggests why findings from studies of words, sentences, and short passages produce different results from those that involve whole texts. It also raises a major issue about research using standardized tests, which utilize words, phrases, sentences, and very short texts to assess reading proficiency.

We believe that reading involved the interrelationship of all the language systems. All readers use graphic information to various degrees Our research demonstrates that low readers in the sixth, eighth, and tenth grades use graphic information more than high readers. Readers also produce substitution miscues similar to the phonemic patterns of text words. Although such phonemic miscues occur less frequently than graphic miscues, they show a similar pattern. This suggests that readers call on their knowledge of the graphophonic systems (symbol-sound relationships). Yet the use of these systems cannot explain why Peggy would produce a substitution such as "day" for "morning" or "job" or "work" (S13). She is clearly showing her use of the syntactic system and her ability to retain the grammatical function and morphemic constraints of the expected response. But the graphophonic and syntactic systems alone cannot explain why Peggy could seemingly understand words such as "house," "home," "ground," and "cream" in certain contexts in her reading but in other settings seemed to have difficulty. To understand these aspects of reading, one must examine the semantic system.

Miscue analysis shows that readers like Peggy use the interrelationships among the grammatical, graphophonic, and semantic systems. All three systems are used in an integrated fashion in order for reading to take place. Miscue analysis provides evidence tht readers integrate cue systems from the earlier stages of reading. Readers sample and make judgments about which cues from each system will provide the most useful information in making predictions that will get them to meaning. S2 in Peggy's excerpt provides insight into this phenomenon. Peggy read the sentence as follows: "One evening when h . . . he came home from work he said to his wife I want you [two second pause] do . . . all day [twelve second pause]." After the second pause, Peggy regressed to the beginning of the direct quote and read, "What do you do all day when I am always cutting wood?" Peggy's pauses and regression indicate that she was saying to herself: "This doesn't sound like language" (syntactically unacceptable; "this doesn't make sense" (semantically unacceptable). She continued slowly and hesitatingly, finally stopping altogether. She was disconfirming her prediction and rejecting it. Since it did not make sense, she decided that she must regress and pick up new cues from which to make new predictions.

In producing the unacceptable language segment "I want you do all day," Peggy was using graphic cues from "what" to predict "want." She was picking up the syntactic cues from "he said," which suggested that the woodman would use a declarative statement to start his conversation. From the situational context and her awareness of role relationships, she might have believed that, since the husband was returning home from working hard all day, he would be initially demanding to his wife. When this segment did not make sense to Peggy, she corrected herself. She read the last part of the sentence, "when I am always cutting wood," confidently and without hesitation. She was probably unaware that "when" and "always" are her own encodings of the meaning. She had made use of all three of the cue systems; her words fit well into the developing meaning of the story; therefore, she did not need to correct her miscues. We believe that both children and adults are constantly involved in this process during their silent reading but are unaware that it is taking place.

There are many times when the developing meaning of a story is so strong that it is inefficient to focus on the distinctive graphic cues of each letter or each word. As long as the phrase and clause structure are kept intact and meaning is being constructed, the reader has little reason to be overly concerned with graphic cues. Peggy read "day" for "morning" in S13 and "job" for "work" in S14. These miscues have a highly synonymous relationship to the text sentence, but they are based on minimal or no graphic cues. In S38 Peggy indicated to an even greater extent her ability to use minimal graphic cues. Her prediction was strong enough; and she was developing such a clear meaning of the situation that "in a flash" was an acceptable alternative to "in a few minutes," although she caught her miscue and corrected it.

Another phenomenon that exemplifies the interrelationships among the cueing systems is the associations readers develop between pairs of words. Any reader, regardless of age or ability, may substitute "the" for "a." Many readers also substitute "then" for "when," "that" for "what," and "was" for "saw" in certain contexts. What causes these associations is not simply the words' look-alike quality. Most of these miscues occur with words of similar grammatical function in positions where the resulting sentence is syntactically acceptable. Differences in proficiency are reflected in the ways readers react to these miscues: the more proficient reader corrects when necessary; the less proficient reader, being less concerned with making sense or less able to do so, allows an unacceptable sentence to go uncorrected. This process can only be understood if researchers focus on how readers employ all the cues available to them. For too long the research emphasis on discrete parts of language has kept us from appreciating how readers interrelate all aspects of language as they read.

Sooner or later all attempts to understand language—its development and its function as the medium of human communication—must confront linguistic reality. Theories, models, grammars, and research paradigms must predict and explain what people do when they use language and what makes it possible for them to do so. Researchers have contrived ingenious ways to make a small bit of linguistic or psycholinguistic reality available for examination. But then what they see is often out of focus, distorted by the design. Our approach makes fully available the reality of the miscues readers produce as they orally read whole, natural, and meaningful texts.

Huey (7:6) once said:

> And so to completely analyze what we do when we read would almost be the acme of a psychologist's achievements, for it would be to describe very many of the most intricate workings of the human mind, as well as to unravel the tangled story of the most remarkable specific performance that civilization has learned in all its history.

To this we add: Oral reading miscues are the windows on the reading process at work.

References

1. Clay, M.M. "The Reading Behaviour of Five Year Old Children: A Research Report," *New Zealand Journal of Educational Studies*, 1967, 2, 11-31.
2. Ewoldt, C. "Psycholinguistic Research in the Reading of Deaf Children," unpublished doctoral dissertation, Wayne State University, 1977.
3. Gibson, E., and H. Levin. *The Psychology of Reading*. Cambridge, Massachusetts: MIT Press, 1975.
4. Goodman, K.S., and C.L. Burke. *Theoretically Based Studies of Patterns of Miscues in Oral Reading Performance*, Final Report. Detroit: Wayne State University, 1973. Eric No. ED 079 708.

5. Goodman, K.S., and Y. Goodman. "Learning to Read Is Natural," in L.B. Resnick and P. Weaver (Eds.), *Theory and Practice of Early Reading*, Vol. 1. Hillsdale, New Jersey: Erlbaum Associates, in press.
6. Hodes, P. "A Psycholinguistic Study of Reading Miscues of Yiddish-English Bilingual Children," unpublished doctoral dissertation, Wayne State University, 1976.
7. Huey, E.B. *The Psychology and Pedagogy of Reading.* Cambridge, Massachusetts: MIT Press, 1968. (Originally published, 1908.)
8. Kintsch, W. *The Representation of Meaning in Memory.* Hillsdale, New Jersey: Erlbaum Associates, 1974.
9. Kirk, S. "Downhole Heave Compensator: A Tool Designed by Hindsight," *Drilling-DCW*, June 1974.
10. Lindberg, M.A. "A Description of the Relationship between Selected Prelinguistic, Linguistic, and Psycholinguistic Measures of Readability," unpublished doctoral dissertation, Wayne State University, 1977.
11. "The Man Who Kept House," in J. McInnes, M. Gerrard, and J. Ryckman (Eds.), *Magic and Make Believe.* Don Mills, Ontario: Thomas Nelson, 1964.
12. Moore, L. "Freddie Miller: Scientist," in E.A. Betts and C.M. Welch (Eds.), *Adventures Here and There*, Book V-3. New York: American Book, 1965.
13. Rader, N.L. "From Written Words to Meaning: A Developmental Study," unpublished doctoral dissertation, Cornell University, 1975.
14. Romatowski, J. "A Psycholinguistic Description of Miscues Generated by Selected Bilingual Subjects During the Oral Reading of Instructional Reading Material as Presented in Polish Readers and in English Basal Readers," unpublished doctoral dissertation, Wayne State University, 1972.
15. Rousch, P. "Miscues of Special Groups of Australian Readers," paper presented at the Annual Convention of the International Reading Association, Miami, May 1977.
16. Smith, L.A., and M.A. Lindberg. "Building Instructional Materials," in K.S. Goodman (Ed.), *Miscue Analysis: Application to Reading Instruction.* Urbana, Illinois: Eric Clearinghouse on Reading and Comprehension Skills and National Council of Teachers of English, 1973.

The Age-Old Controversy between Holistic and Subskill Approaches to Beginning Reading Instruction Revisited

S. Jay Samuels
University of Minnesota

Not to know the past is to repeat history many times over.

All of us are aware of the extent to which humans have fractionated themselves. We have compartmentalized ourselves into nations and nations into political factions. With regard to religious beliefs, the World Almanac lists eighty-one religious bodies in the United States.

If we humans seem divided on issues such as politics and religion, why should the acquisition of a skill as important as reading escape this divisive trend? The answer is that it has not. There are numerous approaches to the teaching of reading, and several of these approaches have taken on the superficial characteristics of a religion. Those approaches which have taken on some of the hallmarks of a religion have a system of beliefs and values which suggest in rather vague ways how to offer instruction. While there is evidence to support some of these beliefs, for many of the beliefs either no evidence exists or the evidence is inconclusive. Between these islands of evidence there are vast uncharted seas where the clinical insights and writings of the high priests of these approaches to reading chart the course to be taken by the followers. What is unfortunate about an approach to reading which takes on the characteristics of a religion is that the believers of each approach often assume that theirs is the true religion which leads to salvation while the other approaches are the false religions which lead to damnation.

Two of the more important approaches which have taken on the characteristics of a pseudoreligion are what may be called subskill and holistic approaches to beginning reading. The subskill approach has gone by other names such as "phonic" and "code breaking" while the holistic approach has been called the "look-say" and "meaning emphasis." The purpose of this article is to extract the strengths of each of these major approaches to reading and to look for ways to improve instruction.

With regard to this controversy, Downing (5) has written:

> Chall's chief contribution in *Learning to Read: The Great Debate* was to sift the rhetoric in the controversy between exponents of "look-say" versus "phonic" methods into logical categories. She reclassified teaching methods into "meaning emphasis" and "code emphasis" approaches, because she found that teachers and authors of reading textbooks placed more importance either on teaching children the meaningful communication aspects of written language or on the technical linguistic elements of the printed code for the spoken language.
> My own studies of the aspect of reading education led me to a similar conclusion. In *Comparative Reading* I reviewed the controversies over methods of teaching reading in fourteen different countries with almost as many different languages. I found that a similar dichotomy of methods existed in every language.... Teachers everywhere discuss the relative merits of what I have termed "meaningful chunking" versus "atomistic decoding" methods. The meaningful chunking teachers use larger chunks of language in instruction because they believe that children learn to read through associating print with the meaning of language. The atomistic decoding teachers prefer to focus on the atoms of written language because they believe that the child needs to know how to work the code that signals the meaning of the message in printed texts. Meaningful chunking methods are concerned mainly with the communication functions of written language. Atomistic decoding methods try chiefly to teach the technical mechanics of the writing system. Why it is felt necessary to emphasize one aspect more than the other is not clear, yet this controversy continues to exist even though the rhetoric appears to change.

Historical Perspective

The debate in educational circles as to whether reading should be introduced more or less as a holistic process with an emphasis on meaning or whether it should be taught by means of a subskill approach is not new. Mathews (18) documented the 2,500 year evolution of different approaches to reading that may be categorized as the holistic, subskill, and mixed methods. Controversy over how to teach reading became dichotomized in the mid-1800s as debate in Europe and America centered on whether to teach by the Greek originated ABC method or the "natural" word method.

In the alphabetic method, the child learned to name letters before learning to read words. After mastering the names of letters, nonsense syllables such as *ab, ib,* and *ob* were introduced. The student first spelled each letter and then pronounced the syllable. He progressed to three letter nonsense syllables, short words, and finally to sentences. With this method the child was required to name each letter prior to pronouncing the syllables or words. A major criticism of the method was that spelling the word before pronouncing it interfered with comprehension which led some educators to advocate a different approach.

In 1840 Josiah Bumstead commented that in the ABC method, the practice of drilling the child month after month on letter names was tiresome to the student and the teacher. Two decades later Horace Mann, the well-known American educator, ridiculed the ABC spelling method. As an alternative, the whole-word method was proposed.

By 1870 the conflict seemed to be resolved in favor of the whole-word method. The method remained dominant until Flesch (7) published his influential work, *Why Johnny Can't Read.* In this book, Flesch argued that children who were taught by the whole-word method had difficulty because of their failure to acquire word analysis skills. This criticism led to a growing emphasis on phonics as a part of the initial reading method.

Looking back on the controversies in reading, we can see that during the mid-1800s the conflict was between the ABC and the whole-word approach, while in the mid-1900s the conflict was over the whole versus subskill methods. These differences regarding reading method were found in Europe also. For example, Friedrich Gedike (1754-1803), one of the most influential Prussian educators of his day, tried to bring the philosophical principle of "naturalness" to the act of reading. He felt that a book was the logical whole with which to begin instruction and that the synthetic method, that is, going from parts to the whole, was reserved for God. Man had to be content with going from the whole to its parts. Other reading methods based on the principle of wholeness and naturalness, where either the sentence or the word was used as the whole unit, were also developed in Europe. Instruction then proceeded from the larger to the smaller units.

Two Views of Instruction

The labels "holistic" and "subskill" are universal and are used to describe whole-to-part and part-to-whole conceptualizations of developmental aspects of reading. Researchers who favor either view would tend to agree that proficient reading represents a highly complex process in which subordinate units are integrated in the formation of higher-order skills. While researchers may share somewhat similar viewpoints concerning proficient reading, they differ in significant ways regarding the best way to instruct beginning readers.

The Holistic View

The most significant characteristic of the holistic view is that from the outset, beginning instruction tends to focus on deriving meaning from the printed page. In this sense, reading and speaking are basically the same process of meaningful communication. From the start the child becomes aware that printed symbols represent meaning and are not a concatenation of meaningless sounds. The unit of instruction, therefore, becomes the word, phrase, sentence, or some unit that carries meaning.

According to Goodman (11) reading can be considered a natural language process that has the potential for being learned with the same ease and speed with which speech is learned. One of the reasons why speech is acquired with some degree of ease is that it fulfills the human needs of communication and of acquiring information. If the environment of reading instruction could be engineered to meet these basic communication needs, reading should also be acquired with relative ease. Regarding the sequencing of instruction, Goodman claims that "Sequencing of skill instruction in reading has often been strongly advocated by publishers and curriculum workers. But the reading process requires that a multitude of skills be used simultaneously. As we have indicated, many of these skills are already employed by the learner in listening. Any sequence will necessarily be arbitrary."

Those who favor the holistic approach believe the a priori assumption that children should be taught subskills is incorrect and may, in fact, be detrimental to the acquisition of fluent reading. It is believed that children learn to speak and listen without formal instruction and that reading—as a natural outgrowth of listening—could, under certain conditions, be learned with equal ease and proficiency. Goodman and Goodman (12) state: "We take as our principal premise in designing initial reading instruction that our goal is to create conditions which help all students to learn as naturally as some do." And, with regard to sequencing of instruction, they write: "Our research has convinced us that the skills displayed by the proficient reader derive from the meaningful use of written language and that sequential instruction in these skills is as pointless and fruitless as instruction in the skills of a proficient listener would be to teach infants to comprehend speech."

It should be pointed out that advocates of the holistic approach would teach subskills under certain conditions. These conditions would arise when the reader fails to get meaning because a particular skill is lacking. Then the instructor would teach the appropriate skill.

The Subskill View

Advocates of the subskill approach look upon proficient reading as the acquisition of a developmental skill. This means that the acquisition of highly complex skills such as reading may be viewed on a continuum that represents beginnings, intermediate, and fluent levels of skill. Thus, beginning and fluent reading are viewed as quite different processes. For example, since so much of the beginning reader's attention is taken up with decoding printed symbols, meaning is not easily derived. On the other hand, the skilled reader is able to decode printed symbols automatically, and, consequently, the limited attention capacity may be used for processing meaning. Smith (26) reflects this view:

I shall occasionally observe that life seems particularly hard for the beginning reader—so many necessary things are difficult for him at the outset that will be easier when his reading skills develop. For example, the mere fact that a child cannot read very fast puts a heavy burden on memory and attentional systems that are both inexperienced and overloaded with all kinds of instructions and rules. By the time the novice has built up enough speed to take some of the strain off his memory, many of the earlier rules have become unnecessary or overlearned and automatic, and the memory load is reduced in any case.

One of the major premises of the subskill approach is that reading is not a natural language process and that learning to read requires specific instruction. Another assumption is that reading, as a complex skill, is comprised of subordinate units that must be mastered and integrated to form higher order skills. Consequently, to accomplish this developmental task, a variety of subskills thought to be essential are taught routinely to students. The order of progression in these skills is from prerequisite smaller units to larger units.

Reading and Speech Acquisition Compared

Since some advocates of the holistic approach to reading emphasize the similarities between speech and reading, whereas advocates of the subskill approach look upon reading and speech acquisition as being quite different, it would be appropriate at this point to examine these counterclaims.

The development of the communication skills of speech and listening takes place over a relatively long period of time. Although they may be acquired in a naturalistic manner without formal instruction, these skills are not developed without considerable time, effort, and practice. Fries (8) has pointed out that the child has developed, and practiced, language skills for over ten thousand hours before formal reading instruction begins.

It should be recognized that the early acquisition of a first language, with its speaking and listening components, is a unique human experience and is different in important ways from other kinds of learning, such as learning to read. A number of arguments support the belief that the child's learning a language involves innate, genetically determined mechanisms operating on information about the structure of language that a child acquires from listening to the speech of adults. The first argument is that linguistic universals such as phonetic systems and syntax are common to all languages. Second, historical investigations of languages reveal that, although spoken languages change, there is no evidence of human speech that can be described as aphonemic or ungrammatical. Third, specific language disability, characterized by the delayed onset of speech, poor articulation, and marked reading disability in which general intelligence remains unaffected, appears to be inherited. Fourth, the developmental schedule of language acquisition follows a fixed sequence so that even if the entire schedule is retarded, the order of attainment of linguistic skills remains constant. Fifth, comparisons of children learning non-Indo-European languages with children learning English indicate a high degree of concordance between the milestones of speech and motor development. Finally, the learning of a second language after cerebral lateralization, which is generally completed by the onset of puberty, occurs with difficulty, usually takes an extended period of time, and normally requires formal instruction. Whereas all children learn communication skills in their first language, not everyone masters these skills in a second language.

Interesting comparisons can be made between the acquisition of speech and learning to read. Learning to speak is generally accomplished with little difficulty whereas learning to read requires considerably more effort. Although the acquisition of speech is gradual, beginning at infancy and extending for a considerable period of time, the introduction to reading is much more abrupt and less gradual. Also, there are strong sources of reinforcement involved with the acquisition of speech, while in the typical classroom sources of reinforcement for reading appear to be much less forceful. The strong reinforcers involved in acquiring speech seem to be applied almost immediately following appropriate speech behaviors, but in learning to read the much weaker reinforcers are often delayed or may be nonexistent. Perhaps the most important difference between acquiring speech and learning to read is that in the latter process intensive periods of concentration are required that may easily take on aversive characteristics.

To summarize the differences between speech and reading, it is indeed accurate to say that for nearly all people the acquisition of a first language appears to be easily mastered, but many people achieve literacy only with difficulty, if at all. Reading is not a behavior common to all humans, and its acquisition frequently requires the expenditure of considerable time and effort.

Thus, this comparison of speech and reading acquisition suggests that there are sufficient differences between the two and that the burden of proof rests on those who claim that learning to read can be mastered as readily as learning to speak.

Role of Subskills in Learning

Critics of the subskill approach have claimed that sequential subskill instruction probably represents improper reading pedagogy. What justification is there, then, for any method of reading instruction that attempts a part-to-whole instructional sequence?

The research of Bryan and Harter (3) on learning Morse code has contributed knowledge regarding requirements for learning a complex task. They noted that in developing skill in Morse code there were plateaus in the learning curves during which practice did not lead to further improvement. Their interpretation of this finding was that in learning Morse code numerous lower order skills had to be learned and integrated. These plateaus, they thought, indicated temporary periods devoted to learning the component skills or to organizing component skills into higher order skills. Thus, before one became skilled in Morse code the subordinate skills had to be mastered and integrated.

Guthrie (13) has provided additional support for the view that complex skill development requires the learning and integration of subordinate skills. He examined the intercorrelations among reading subskills for good and poor readers. With the good readers the intercorrelations among the skills were highly significant, suggesting that these readers had integrated the skills into higher order units. With the poor readers, the intercorrelations were low, suggesting that these readers were still at the level of separate skills. Guthrie concluded that one source of disability among poor readers was the lack of subskill mastery and the lack of integration of these skills into higher order units.

Hilgard and Marquis (*14*) have written that most learning is complex and requires the simultaneous learning of several components. A question remains about simple learning, such as associational learning: is the formation of simple associations influenced by subsystems?

Associational learning was traditionally believed to be a simple, single stage process, but as psychologists continued to investigate its nature, they discovered that stimulus-response learning was anything but a simple, single stage process. Research in associational learning over the past twenty-five years has revealed that there are stimulus learning stages, response learning stages, and associational stages. And these stages are influenced by other factors such as overt attention, perceptual learning, memory, and mediational strategies.

Thus, even the so-called simple learning tasks have their complex aspects, and fractionating a simple associational task into subskills can facilitate the learning process. For example, in an associational task such as learning letter names, it appears that breaking the task into subskills facilitates learning. In Samuels' experiment (*20*), an experimental group received visual discrimination training on noting distinctive features of letters. Following perceptual training, they learned the letter names. A control group was taught using a holistic approach; this group did not get perceptual pretraining. They were shown the letters and were told to learn their names. The experimental group that received subskill training learned in significantly fewer trials, and the savings were sufficient to make a practical difference as well.

In what is now considered to be a classical study on instruction, Gagne (*9*) took a mathematics skill, fractionated it into subskills that were ranked from lower order to higher order, and developed tests for each level. Following instruction on the mathematics skill, he tested the students and found that those who failed a lower order task were unable to pass a test at the higher level. He then taught the unit again requiring the students to master each of the subordinate skills. All the students were able to complete the terminal task after having mastered the subordinate tasks.

An example from the psychomotor domain can illustrate how a subskill approach can be used to facilitate the attainment of goals. To support the notion that one learns to read by reading meaningful material, some advocates of a holistic meaning approach point out that one learns to ride a bicycle by getting practice riding the bicycle. It should be pointed out, however, that children often go through a graded series of experiences of increasing difficulty before they learn to ride a large frame, two wheel bicycle. They frequently practice first on a tricycle, graduate to a two wheeler with a small frame, and practice getting their balance on the small frame bicycle before they use the pedals on the large frame two wheeler. One might inquire into the most desirable method to use in teaching a child to ride a bicycle. Would it be preferable simply to place the child on a two wheeler or to allow him to gain experience on a graded series of activities, each somewhat more difficult, before encountering the two wheel bicycle?

There is evidence that perceptual learning also seems to follow a pattern from smaller to larger units. At one time, it was believed that when a beginning reader encountered a word, the perceptual unit was the whole word. Contrary to this belief, however, research has indicated that children tend to select a single letter rather than the whole word as the cue for word recognition (17, 21). In fact, it is usually not until the tenth grade that a single eye fixation suffices to take in the whole word at once (28).

One can find examples from perception and reading to illustrate the principle that smaller units are mastered prior to larger units. The model of perceptual learning developed by LaBerge and Samuels (16) is hierarchical and suggests that the sequence of learning is from distinctive features, to letters, to letter clusters, and to words. In the process of leaning to recognize a letter, the student must first identify the features that comprise it. For the lower case letters b, d, p, and q, the features are a vertical line and a circle in a particular relationship to each other; that is, the circle may be high or low and to the left or right side of the vertical line. Having identified the parts and after an extended series of exposure to the letters, the learner sees it as a unit; that is, the parts are perceptually unitized. We have recently gathered evidence at our laboratory that skilled readers appear to have perceptually unitized—or chunked—digraphs such as *th, ch*, and *sh*. These are not processed as *t + h, c + h*, or *s + h*, but as a single unit. Evidence gathered elsewhere indicates that units longer than the letter, such as affixes *ed* and *ing*, can become perceptually unitized. These findings from different laboratories suggest that perceptual learning seems to follow a pattern from smaller to larger units.

Additional evidence illustrates the point that subskill mastery may be essential for achieving reading fluency. Shankweiler and Liberman (22) investigated whether the main source of difficulty in beginning reading is at the word level or at the level of reading connected text. In other words, how well could one predict a child's fluency in oral reading of paragraph material from his performance on selected words presented in tests? The average correlation was .70 between reading individual words on a list and reading connected discourse. Thus, roughly 50 percent of the variability in oral reading of connected words is associated with how well one can read these words in isolation. The authors concluded: "These correlations suggest that the child may encounter his major difficulty at the level of the word—his reading of connected text tends to be only as good or poor as his reading of individual words."

A similar conclusion was reached by a classroom teacher (27), with perceptive insights into problems children have with reading, who wrote:

> ...there has been great emphasis put on developing the child's comprehension ability. It is true that poor readers in the upper grades wrestle with comprehension problems. I have found this problem stems mainly from the student's lack of word-decoding skill. The comprehension cannot improve until the reading process becomes automatic, a development that takes place after the conscious analysis skills have been mastered. Therefore, though you want the child to understand the story he is learning to read, his ability will not be perfected until the child actually learns to read accurately.

The importance of a subskill approach in reading was made by Goldberg (10) who conducted a large scale study of beginning reading of disadvantaged children. She observed that, while teachers may be stressing comprehension, the children were devising ways of breaking the sound-symbol code and trying to figure out what the printed material says rather than what it means.

Still other investigators have discovered the importance of reading subskills. Silberman (*24*) reported on an experimental program used to teach beginning reading. He found that the brighter children acquired the necessary reading skill he wanted them to learn, but that the less bright seemed unable to transfer their knowledge to words not specifically taught. Classroom teachers brought in to evaluate the program discovered that a necessary subskill had been omitted. Only after that subskill had been included in the program were all the children able to master the transfer to untaught words. It is interesting to note that, even with an important subskill missing, the brighter children were able to surmount this obstacle. Silberman's study suggests, therefore, that brighter children may be able to overcome an inadequate program, but the less bright have great difficulty.

Another example of how children were able to overcome an inadequate teaching program is reported by Feitelson (*6*) in her review of reading instruction in Israel. Prior to the 1950s, reading pedagogy in that country was dominated by an official viewpoint: the child's own interest was the major factor to consider in constructing a reading program, and it was assumed that as long as the student was motivated, he would acquire the necessary reading skills. According to this viewpoint, in order to maintain motivation it was necessary for the child to read in units larger than the word, mostly in phrase units. This approach may be called the "holistic approach." Feitelson said that, until the 1950s, this way of teaching reading was widely used, and the results, in general, were satisfactory.

Subsequent to the 1950s, there was large scale immigration from Arab countries, and schools began to report rates of failure of 50 percent at the end of first grade. It would have been easy enough to attribute the cause of failure to the influx of a foreign group into Israel. A study was made, however, to determine the possible causes of failure. One of the more startling findings emerging from this study was that failure to acquire reading was not evenly dispersed. An entire classroom would either be successful in acquiring reading skills or unsuccessful. Successful classrooms were found to have teachers who did not use a holistic approach and who devoted much time to systematic phonics drills and to the breaking of words into smaller components. A second finding of interest was that parents were very helpful in overcoming the harmful effects of the holistic approach by teaching phonics themselves. Thus, what the child was not offered in school, the parents were teaching at home. Whereas many teachers taught in holistic units, at home the parents were drilling the children on the components of words so that the children could attack new words based on letter-sound correspondences and blending. In Israel, then, we find that an inadequate program was overcome by the teaching of essential decoding skills.

Before concluding this section, we wish to describe two laboratory studies that investigated a problem of some importance to reading. This problem concerned the type of initial training in reading—phonics versus the whole-word approach—that provides the best basis for transfer to reading new words. One of the studies used children who were nonreaders (15), and the other utilized adults who had to employ an artificial alphabet in reading (1). Both studies came to the same conclusion: that specific training on letter-sound correspondences was superior to whole-word training for transfer to recognizing new words.

This section on the role of subskills in learning has examined complex cognitive skills, such as learning telegraphy and transfer tasks in reading, and "simple" cognitive tasks, such as associational learning of letter names, perceptual learning, and psychomotor learning. Psychologists have discovered that these tasks are comprised of lower order skills, that mastery of higher order skills may be contingent on mastery of lower order skills, and that successful attainment of the final task may be facilitated by helping the student to master the lower order units.

Role of Context in Word Recognition

Advocates of the holistic meaning emphasis believe that there are syntactic and semantic cues in a sentence which can help beginning readers recognize words. There is ample evidence to indicate that word recognition is facilitated in sentences which are specially designed for experimental purposes. For example, recognition of the word "pepper" is aided when it is preceded by a phrase such as "Bring me the salt and _____ ." To a certain extent, the experimental evidence showing that sentence context can facilitate word recognition is irrelevant to the needs of beginning reading instruction. First, the experimental evidence was gathered with reasonably skilled to highly skilled readers and not beginning readers. Second, like the above sentence which utilizes associations between words such as salt/pepper, the sentences used in experiments frequently contain greater constraints between words than one finds in sentences used in beginning readers. Therefore, the syntactic and semantic cues found in beginning reading texts may not be very useful to the unskilled reader.

Two important arguments are being made here. The first is that beginning readers have great difficulty in using context. The reason is that in decoding the text the beginning reader's attention is focused upon elements smaller than the word. Buswell's (1922) eye-movement studies of poor readers reading text have demonstrated this. Also, studies of the unit of visual perception have found that even by the second grade the unit appears to be as small as the letter, whereas by the sixth grade the entire word seems to be processed as a single unit (22). With attention on units smaller than the word, despite efforts to get the student to read in meaningful larger units, the student's short-term memory gets filled with the nonmeaningful parts of a word and, hence, the meaningful context cannot be used.

The second argument being made is that the syntactic and semantic cues found in beginning reading texts are so weak that even if the student could read the words as single meaningful units, the context would not help much. If you doubt this statement, go to a beginning reading text and delete every fifth word. Then have someone else, preferably a beginning reader, attempt to fill in the deletions. If you give credit only for exact replacements, you will notice that the cues are not particularly powerful. If, however, you retain the first letter in each deleted word, as in "The man drank his c _____ ." the task becomes somewhat easier, since the first letter in a word contains more information as an aid to recognition than any other letter position.

A study by Wood (31) illustrates how difficult it is for beginning readers to use context. Starting with the view that reading should be taught with a holistic meaning emphasis,

Wood endeavored to test the hypothesis that word recognition was best learned in the context of a sentence. Previous studies by Samuels (1967) and Singer, Samuels, and Spiroff (25) had shown that words were learned best when presented in isolation. As a test of her hypothesis, Wood had all the experimental groups attempt to recognize the previously learned words when they were embedded in a story context. The results showed no difference for any of the experimental groups. Wood's explanation was that the story provided very weak cues. A follow up study by Brown (2), who is Wood's advisee, also failed to show superiority for any teaching method when target words were in a story context, even though more powerful cues were built into Brown's story. These failures suggest that the syntactic and semantic cues used in children's stories are not very useful to the beginning reader and that the beginning reader's attention, which is focused on the internal components of words, inhibits the student from using context.

Practical Implications for Reading Instruction

The current debate concerning the holistic versus the subskill approach may be somewhat overdrawn and may have established a false dichotomy, especially if one realizes that many teachers are eclectic in their approach to reading instruction. Furthermore, despite the claims of some teachers regarding their adherence to a particular approach to reading, there may be a significant gap between what they say and what they do.

Our problem may be reduced to one of focus, emphasis, and sequence. Regardless of which size unit one uses for beginning reading, one must include units at the other end of the scale. As Venezky (1972) points out: "almost all methods for teaching reading include letter-sound learning somewhere in the teaching sequence, although the amount and exact placement of this training account for the central disagreement between methods." This view was expressed by Singer, et al. (25) who state: "While this study has demonstrated that for the purpose of teaching children to identify a word it is best to present that word in isolation...the child [also] needs to get ample practice reading meaningful and interesting material in context so that he will develop strategies for using semantic and syntactic constraints in passages as aids in word identification."

Regarding the controversy over holistic and subskill approaches to reading, Weaver (*30*) said

> When researchers discuss reading as a single process, they say that it is holistic in nature. The term holistic implies that reading is more than just the sum of its parts. Those who hold this opinion might assert for example that reading is much more than decoding plus comprehension and that it cannot be subdivided even for teaching purposes. When the term subskills is applied to reading it implies that reading is comprised of different components. Reading and understanding what is read are seen as the outcomes of a number of separate skills that are interrelated and become integrated during the act of reading.
>
> If reading were viewed holistically, how would you teach beginning readers to read? We don't think it would work just to say "Watch and listen to me read and then you do just what I did." Although we highly recommend reading to children in order to expose them to reading and to literature this certainly is not sufficient for most children to learn to read. An example from teaching sports helps. In learning to play tennis, a very complex activity, students are taught components of the skill. They learn foot work, how to grip the racket, how to hit backhand and forehand shots, how to serve and so on. Most of these components are broken down further into even smaller steps for teaching purposes. Even though the instructor may often demonstrate the whole skill, more demonstration is never the only means of teaching.
>
> Although some research suggests that skilled reading is a single, holistic process, and some suggest that it is a set of processes carried out so fast that it appears inseparable, there is no research that we know of to suggest that children can learn to read and develop reading skills by teaching them reading as if it were a single process. For teaching purposes, we think that it is probably best to think of reading as a set of interrelated subskills. These separate skills should be taught, practiced, and integrated with the other skills being taught and those that have already been learned. The important thing to remember is that although reading may be taught subskill by subskill, students should always have an ample opportunity to practice the whole activity.

Resnick (*19*) reviewed the evidence for code and meaning oriented approaches to reading and concluded, "First, as a matter of routine practice, we need to include systematic, code-oriented instruction in the primary grades, no matter what else is done. This is the only place in which we have any clear evidence for any particular practice.... The charge, made by some who espouse language-oriented approaches and who view reading as an autonomous communication system, that too early or too much emphasis on the code depresses comprehension, finds no support in the empirical data. On the other hand, neither is there support for the claim of code proponents that once the code is learned other reading problems will disappear."

A major point made by critics of the subskill approach is that fractionating the reading process interferes with the essential characteristic of reading, which is comprehension. This point is well taken. Many teachers who use the subskill approach have lost sight of the fact that the approach is simply a means to an end. In many classrooms there has been a displacement of goals, and the means have become ends. In the subskill approach, care must be taken to prevent the subskills from becoming the focal point of instruction. Once again, perhaps, the point should be made that it is important for the child to get ample practice reading meaningful and interesting material in context.

We agree with the critics of the subskill approach that too much emphasis can be placed on these subordinate skills. The critics probably are in error, however, in failing to recognize the importance of subskills in the developmental sequence of skill attainment. Just because fluent readers are able to determine the meaning on a printed page is no reason to believe that beginning readers can do the same or that we can transfer the sophisticated strategies of the fluent reader to the beginning reader. Downing (5) shares this view: "It seems quite unlikely that the learning-to-read process is directly derivable from the behavior observed in a fluent reader as is assumed in the theories of Smith and Goodman."

Both the advocates of holistic and subskill approaches recognize that reading is comprised of subordinate skills. There is a problem, however, concerning who determines which subskills should be taught and when they should be introduced. According to one school of thought, when the student encounters a problem, the teacher should analyse the nature of the difficulty and remedy it. This approach places the teacher in the role of a troubleshooter. Thus, the particular subskills that are taught are determined by the student, that is, by an analysis of the student's weaknesses, and the skills are introduced after the problem is uncovered. According to the other school of thought, certain subskills must be mastered in the reading acquistion process, and these skills can be taught routinely before the student shows signs of having a problem. Thus, with this approach, it is the teacher or curriculum expert who determines a priori which skills are to be taught and when.

Many critics of the subskill approach suggest that meaningful reading material should be given to a child and that subskills should be taught when the student asks for help or shows evidence of needing particular skills. The short-comings of this approach become obvious when one realizes the logistical and managerial problems facing the teacher with a large number of students. With regard to this last point, it is important to realize that many students do not know what kind of help to request, and a good number of teachers are not sufficiently trained to pinpoint the cause of the student's difficulty. Even when the teacher is able to diagnose accurately the cause of the problem, the managerial problems of providing individual help are so large as to make the system difficult to operate, if not unworkable. It would seem more manageable to assume on a priori grounds that beginning readers require certain subskills, which would be taught routinely to students. For those students who fail to master these skills, additional time could be allocated, and different methods could be tried.

We made the point earlier in this chapter that the adverse relationship between holistic and subskill approaches may not exist. Both approaches recognize these are subskills. Subskill approaches start with smaller units and move to larger and more complex units. The holistic approach, on the other hand, begins with the larger unit and moves to smaller units. Thus, one of the important factors differentiating the two approaches is that of sequencing. In considering this factor, we must think about which tasks and which unit size one would use to start instruction and how one would program the sequence of skills to be taught as the student progresses in skill. Another similarity between the two approaches is that both recognize the importance of diagnosis of difficulty in reading and the need to remedy the problem. The subskill approach, however, attempts to reduce the number of students who will experience difficulties in reading by teaching the prerequisite skills before a problem appears.

In summary, we must keep in mind that reading is a developmental skill and, while the goal of reading is to acquire meaning, there are certain prerequisites. One important prerequisite is the development of decoding skills. These skills must be brought beyond the level of mere accuracy to the level of automaticity. When these skills become automatic, the student is able to decode the printed symbols without the aid of attention, thereby freeing attention for the all important task of processing meaning.

References

1. Bishop, Carol N. "Transfer Effects of Word and Letter Training in Reading," *Journal of Verbal Learning and Verbal Behavior*, 3 (1964), 215-221.
2. Brown, Mavis. Personal communication, 1977.
3. Bryan, William L., and Noble Harter. "Studies in the Physiology and Psychology of the Telegraphic Language," *Psychological Review*, 4 (1897), 27-53.
4. Buswell, G.T. *Fundamental Reading Habits: A Study of Their Development*, Supplementary Education Monographs, No. 21. Chicago: University of Chicago Press, 1922.
5. Downing, John. "The Child's Understanding of the Function and Processes of Communication," unpublished paper, University of Victoria, Canada, 1977, 25-26.
6. Feitelson, Dina. "Israel," in John Downing (Ed.), *Comparative Reading*. New York: Macmillan, 1973.
7. Flesch, Rudolf. *Why Johnny Can't Read and What You Can Do About It.* New York: Harper and Row, 1955.
8. Fries, Charles C. *Linguistics and Reading.* New York: Holt, Rinehart and Winston, 1963.
9. Gagne, Robert M. "The Acquisition of Knowledge," *Psychological Review*, 69 (1962), 355-365.
10. Goldberg, Mariam L. "The Effects of Various Approaches to Beginning Reading," Final Report, Beginning Reading Project. New York: Teachers College, Columbia University, 1973.
11. Goodman, Kenneth A. "Literacy in a World View: Who Skilled Cock Robin?" paper presented at the Sixth IRA World Congress on Reading, Singapore, August 1976.
12. Goodman, Kenneth A., and Yetta Goodman. "Learning to Read is Natural," paper presented at Conference on Theory and Practice of Beginning Reading Instruction, Pittsburgh, April 1976, 21.
13. Guthrie, John T. "Models of Reading and Reading Disability," *Journal of Educational Psychology*, 65, (1973), 9-18.
14. Hilgard, Ernest R., and Donald G. Marquis. *Conditioning and Learning*, Second Edition. New York: Appleton-Century-Crofts, 1961.
15. Jeffrey, Wendel E., and S. Jay Samuels. "Effect of Method of Reading Training on Initial Learning and Transfer," *Journal of Verbal Learning and Verbal Behavior*, 6 (1967), 354-358.
16. LaBerge, David, and S. Jay Samuels. "Toward a Theory of Automatic Information Processing in Reading," *Cognitive Psychology*, 6 (1974), 293-323.
17. Marchbanks, Gabrielle, and Harry Levin. "Cues by Which Children Recognize Words," *Journal of Educational Psychology*, 56 (1965), 57-62.

18. Mathews, Mitford M. *Teaching to Read: Historically Considered*. Chicago: University of Chicago Press, 1966.
19. Resnick, Lauren B. "Theory and Practice in Beginning Reading Instruction," paper presented at National Academy of Education, New York, 1977.
20. Samuels, S. Jay. "Effect of Distinctive Feature Training on Paired Associate Learning," *Journal of Educational Psychology*, 64 (1973), 164-170.
21. Samuels, S. Jay, and Wendell F. Jeffrey. "Discriminability of Words and Letter Cues Used in Learning to Read," *Journal of Educational Psychology*, 57 (1966), 337-340.
22. Samuels, S. J., C. Bremer, and D. LaBerge. "Units of Word Recognition: Evidence for Developmental Changes," *Journal of Verbal Learning and Verbal Behavior*, 17 (1978), 715-720.
23. Shankweiler, Donald, and Isabelle Y. Liberman. "Misreading: A Search for Causes," in J.F. Kavanagh and Ignatius G. Matting (Eds.), *Language By Ear and By Eye*. Cambridge, Massachusetts: MIT Press, 1972.
24. Silberman, Harry F. *Exploratory Research in a Beginning Reading Program*. Santa Monica, California: System Development, 1964, 430-432.
25. Singer, Harry, S. Jay Samuels, and Jean Spiroff. "Effects of Pictures and Contextual Conditions on Learning to Read," *Reading Research Quarterly*, 9 (1974), 566.
26. Smith, Frank. *Understanding Reading: A Psycholinguistic Analysis of Reading and Learning to Read*. New York: Holt, Rinehart, and Winston, 1971, 3.
27. Stevenson, I. *The Natural Way to Reading: A How-To Method for Parents of Slow Learners, Dyslexic, and Learning Disabled Children*. Boston: Little, Brown, 1974.
28. Taylor, Stan E., Helen Frackenpohl, and J.L. Pettee. *Grade Level Norms for the Components of the Fundamental Reading Skill*. Huntington, New York: Educational Development Laboratories, 1960.
29. Venezky, Richard. *Language and Cognition in Reading*, Technical Report No. 188, University of Wisconsin at Madison. Washington, D.C.: U.S. Office of Education, 1972, 19.
30. Weaver, Phyllis. *Research within Reach: A Research Guided Response to Concerns of Reading Educators*. St. Louis, Missouri: CEMREL, 1978.
31. Wood, Martha W. "A Multivariate Analysis of Beginning Readers' Recognition of Taught Words in Four Contextual Settings," doctoral dissertation, Texas Woman's University, 1976.

Active Comprehension: From Answering to Asking Questions

Harry Singer
University of California at Riverside

Comprehension has three dictionary definitions (*4*): 1) the act or action of grasping with the intellect; 2) knowledge gained by comprehending; 3) the capacity for understanding. These definitions imply that the term *comprehension* can refer to a process, a product, or a potential. These different conceptions of comprehension intermingle, whether the focus is on teaching, testing, or on a theory of comprehension. Thus, I will touch on each aspect of comprehension, although my emphasis in this article will be on teaching a process of comprehension.

The main strategy for teaching comprehension is to ask students questions before, during, and after reading. Questions asked before reading, preposed questions, direct and focus students' thinking on the information in the text that will answer the questions, but other information in the text is not attended to as well. Hence, recall of the selection will be as narrow as the preposed questions have been unless students have been highly motivated to remember all that they have read (*1*). But the value of preposed questions for comprehension is that they maintain a searching attitude on the part of the reader.

Postposed questions, which come at the end of a reading selection, lead students to have a broader focus in reading. Thinking that all information is equally relevant, they try to

Adapted from *The Reading Teacher*, May 1978, 901-908.

store all information and recall it at the end. Hence, their process of reading is slower and their recall is better than when preposed questions are asked (1, 8).

Most of the questions teachers ask, whether preposed or postposed, are directed at the literal level of comprehension (3). These are the "how, what, who, when, where" types of questions. They aim at memory or direct recall of information. Information at the literal level, of course, is necessary before asking higher level questions, such as questions that lead to inferences, interpretations, generalizations, and evaluations, but how many literal questions would be appropriate or necessary for establishing a basis for higher level questions probably cannot be established. Certainly literal questions should not be the sole level for teacher posed questions.

However, some teachers are prone to stop at the literal level in their question asking behavior, even though textbooks for teaching teachers how to teach students to comprehend printed materials emphasize preposed and postposed teacher questions that are designed to stimulate students' thinking at various levels. For example, as shown in Figure 1, Spache and Spache (12) stress seven types of questions: memory, translations (paraphrasing), interpretation, application, analysis, synthesis, and evaluation. While these questions stimulate students' thinking, they stress products of thinking, that is, answers to teacher posed questions. Although process of thinking can be inferred from responses to teacher posed questions, such questions do not stress processes of comprehension.

Processes of Comprehension

However, Taba (13) has formulated questioning procedures that do guide the processes of comprehension. She pointed out that teachers could ask questions in a sytematic sequence that would lead to the formulation of generalizations. In following this sequence, the teacher starts by asking a question that initiates a discussion. For example, "Would you summarize the story for the class?" An extending question then keeps a discussion at the same level in order to obtain more information or more data. For example, "What additional information is there on this topic?" After enough information,

Figure 1
Questions directing students' thinking in reading

Memory: recognizing or recalling information.

   Who did _____ ? What is meant by _____ ? What events led to _____ ?
   What kind of boy was _____ ?

Translations: expressing ideas in different form or language.

   What does the writer mean by the phrase _____ ?

Interpretation: perceiving relationships among facts, generalizations, values.

   How is _____ like _____ ? What would happen if _____ ? What events
   led to _____ ? What conclusions can you draw from the graph? Why
   did _____ happen?

Application: solving a problem that requires the use of generalizations, facts, values.

   How can we show we need a police officer at the crossing in front of
   the school?

Analysis: applying rules of logic to solution of a problem.

   Do you thing boys can run faster than girls? Why?

Synthesis: using original, creative thinking to solve a problem.

   What other ending could you think of for this story?

Evaluation: making judgments by applying criteria.

   Do you approve of the boy's actions?

Adapted from Spache and Spache, 1969, pp. 475-478.

data, or evidence has been made explicit through these types of questions, the teacher asks a lifting type of question which raises the discussion and causes students to think at a higher level. Perhaps the question is one that requires the students to abstract common elements from a variety of examples. For instance, the teacher might ask, "We now have enough examples. What do they have in common?" After the class has progressed through at least two discussions, resulting in the formation of two concepts, the teacher can then ask a question which leads students to perceive and formulate a relationship between the two concepts.

Ruddell (9) has adapted Taba's thinking process strategy, which he refers to as an interaction between the teacher and the students. As shown in Figure 2, Ruddell stresses that the interaction role of the teacher is to ask questions and the student's task is to respond with answers.

Although interactions between teacher and student emphasize sequential steps in processes of thinking, the teacher is directing students' processes of thinking. While such

Figure 2
Teacher-Student Interaction

Teacher-student
interaction

Who talks	*Function*
Teacher	Question
Student	Response

Questioning strategy

Type	Purpose	Question
Focusing	Initiate discussion or re-focus on the issue.	What did you like best about the story? What was the question we started to answer?
Controlling	Direct or dominate the discussion.	First, would you review the plot?
Ignoring or rejecting	Maintain current trend in discussion. Disregard a student's interest.	Would you mind if we don't go into that now?
Extending	Obtain more information at a particular level of discussion.	What other information do we have about the hero?
Clarifying	Obtain a more adequate explanation. Draw out a student.	Would you explain what you mean?
Raising	Have discussion move from factual to interpretive, inferential, or abstraction and generalization level.	We now have enough examples. What do they have in common? (Abstract) Was it always true for his behavior? (Generalization)

Response level

Factual or literal (What the author said)
Interpretive (Integration of ideas of inference)
Applied (Transfer of ideas or judgment that idea is subsumed under broader generatization)
Evaluative (Using cognitive or affective criteria for judging issue)

Adapted from Ruddell, 1974.

teacher posed questions may serve as a model of the way processes of thinking during reading should occur, this interaction strategy does not achieve what I believe should be the main objective of teaching comprehension: to have students learn to ask their own questions and to guide their own thinking. While some transfer may occur, perhaps through imitation of the teacher's questioning behavior, the evidence from numerous transfer experiments in education is that transfer is more likely to occur if we teach for it. To do so, three concepts are necessary for guiding instruction: modeling behavior, active comprehension, and phase-in and phase-out strategies.

Modeling behavior. Teacher posed questions are necessary as models of what questions to ask in a particular content area. However, the teacher must also teach students to ask their own questions. Consequently a lesson, unit, or course should progress from teacher-posed to student-posed questions. This progression involves phasing out the teacher and phasing in the student.

Phase-out/phase-in strategy. The phase-out and phase-in procedure starts with teacher-posed questions. The teacher first takes students through an entire lesson, a unit, or a chapter, demonstrating what questions to ask and what process of thinking to go through in reading and comprehending text. This stage of the phase-out/phase-in strategy involves doing what Spache and Spache advocate in developing products of thinking and what Taba and Ruddell stress in promoting processes of comprehension.

But teacher posed questions, which only direct student thinking, are inadequate for development of comprehension in students. To complete the instructional procedure, the teacher must go through a subsequent lesson, unit, or chapter in which students are stimulated to formulate their own questions before, during, and after reading. Eventually, the teacher is phased out and students are phased in in asking questions. As the students start to ask their own questions, they are developing active comprehension.

Active comprehension. The objective of teaching comprehension is to have students learn to ask their own questions and guide their own thinking so that they can become independent in the process of reading and learning from text. This process involves reacting to the printed page with questions or hypotheses that are answered or confirmed by the text as the student reads and interacts with it. But unlike Robinson's study skill technique (6) known as SQ3R (survey, question, read, recite, and review) which emphasizes asking questions before reading, active comprehension is a continuous process of formulating and searching for answers to questions before, during, and after reading.

The purpose of teaching students to formulate their own questions is not just for attaining the goal of having students select and retain information, although this goal will be achieved in active comprehension, but also to teach students a process of reading and learning from text which emphasizes the reader's purposes and the dynamic interaction between the reader and the printed page, including selective attention to those aspects of text that are relevant to satisfying students' curiosity.

Teaching Active Comprehension

Various techniques can be used to teach active comprehension. One of them is to ask students a question that gets a question, not an answer, in return. Although the change in instruction is slight, I believe the difference attained is profound. For example, imagine the following scene: A kindergarten teacher holds up a picture for a group of children to look at. The picture is from a reading readiness book. It shows a house with a walk leading from the house to the sidewalk. Coming down the walk is a boy on a bicycle. On the sidewalk a little girl is roller skating towards a little boy on a wagon. It appears that all three of them are likely to reach the intersection of the walkway and the sidewalk at the same time. Now, instead of asking questions that yield answers, such as "Who is on the bike?" "What is going to happen?" the teacher says to the class: "Look at the picture. What would you like to know about the picture?" The questions children ask in response to this question are quite varied and sometimes surprising.

Since most pictures in beginning reading books are complex and richly colored, children can ask a multitude of questions reflecting their own perceptions, levels of cognitive development, and processes of thinking. Some children may first ask about small details and then go on to the main idea portrayed in the picture while others may start there and progress to the details. Thus, children might ask these questions: "What is this worm doing?" "Why is the boy on a bicycle?" "Does the little girl see the boy on the bike?" "Will they crash?" The teacher can direct the class's question back to the group, causing the group to listen to each other and answer each other's questions. The teacher might then ask, "What would you like to know about what happens next?" Or the teacher can switch to directed thinking and conclude this part of the lesson with a directed question: "How would you avoid the crash?"

Figure 3
Lesson on teaching active comprehension[1]

Passage
"Filming a Cannibal Chief," by Osa Johnson[2]

My husband and I wanted to make a moving picture of savages, and Martin finally decided on Malekula, second largest of the New Hebrides Islands. We started from Sydney, Australia on a small ship. Soon a storm of warning broke around us.

Teacher-student interaction

Teacher questions to elicit student questions:
"Look at the title. What questions could you ask just from the title alone?"

Student questions on the title:
"How do you film a cannibal chief?" (Often implicit in this question is the idea of how do you film a cannibal chief and get away with it.)
"Were they successful?"
"Why film a cannibal chief?"

Teacher techniques for eliciting questions in the paragraph:
"What would you like to know about Martin?"

Student questions:
"Who is Martin?"
"Is Martin the husband?"
"Why did Martin decide?"
"Did Martin have trouble making up his mind?"
"Is Martin deliberative?"

Teacher elicits answers to questions after each block of questions:
"Who would like to answer a question about Martin?"
"Does anyone have another answer to this question?"
"What is your reason for your answer?"
"Do you need additional information to support your answer?"

Teacher question:
"Is there anything you would like to know about the relationship between the writer and Martin?"

Student questions:
"Is she frustrated by Martin's indecision?"

"Is he the domineering person in their relationship?"
"Is she a nagging type of person?"
Teacher question:
"Does the ship make you wonder about the trip?"
Student questions:
"Why were they going in a small ship?"
"How small was the small ship?"
"Why didn't the author describe the ship?"
Teacher question:
"Look at the last sentence. What questions pop into your mind as you read that sentence?"
Student questions:
"What is a storm of warning?"
"What kind of danger are they about to encounter?"
"Will they survive?"
"What was the warning?"
"Did they still go ahead with the trip?"
Teacher phases out/students phase in:
"Now read the rest of the story, asking and answering your questions as you go."

[1]Adapted from Singer and Donian, 1977.
[2]Quoted from Osa Johnson, "Filming a Cannibal Chief," in *Reader's Digest Reading Skillbuilder VI, Part I*. Pleasantville, N.Y.: Reader's Digest, 1950. Permission granted for quotation.

This question puts the children into a problem solving situation. Their thinking is now directed toward a solution to a problem. After several solutions have been elicited from the group, the teacher can say, "Let's turn the page and see how the person who drew these pictures solved the problem." After turning the page and understanding the author's solution, the teacher can initiate an evaluation of the author's solution with the question: "Is this the best way to stop a crash?" Or, "Do you like the way the children in the picture stopped from crashing into each other?" The class can then compare its solutions to the author's. Thus, the class can engage, even at the kindergarten level, in critical and affective reactions. Also, the switch from teacher elicited to teacher directed questioning can be used to demonstrate and teach the class the kinds of questions it can ask. As the class asks these questions themselves, the teacher can phase out or gradually stop asking such questions.

Another technique a teacher might use to develop active comprehension is to ask the class to take turns pretending to be the teacher and ask the group questions. Or the teacher could draw attention to a particular feature of a book and then elicit questions. For example, a third grade teacher introduced a book by having someone read the title and then asked the class what students would like to find out about this book. Or some group dynamics can be used to elicit questions. For instance, a ninth grade teacher arranged for a competitive situation in which the class was divided in half, with two students at the blackboard to write down questions. The students filled up two blackboards with their questions. The group then tried to outdo each other in asking and answering its own questions raised in the title and in the first paragraph of the story.

Teachers' manuals which accompany basal readers or anthologies usually have questions for teachers to ask the class. These questions and lesson plans in teachers' manuals can be transformed into active comprehension lessons. But instead of simply asking the questions and having students seek answers to them, the teacher can use them as examples of the kinds of questions to elicit from students.

To make the idea of active comprehension more vivid, I shall take you through a lesson on active comprehension that I have used for teaching teachers how to teach comprehension. In this lesson, the teacher asks questions that get questions in return. The lesson, shown in Figure 3, starts with a relatively easy reading passage. Following this passage, the teacher asks questions, not answers, in return. After each set of questions, the teacher asks for answers to the questions and the reasons for them. Note: the teacher elicits the entire range of answers to a question by not stopping after one answer, even if the answer agrees with the teacher's answer. The teacher notes that some answers are hypotheses or answers that may turn out to be right or wrong as the class reads on and gets more information. At the end of the passage, some questions are still unanswered.

Motivated by their own questions, students go ahead on their own, reading the rest of the story rapidly to answer their own questions. In the process, they also answer other questions. As they reach answers to their own student questions, they have a positive feeling, tantamount to saying, "That's an answer to my question!"

In subsequent lessons, the teacher has the class ask questions at the end of each section. Then the teacher fades out and students fade in, initiating their own questioning behavior throughout the story.

Research on Active Comprehension

The process of active comprehension emphasizes and puts a premium upon the reader's curiosity. It stresses reading for the purpose of satisfying the reader's curiosity. Because it is a continuous process, I anticipated it would not narrowly focus students' attention as the teacher's preposed questions do. Rhodes (5), one of my graduate students, then did an unpublished study in which he found that students who were taught to actively comprehend short stories resisted the narrowing effects of teacher preposed questions on comprehension products. They also performed significantly better on a comprehension test consisting of literal, interpretive, and general questions than control groups who had teacher preposed or teacher postposed, or no teacher formulated questions.

We have also carried out an exploratory study on the effects of active comprehension on reading achievement. Doris Doskocil, a reading specialist in the Riverside, California Unified School District, taught third graders to formulate their own questions and read to answer them. At the beginning of a passage she asked them to tell what they would like to know about the story. Then they read to answer their own questions. If their books did not answer their questions, they were directed to get their answers from reference reading. This small group of nine children was then matched with a control group tested at the end of the year. The difference on the Stanford Reading Achievement between the two groups favored the experimental group. However, the difference did not attain our preset criterion for statistical significance, the 5 percent level. Had we been more lenient and used the 10 percent level, the difference would have been statistically significant. We are now planning to redo this experiment with a better design.

Other researchers have found that students can learn to imitate teacher questions (7) and that students who ask one another questions earn significantly higher achievement test scores than students who study alone (2). As research results accumulate to indicate that teaching for active comprehension significantly improves students' achievement, we shall have to formulate tests that assess this process and design theories and models which go beyond our current theoretical models and processes of reading (11). Our new model will have to emphasize a two-way or an interactional process of reading. This model would represent what we refer to as active comprehension.

References

1. Frase, Lawrence T. "Effect of Question Location, Pacing, and Mode on Retention of Prose Material," *Journal of Educational Psychology*, 59 (1968), 244-249.
2. Frase, Lawrence T., and Barry J. Schwartz. "Effect of Question Production and Answering Prose Recall," *Journal of Educational Psychology*, 67 (1975), 628-635.
3. Guszak, Frank J. "Teacher Questioning and Reading," *Reading Teacher*, 21, (December 1967), 227-234.
4. Merriam-Webster. *Webster's Seventh New Collegiate Dictionary*. Springfield, Massachusetts: G. & C. Merriam, 1963.
5. Rhodes, Alan. "Active Comprehension: Improving Reading Comprehension through Reader Generated Questions," unpublished research investigation, University of California at Riverside, 1977.
6. Robinson, Francis P. *Effective Study*. New York: Harper and Row, 1946.
7. Rosenthal, Ted L., Barry J. Zimmerman, and Kathleen Durning. "Observationally Induced Changes in Children's Interrogative Classes," *Journal of Personality and Social Psychology*, 16 (1970), 681-688.
8. Rothkopt, Ernest L., and E. Besbicos. "Selective Facilitative Effects of Interspersed Questions on Learning from Written Material," *Journal of Educational Psychology*, 58 (1967), 56-61.
9. Ruddell, Robert B. *Reading—Language Instruction: Innovative Practices*. Englewood Cliffs, New Jersey: Prentice-Hall, 1974.
10. Singer, Harry, and Dan Donlan. *Reading and Learning from Text*. Boston: Little, Brown, 1980 (in press).
11. Singer, Harry, and Robert B. Ruddell (Eds.). *Theoretical Models and Processes of Reading*, Second Edition. Newark, Delaware: International Reading Association, 1976.
12. Spache, George, and Evelyn B. Spache. *Reading in the Elementary School*, Second Edition. Boston: Allyn and Bacon, 1969.
13. Taba, Hilda. "The Teaching of Thinking," *Elementary English*, 42 (1965), 534-542.

Operant Conditioning in Reading

George D. Spache
Sarasota, Florida

We are being snowed under now by engineers and the like who are going to put us on an assembly line in the teaching of reading; and we are going to turn out robots who read, under the premise that this infinite, detailed analysis of the process of reading is individualized. It is individualized in the sense that every child uses the same skills in the same sequence through the same modality; it's individualized because he's at his own desk.

Another of the outstanding claims is that of a systematized set of materials for skill development; the learning is more efficiently managed, and its concentrated faults reinforced; it is evaluated at each step, and it's self-pacing. Furthermore, its system apparently provides a complete tonic to skill development in the reading process for the teacher.

Of these things, only the last one really has any merit or validity. And even that is very doubtful.

What are two other advantages that the purveyors tell us about? Well, teachers can learn a great deal about the nature of the reading act as the engineers see it, especially when they work on spelling out details, behavioral objectives, and devising the related tests of unknown validity and reliability. Because of this growth in knowledge, instructional practices become even more diversified and individualized. And, finally, if the battery of accompanying criterion referenced tests is given to a class, the individual needs of each pupil for instruction can be determined; and, of course, we have the worksheets for those needs. Thus, the child's individual development is mainly assessed hour by hour, and guided minute by minute.

What are some of the assumptions in this so-called approach to the teaching of reading? We have to assume, first of all, that the process of reading or of learning to read is entirely one of skills development; and, as the engineers tell us, there are hundreds of these little skills that must be learned— 300, 500, pick a round number, have your choice. They tell us that all children will learn to read by building this series of skills in the order planned, and that all children need training in *all* these skills in order to read successfully. These skills *must* be real because the authors have told us so. These objectives *must* be real because, after all, the authorities have written them; or in Orange County, California, the teachers wrote them—which makes them even more real.

The identity and the interdependence of the subskills have been established, apparently. The tests that accompany each series are valid and reliable samples of the skills named in their titles. The a priori standards for these tests are defensible or legitimate. It is perfectly all right to decide what the children are going to have to do with the tests. Identifying the child's deficiencies in this fashion and then teaching to eradicate them are the best ways of conducting reading instruction, the most logical, the most effective, and so on.

I do not buy any of these assumptions. For example, all children do *not* use the same skills in order to read, even with the same degree of comprehension. Some are highly dependent upon phonic analysis; others don't know beans about phonic analysis and still read within their limits well enough to be acceptable. Some use word forms—although that's not supposed to be a good clue, but it is for some people or some children.

All I have to do is put upon the blackboard two letters, WW, and ask you for whom this stands. What statesman? What president? Remember? Sure. How much of a word do you need? A context and even an initial blend is enough for some of us.

Good readers do not differ from poor readers in that the good readers have learned all the skills to read successfully. Or, to put it another way, that good readers use only skills while poor readers do not. It's much more mixed than that. Some good readers lack certain skills; some poor readers have certain skills.

At a recent national reading conference, a paper was presented which described a study of sixth graders who were reading satisfactorily and discussed their performance on five of the word attack tests in the Wisconsin design—one of the prominent systems. Sixty percent of the children failed three of the five word attack skills tests and, therefore, should not have been able to read. But they did read.

We found the same thing when Hackett was first making her system, now called Criterion Reading. They gave these poor kids hundreds of tests. The children failed, you know, and the teachers were most discouraged. "This child is reading at grade level or above grade level. Why should I go back and fill in that little bit or piece that I don't even understand myself?"

It has not been demonstrated that all the skills identified actually exist or are significant for ultimate reading ability. For example, phonic skills are helpful at primary levels and in recognition of words the child already knows. They do nothing for him on a word for which he has no associations, no semantics.

For example, there is a delightful French phrase, *coup de grace*. Now, it's spelled c-o-u-p, but the *p* is silent in French like most final letters except *c, r, f,* and l. So, although spelled c-o-up, it is not a coupe. It's a coo. De is duh, and g-r-a-c-e sounds like the stuff the Bostonian cuts on his lawn, "coo d' grass." The *c* is soft and the *a* is long as in father.

Now you know something about French phonics. Tell me what it means. You are no further along than you were before. You've got good verbalism, but phonics does not unlock meaning except in breakfast type words. Phonics doesn't function from about fourth and fifth grade on in the technical terms the child is meeting in history, geography, and social science. Yet we tutor junior high, senior high, and college students in phonics as a remedial effort. Children who are reading at about fourth grade or higher don't use phonics. In fact, the research studies show that in the relationship of any of six phonics tests on the market, from the fifth grade on, phonics plays no part in comprehension. Yet these skills are in there—dozens of them—more than I ever dreamed of.

All right, since the significance of many other subskills tested is dubious, the validity or the meaningfulness of their tests is suspect. Moreover, the tests are so brief, they have very little reliability. They do not measure permanent learning. They are not dependable. They can't tell you what the child will be able to do two weeks from now because of lack of reliability. Nor do the tests necessarily prove that the child is lacking in these skills because they *can* be subject to chance behavior.

As your children get test sophisticated, and they certainly will under this kind of system, it won't be long before they'll be managing tests very easily but not learning anything. We found that in private schools. They did so much testing that by the sixth grade all the children were three years accelerated.

A priori standards are theoretical or ideal, but certainly not criteria that we set for success or failure or promotion. How can one tell how little children should do in a test, a test that has never been tried on any child? Can you justify this kind of thinking? I can't. It doesn't even make common sense, much less good test construction, to decide beforehand that 85 percent is the normal behavior when you haven't even tried it on any child of any age or any ability.

The underlying theory of teaching-to-deficiencies has never been scientifically tested. It is no more logical than the contrasting approach of instruction intended to create interest, positive self-concept, and personal involvement in reading. Those of us who have some humanistic feelings lean toward that as a better approach, rather than correcting the supposed deficiencies—building on the strength of a child, showing how he can be successful, using his own language as in the language experience approach, for example. He can't fail because, if he can talk, we can get it on paper; and if we get it on paper, he can manage to read it; and he can go on from there indefinitely, regardless of his age.

This fractionating of the reading process tends to separate learning to read from the true act of reading. It tends to emphasize bits and pieces which may not be relevant to the abilities to reason, to use information for the *reader's* purpose, or any other long range results of instruction. Reading is not solely skill development, nor is it solely a matter of a performance in judgment, reasoning, and critical evaluation; but it certainly moves toward the latter.

In other words, while word recognition, vocabulary development, and word analysis *help* to develop the basic reading ability, the child goes on developing new and more sophisticated reading behaviors far above the lower level behavioral objectives and subskills identified in the systems. He moves out from there to cope. Our concern should be in creating interest in reading, creating personal reading habits, judging whether the children are using books in a way this year that they didn't last year, rather than whether they can fill in two words on a test as a measure of the year's growth, and other such nonsense.

Key Issues Facing Reading Consultants:
Practical Solutions to Common Dilemmas

Larry J. Mikulecky
Indiana University at Bloomington

Patricia L. Anders
University of Arizona

Linda Ramig
Georgia State University

Norma Rogers
Monroe County Community School Corporation
Bloomington, Indiana

Role Definition of the Reading Consultant:
Administrator, Teacher, or Somewhere Inbetween?

Overview

As a reading consultant you are probably expected to be an administrator as well as a teacher, depending on the time of day. The problem becomes one of credibility. Much organization goes into any good educational program and that means time in flexible quantities. While all this organizing is being done, classroom teachers are found to mumble, "What difference does it make anyway? It's actually working with these kids every day that counts. How can any idea work when it is thought up by someone who doesn't really teach?"

To establish that much needed and often elusive credibility, you must spend time with kids as well as time organizing and planning programs. That puts you with a foot in two camps; it can turn out to be the best of both worlds or it can be the biggest frustration of your career. You're in a position to get a first hand look at classroom practices in your building. Some are terrific, and others are, well, terrifying. How do you handle this kind of information? Are you a teacher with all the things you can't control to complain about, or are you an administrator with power to evaluate? You are a specialist and expected to keep up with new trends and research. Are you an administrator with time for professional conferences and meetings or are you a teacher tied to the daily classroom routine? Everyone needs to have professional friends, many of whom may become social friends. Do you choose other administrators for those special people; do you choose other teachers? Or do you end up feeling isolated with neither group feeling free to "trust" you with their friendship?

Answers to these questions should not be for today or even for tomorrow. Some of these decisions, once made, may become irreversible immediately. The decision is ultimately yours, but think carefully about possible results and know what you're doing.

Situation

The system in which you work has a very strong local teacher's organization. You have been fairly successful at skirting the issue, but this year contract negotiations have been very difficult. Tomorrow the people in your building are taking a strike vote. What do you do?

Reaction

You will have to declare yourself very soon—either as an administrator, who usually has his own professional organization which is management oriented and automatically is assumed to be "above" a strike, or as a teacher, whose organization is in the throes of an important decision that will affect everyone in the system. You have inside information about the situation. Superficially, it seems that there are basically two ways to go.

One, you can make a judgment purely on a majority rule basis. If you feel most teachers will strike, then you'd better go out with them. This will place you in the teacher category and not administrator. Any staff that is split will live with hard feelings for a year or so but, given your position and job, you may be better off siding with that majority.

Two, you may feel the need to make a purely moral decision about the situation. To be in this position is highly desirable, but unfortunately not always the case. It may be difficult to convince some people that a decision not to strike is a moral one and not a decision to side with the administration. You must choose very carefully. Whatever decision you make will affect your future effectiveness.

Situation

As a reading consultant, you must attend many local job related meetings as well as several professional meetings. How do you cope with the feeling of resentment which may quickly develop as a result of your "out of building" time?

Reaction

Since you are a specialist, your role potentially puts you on many committees. You should keep the staff informed, at least informally, of these meetings—their purposes and outcomes. This will keep people from wondering what you're really up to. Be sure to tell them before they ask.

In case of professional meetings which may require more than an afternoon's absence, again explain where you're going, when, and why; be sure to notify personally all teachers/students of cancelled appointments. Don't rely on a note. Someone always gets missed that way. Upon return, share, informally with small groups of teachers, one or two ideas you picked up *especially for them*. This is usually more successful than a formal large group presentation.

As a final word for eliminating resentment, be sure to *request* your fair share of jobs, such as hall duty, bus duty, or lunchroom patrol. Having other teachers see you do nuisance jobs just as they do helps your credibility. If you must miss duty, be sure to trade with someone or make the time up. Any special concessions made for you will just serve to make you one more step removed from the teachers and their classrooms.

Situation

As part of a local administration reading campaign, each teacher must be evaluated in terms of teaching reading. Based on these evaluations, inservice programs will be developed locally for all teachers. You, as the reading consultant, are responsible for this evaluation information. How do you carry out the program tactfully and positively?

Reaction

A first priority item is to get the teachers themselves involved in this whole process. Almost anything which comes directly from the administration is looked upon with some degree of mistrust. Don't offer the excuse, "I have to do this because somebody told me to." Set up positive reasons as quickly as you can.

When people are informed of the *why*, begin involvement on the *how*. You are ultimately in charge, but that's probably not meant to exclude others from the process. You may be able to get a volunteer committee together to work up a special form for evaluation purposes. This might include such things as a checklist of strengths and weaknesses and open-ended questions for same; an observation form with criteria for observing; a list of possible inservice ideas for a priority ranking; a section for student responses to reading and how it is being taught in their own classrooms; suggestions for how your time could be used to best help them; and random comments regarding the teaching of reading. Given a variety of ways to evaluate their own teaching of reading, consensus can usually be reached as to the form(s) such evaluation should take. Include some items for everyone to respond to successfully.

After the forms are completed, again work with the teachers in identifying areas for the inservices so that nothing is felt to be secretive. Don't let it be *your* decision alone. Force teachers into taking a stand. If they have been involved thus far, chances are they won't complain about the outcomes. As a last positive note, you might even suggest some of your own teachers as potential planners/leaders for the sessions. This would insure willing participation of many of your staff members and help foster a feeling of pride in what your teachers and school do.

Situation

As a reading consultant in your building, you are in a position to see many classroom practices, ranging from good to mediocre to bad. Your principal asks you for information about a particular teacher who is thought to be not doing the job. Your "report" will be essential in decisions concerning dismissal of this teacher.

Reaction

You have probably already informally evaluated the teachers in your building in order to construct your reading program. These evaluations tended to be general observations unless a teacher has specifically asked for help in some area, or you have worked in the same classroom along with that teacher. Even then it seems any negative impressions/ attitudes gathered about that teacher should be shared only with that teacher and not be made public. You cannot assume a major role in evaluating teachers. You do it, in fact, as a matter of course in doing your job, but it seems important to keep it within that context if you are to remain effective.

Consider another aspect; this problem is not yours but your principal's. It may be easiest for him to involve you in the process of contract nonrenewal, but the minute you become involved you will lose ground with the other teachers. "Who's next?" is likely to be the big question in the teacher's lounge. The principal should know himself what goes on in the classroom and should not depend on you for this job. Let him make his own observations.

Two other approaches, though not necessarily solutions, can be considered. Having people know that you are observing for a special purpose (which *you* have already set up to include *everyone*) may stimulate some people to improve. Teachers feel peer pressure and putting classrooms on display for *each other* (that is, having teachers visit in their own building) has brought about interesting results. This again takes the evaluation aura away from you, and at the same time allows you to be an observer like everyone else.

Another much broader side of the issue is that we, as professional educators, must take an active role in how people are admitted to this profession and almost more importantly how those who prove unworthy are removed. All of this goes far deeper than our immediate roles as reading consultants, but yet we must face the issue with our own actions in the all too common situation presented here.

Situation

Since you do not have a homeroom, i.e., regular classroom, you are likely to be asked to fill in for someone. If you do it, then your job becomes part time substitute, not full time consultant. But how do you refuse without giving others the feeling you're afraid to teach someone's class or are not willing to help?

Reaction

This is a matter for you and your principal. You must be firm in letting him know you are not a substitute. You have your own job to do. Ask him who will substitute for you while you're doing someone else's duties. In case of an emergency, he should understand however that you're willing to step in and help when and where necessary, but only in such a situation. You are likely to end up "on call" for just about everyone if you're not careful.

Substitutions in classrooms are not always to be avoided and may be used wisely in conjunction with your own program. You may voluntarily be able to free another teacher to attend a meeting related to reading or for some extra planning time for someone helping you prepare an inservice for the rest of the staff. You may be able to allow some intra-school visitations by taking someone's class while he observes a colleague. Substituting in this manner would only put you in the position of being viewed as willing to help the classroom teachers. You aren't compromising by spending days substituting for the sake of convenience only.

Reading Consultant:
Director, Facilitator, or Manipulator?

Overview

A reading consultant's mode of operation changes many times throughout a single day. At times one may be called upon to be director of a schoolwide literacy task force or of a student tutoring program, or perhaps of volunteers in a reading laboratory. More often, the subtle skill of helping teachers and administrators define their reading-related needs and goals and then facilitating cooperative work among faculty members is what is called for. Sometimes, since very little administrative power is delegated to reading consultants, careful political analysis and manipulation of situations is called for if good ideas are to become operating realities within a school district.

Many teachers and administrators may have preconceived notions of how a reading program or how a reading consultant is supposed to operate. The fact that some of these notions are not particularly well thought out doesn't diminish their strength. Some colleagues will expect the consultant to always be in a classroom working with poor readers, while others will demand a more directive role as the dictator in charge of reading who will bring those other teachers back into line. Because so many people "think" they know what the reading consultant should be doing, it is important for the reading consultant to have thought through the appropriate mode of operation for a variety of situations. Sometimes doing what people say they expect can run counter to meeting the reading needs of a school. At other times, complying with others' expectations while facilitating attitude change is the only sensible course to take. A good reading consultant needs to know when to be a director, facilitator, or manipulator and when to use a variety of other operational modes.

Situation

You are frequently asked, "What is the best test (material)?" How can you share some of the decision making process with teachers?

Reaction

You are the reading expert on your staff. It would be very easy to assume an authoritarian role and simply tell people what you think they ought to hear—especially when they ask you! When things do not work out properly, however, you may be blamed since it was *your* decision.

One approach might be to plan definite teacher involvement. Respond to their inquiries about materials with questions: "Why do you want this at all?" or "What do you want to accomplish?" Use of any test ought to imply or state some use(s) or results. Begin there. If teachers can justify no valid use of the results, then why bother with time and money to test at all? If and when the reason for giving a test is established, that will automatically limit the type of instrument you might use. Make copies of the available tests which you initially suggested and meet with teachers to discuss how each will meet the needs they have already defined. By following this procedure, chances are much greater that the outcomes will actually prove to be useful.

The same basic procedures used for tests are applicable to materials. You cannot assume that all teachers know how to properly evaluate instructional material. You should be in a position to recommend a variety of materials according to the specific needs defined by teachers and, in case of unfamiliar material, do some research into what this material will and will not do. Here again, teachers should state their need for this material.

Since there are poor materials as well as good materials on the market, the job of facilitator will be to screen certain materials and then match up teaching styles with those materials. You may have already received teachers' very good reasons for requesting materials and now you may be able to get some teachers to try new materials which will help them to make some adjustments in their teaching styles.

Situation

A teacher with whom you have not worked directly asks what you can do to help her students in reading. In the past you've found that simply giving advice doesn't work.

Reaction

A first priority is to find out what is going on in the classroom now. This can be accomplished through planned classroom observation of the teacher. (Don't rely on what the teacher tells you; see for yourself.) Meet together to discuss what seems to be missing in the current program, and define what that teacher's goal is for the students. This should help outline the problem(s) that will need to be tackled and may turn out to be the easy part as you play the role of director.

Since giving advice or recommending does not work well, you must be careful and realistic. Consider the teacher. You'll need to fit the problem's solution to the personality and style of the particular teacher you're working with. The solution may require more and/or different materials. You're the one to collect and organize them. Once you've gotten materials together, the teacher must be aware of how to use them properly. The key lies in planning with that teacher and actually helping in the classroom when appropriate. Your second role, then, is that of a facilitator.

If the solution involves a new method rather than material, then it is essential that you be in the classroom demonstrating for the teacher all the things you have said for someone else to do. This should not mean a one time only situation. The most important thing is to let the teacher know that you're there to back up all those suggestions that, though clear to you, are still hazy or threatening to the classroom teacher. Once you've gotten someone interested and involved, you simply can't let them down. That's only the first step; it's a long range, action filled plan if you are to succeed in bringing about change.

Situation

As a reading consultant in your building you work for and with an entire staff. How do you create a feeling of fairness or equality among teachers when the tendency is to help those who are most open to suggestion and value your help?

Reaction

The balance is delicate and, at best, difficult to maintain. How successful you are will depend a great deal on your particular situation and the people you work with. Even though you may develop personal friendships, you must be very careful to treat everyone the same within the context of your job. Offer the same services to all teachers and be just as available to someone you don't particularly care for as someone for whom you do. It may sound easy, but it's not.

The social friendships you develop will most likely be with teachers you tend to agree with professionally. The automatic reaction is to share professional and outside interests with them. Any new materials or ideas are best shared with teachers who you know are going to use them wisely. It is difficult to remain neutral when you know a number of teachers won't (or can't) use the ideas/materials you have available for teacher-sharing. You might work out a schedule to keep material circulating or operate on a checkout basis for sharing. You may also consider telling people who have the chance to try out the new material that you'd like to see it being used; better yet, volunteer to help them set it up. Be sure that *everyone* knows the materials you're offering are available. Then, even though you may have arranged some sharing previously, everyone will or should be aware of what is available.

Remaining neutral helps in your attempt to predict responses to things you do so that you are not unintentionally causing friction or seemingly doing your job without keeping classroom teachers—all of them—and their problems in mind. This may mean you spend some time "running interference" for and with people by laying the groundwork for some future plan before you actually attempt to carry it out. This is where you might take time for small talk; eat lunch with different people; get to know all your teachers. Consider everyone's reactions, not only those you know best and work with most frequently.

Situation

The principal at your school is in charge of everything. You have just been hired to direct the reading program.

Reaction

First, you are going to have to earn the respect of your principal. If he has been in charge of all programs in the past, you will probably not be a very welcome addition unless he has not enjoyed his powerful role—and that's not likely. Find out in a nonthreatening way as much as you can about his biases and prejudices and why he holds the views he does. You will also need to predict his reactions to many things you do. Just keep in mind that you are the reading specialist and perhaps gently, but firmly, remind the principal of that periodically. At first you may need to cite research or references to support your viewpoint and to reinforce the idea that you *do* know what you're talking about. You might even use a past experience to describe something you wish to try in your current situation.

Assume some responsibility for yourself. Do some things on your own. The saying, "It's easier to ask forgiveness than to ask permission," is often true. By asking for or about everything, you are reinforcing the power role your principal has always played. One word of caution is in order, however. Be sure to keep your principal informed of everything you do whether it includes him directly or not. He should never be put in the position of not knowing what is going on in his school. Notify him of all meetings, give him copies of all memos, letters, etc., and spend time just talking with him. Don't make every time you meet with him a request for something or a business meeting. In short, employ some good public relations techniques. Leave him in a position of knowing, but not necessarily directing.

Be very careful never to put teachers in the position of having to choose between you and the principal. It's certainly awkward at best for the teachers, and it won't do much for you either. This is where it really pays off to know your principal well and be able to predict his reactions/responses to things you might do.

Don't expect miracles overnight. It may take you a year to really get your bearings with the principal and staff before you're ready to talk in terms of a program without compromise. Compromise may come later, but you may not have to begin there once you have structured a good working relationship with your principal.

Situation

Many of your teachers are far removed from your plan of how reading ought to be taught. They want to send you their remedial readers and keep you in your own reading room. How can you work to change their reading approach?

Reaction

The most common attitude of classroom teachers is to view any reading specialist as a remedial reading teacher who sets up a separate room for the poor readers; what goes on there doesn't really concern them. As a reading consultant, your role is essentially program oriented. You work with and for the students but you must work directly with the teachers and support them in order to bring about real change. You must work with students in the classroom setting as much as possible so that there is no mystery about what goes on in a closed reading room setting. This puts you in the situation of demonstrating good reading practice where other teachers can see you. It also does not remove or relieve their responsibility for teaching reading to everyone. Often, one reason teachers give for not teaching reading at all (in high school) or not doing a better job (in elementary school) is that someone else does it for them in remedial reading classes. To get anyone to change, you must first have him realize what he's doing now probably isn't as relevant or useful as it should be. One subtle way to do this is to set yourself up in reading-within-the-classroom situations and begin by being a good example of what you'd like others to do. In other words, remain highly visible and be sure *you* practice what *you* preach.

There is need for everyone to be involved in learning activities—even teachers on their own level—if positive results are to come about. Informal meetings/activities by grade level or department to plan for continuity of students as they move through the curriculum are useful. Most teachers are willing to make adjustments if they can see good reason for such change, and your job is to make them see that necessity. Stress both student and teacher learning. Keep abreast of new trends and, depending on the teacher-student needs, provide the relevant information. You must use finesse to get teachers to question their own teaching. Once questions start, you are free to provide all the possible answers and that is the position to set as your goal if change is to take place.

Elementary Consultant Role versus Secondary Consultant Role: The Great Divide or Is It?

Overview

Are there any substantive differences between being a reading consultant at the elementary school level and being a reading consultant at the secondary school level? What sorts of training should one have in order to work effectively at either of these levels? Should the training be the same with minor modifications to accommodate the differing ages of students or should elementary and secondary training be substantially different?

Additional questions about similarities and differences emerge when one considers the major emphases of elementary or secondary consultants' jobs. Are there differences in how much time is student-oriented and how much is teacher-oriented? Does level make a difference in deciding whether one's major emphasis should be toward developmental or remedial reading? Does a secondary consultant need to know a bit about chemistry, sociology, auto mechanics and driver education while an elementary consultant needs to know a bit about child psychology, constructing games, raising gerbils, and nurturing children?

Since personality and social skills are as important in determining success as is training, questions need to be asked in these areas. Are the personality attributes which enhance success at the elementary level the same as those which enhance success at the secondary level? Is assertiveness prized more one place than another? Do political and administrative skills differ according to teaching level or are they basically the same? All of us are leaders sometimes and followers at other times. Does the degree to which one is a leader or a follower influence the likelihood of success at either level?

As demands increase for secondary reading help, it becomes increasingly important to answer these questions. Search committees and directors of personnel should have more to base decisions upon than a candidate's degree in reading.

Situation

You are an experienced elementary reading consultant who finds herself at the secondary level. You were quite good at your elementary level job and prided yourself on being able to teach nearly anyone how to read. You have an uncomfortable feeling, however, that different expectations may exist in your new job.

Reaction

Your discomfort is over a very real issue: Part of your competence as an elementary consultant was your ability to help students *learn to read.* Your mastery of several teaching techniques, your knowledge of a warehouse full of materials, and your ability to motivate and encourage discouraged children all aided you in accomplishing your goal. Learning to read can be a process that is enjoyable and possible for nearly every student if help such as you were able to give is available.

Some of the expectations of your secondary level job as a reading consultant will be much the same. You will find *some* students who read poorly or not at all. Your knowledge of teaching techniques will gain respect from these students. You may have to become familiar with new sets of high interest, low readability material for these students; but you can do that, given time. Since many of these secondary students have failed for a longer period than the elementary students you've taught, you may have to motivate, encourage, and reinforce a bit more; but you know how to do that already. Basically, with these students, you are still helping them *learn to read.*

There is, in addition, a new expectation at the secondary level. You must help students and aid teachers in helping students *read to learn.* Most secondary students can already read, to a degree. At this point they need training in how to handle the widely diverse styles of writing they encounter in each new class (chemistry, biology, sociology, poetry, essays, fiction, economics, auto mechanics). Each content offers its own problems and you must work with both students and teachers to overcome these difficulties. Another aspect of *reading to learn* is mastering the ability to read flexibly according to the demands offered by reading material and mastering the ability to study efficiently. You may choose to teach some classes in reading rate and study skills.

You will still be helping some students *learn to read* in your new job. The major emphasis, however, will be in helping everyone at the secondary level foster an environment in which students can more efficiently *read to learn*.

Situation

As an elementary trained teacher, you are asked to help out in a chemistry class. You nearly flunked that subject at the university.

Reaction

Try to fight down your panic and realize that your role as a reading consultant doesn't demand that you be an expert in each content area. As a matter of fact, you can use your lack of expertise in chemistry to the advantage of both the chemistry teacher and his students.

Initially, make it clear to the chemistry teacher that you consider him the authority on chemistry. Your area of expertise is in using reading as a vehicle for learning. If he has a text or printed material in his course, perhaps you can help to make the information in that text more accessible to his students.

Get the chemistry teacher to take home a reading assignment he plans to use next. Have him identify and locate key ideas he considers absolutely necessary to understanding the lesson. You, in turn, should examine the assignment from the point of view of a student with reading difficulties. Which concepts, passages, vocabulary, or graphs are difficult to comprehend? Your lack of chemistry knowledge should prove helpful to you here.

When you and the chemistry teacher again meet, you will have a sound idea of how each of you can contribute to a cooperative effort. You can point out areas where students might have difficulty, while suggesting word-attack strategies (context, structure, sounding out words, glossary), advance previews of the chapter, or purpose-setting questions. Let the chemistry teacher create the purpose-setting questions or decide which preparatory information he must provide and which is available in other parts of the text. The point here is to get the chemistry teacher to identify what is *really* important and then decide what he must do to bring his students to those important ideas. You can supply vocabulary and comprehension techniques. You can identify areas of difficulty he might pass over or neglect. A modified Directed Reading Activity, such as is used with elementary students, can be developed for a content area class once the teaching goal of the reading material is understood. Later, if your initial contact is successful, you and he together might work with the class on better study skills and use of the text (index, glossary, table of contents, subheadings, footnotes, italics). You might even seek more readable supplementary material.

The key here isn't that you must teach chemistry. The key is that you must get the chemistry teacher to think of the text from the point of view of a student with reading difficulty. Once the teacher can do that, your suggestions about vocabulary, comprehension, and study techniques are more likely to be listened to. They can then be seen as effective ways of dealing with impediments to learning. As the teacher incorporates more techniques, you can pull back to help others.

Situation

You are a central reading administrator who needs secondary reading help. You can't afford a new person. Mrs. Jones, a fourth grade teacher, has a reading certificate. How do you decide whether she should be moved to the secondary reading level?

Reaction

You should first have a conversation with Mrs. Jones in which you explore a) her desire to work at the secondary level, b) her training and experiences with adolescents, c) how she envisions her role, d) her ability to get along politically and socially with other teachers, and e) her willingness to continue learning. Many of Mrs. Jones' experiences working with the reading of younger children will be useful to her at the secondary level. She is also likely to face a totally new set of expectations, however, which will call for personal resources not evident upon a transcript.

Desire. Moving from a situation in which one is comfortable to something new and somewhat unknown can be disconcerting. A certain amount of anxiety on Mrs. Jones' part would be natural. If, however, the anxiety is so great that you need to coax and persuade, she may be wrong for the job. She should be excited enough by the challenge of a new job to take on that job without constant support.

Secondary role. Mrs. Jones has had experience with students who have had reading difficulties at a fairly early level. This experience will aid her in dealing with adolescents with remedial problems. She should also, however, see her role as working with content area teachers in their classrooms or while planning units.

One remedial reading teacher in a large high school is a waste of resources if that teacher works only with students. Daily time, divided between students and working with content teachers, ensures that reading aid with textual material will reach a far larger number of students.

In addition, as an elementary teacher, Mrs. Jones may have become quite proficient at creating teaching materials. Trying to make materials for secondary teachers can be a trap for reading consultants. A great deal of time can be expended on material production with little guarantee of use. It is far better when teachers meet the reading consultant half-way and invest some of their own time in the creation of materials. It is highly important that a secondary reading consultant truly envisions her role as a participant in a cooperative venture with other teachers.

Training and experience with adolescents. It would be best if Mrs. Jones had had some experience teaching adolescents at the secondary level. That is not always possible, however. Short of that, Mrs. Jones should have some experience in dealing with adolescents. This could be as a parent or perhaps as an advisor to community groups. In addition to reading problems, some of the students she deals with will have become discipline problems. Challenging authority is typical, to a degree, among some adolescents. For students failing several classes because of reading difficulty, such challenges may be the only successful experiences available in school.

Political and social ability. A secondary reading consultant should be well versed in the area of persuasion and should be able to put fellow teachers at ease. Reading consultants rarely have administrative authority over teachers or over schoolwide curricular decisions. Effective change to improve reading only occurs if teachers from a variety of political and philosophical viewpoints can be convinced to attempt new teaching methods and consider reading improvement when ordering books, planning classes, and setting goals. These changes occur best if the reading consultant and secondary teacher can comfortably work closely together. A reading consultant who can't effectively deal with all sorts of teachers will have a difficult time accomplishing the most important part of his or her job.

Willingness to continue learning. Willingness to continue learning is especially important in Mrs. Jones' case. She must polish her ability to deal with content area reading, critical reading, comprehension improvement, study skills, rate, program organization, and a host of other aspects of secondary reading. Enjoying learning about new things is important and necessary for any secondary reading consultant. To effectively work with texts ranging from auto mechanics to calculus, a reading consultant must be willing to learn a little about many different subjects. In addition, keeping up with new ideas for each of the content fields calls upon a consultant to continue reading and learning through university classes, professional journals, and conferences.

Situation

As a new reading consultant in a small district, you are asked to design an inservice on reading for all teachers. You will work with elementary teachers in the morning and secondary teachers in the afternoon. In what ways should your presentations differ?

Reaction

Elementary. Since you are new, you can count on both groups being initially skeptical about your ability to make useful classroom suggestions. The elementary group will be waiting for some indication that you really know what it's like to work with a group of younger children. On the positive side, the elementary teachers, in all likelihood, view the teaching of reading as their responsibility and will be ready for help in meeting that responsibility.

If at all possible, you should survey the elementary teachers before the inservice to determine what they view as their primary reading needs. Depending on your situation, the previous training of the teachers, and the time you have available for the inservice, you may select from among several topics:

- Methods to individualize and set up learning stations.
- Availability and use of supplementary reading materials.
- Use of directed reading activities at a variety of grade levels.
- Methods of working with slower readers.
- Use of a language experience approach.
- Use of a skills management system.
- Supplementary use of a variety of programed instruction.
- Methods for incorporating tutors (parents or older students) into elementary classrooms.

Secondary. Like the elementary teachers, the secondary teachers may be skeptical about your credibility in the classroom. In addition, you are likely to encounter a number of myths about reading which need to be confronted and dispelled. Among these myths are

- Now they expect us secondary teachers to teach phonics.
- If the elementary teachers had done their job, we wouldn't be in this fix.
- The English teacher ought to handle the reading problems.
- If we could only get a remedial reading teacher, we could send all the reading problems to that teacher.

After dispelling these myths, suggest that each teacher handle some reading considerations that directly relate to the subject he or she is teaching. Draw on the fact that many good teachers have been addressing content area reading considerations for years. At this point, both the reading consultant and the secondary teachers can share practical suggestions on how best to:

- Handle the teaching of special content area vocabulary.
- Set purposes for reading and design reasonable assignments.
- Address teaching to students who range in reading ability from third grade to university level.
- Find useful supplementary reading material at various difficulty levels.

Later secondary inservice sessions can deal with developing an all-school reading program and meeting the special needs of each department. The initial inservices with secondary teachers, however, should dispel myths and provide practical classroom suggestions that are likely to be used.

Situation

Content area teachers seem to use you fairly consistently when you offer to prepare materials, yet rarely seem to apply ideas unless you do the leg work.

Reaction

This situation is one that is quite common at the secondary level and is a difficulty that can be especially dangerous for an elementary trained reading consultant. For the most part elementary teachers are quite competent at creating their own materials and trading them with other teachers. This sort of cooperation works to the advantage of students and usually follows the unwritten rule that you give as much as you receive. A reading consultant is just one more teacher who has some good ideas and materials for teaching reading.

Secondary teachers, however, are not as familiar with constructing their own materials and may even have some mistaken idea that such activity is inappropriate for higher grade levels. In addition, such teachers may choose to see the reading consultant as the person who ought to single-handedly solve all the reading problems of their students. These two factors make a zealous, materials-creating reading consultant an easy mark for some secondary teachers.

A reasonable rule of thumb for a secondary consultant is to begin working with people who will help in both planning and creating materials. Teachers are much more likely to use materials they've helped create. More to the point, however, is the fact that the consultant has a great deal of reading information that ought to be distributed to the teachers. His or her time shouldn't be swallowed up making materials when it is more productive to train others (students or fellow teachers) in how to construct their own materials.

The Reading Consultant's Relationships with other Specified Staff: Learning Disabilities Teachers, Special Education Teachers, Speech Therapists, School Psychologists, Social Workers

Overview

The reading consultant is one of several specialists employed by most school districts. Since problems rarely stay as compartmentalized as our administrative structures, there is likely to be a great deal of overlap in the tasks of a district's specialists. There is very little chance that such overlap can be avoided.

The overlap has both positive and negative aspects. The increased resources of several specialists, each with unique insights and viewpoints, can be a valued strength in problem solving. On the other hand, the possibilities for competition, political maneuvering, and misunderstanding are also a drawback of such overlaps.

A reading consultant, in order to succeed, must become familiar with the professional and personal strengths of other specialists. Anticipating and preparing for both positive and negative possibilities are unwritten parts of the reading consultant's job description.

Situation

As a districtwide consultant at the secondary level, you find Mr. Forest, a building level principal, threatened by your power over federally financed programs in his building as well as your needs assessment and evaluation data. He seems to be uncooperative at times in providing space and office help. This makes it difficult to implement a needed project. What approaches can you take to minimize this problem?

Reaction

Learning to successfully live with and respect those with whom one works is a fundamental component of success. The first step in such a situation is to look at oneself to discover specifically what might be eliciting a response of fear and resentment. What can be done to reassure (convince) Mr. Forest that there is no threat to his prestige or power and that, in fact, he will be greatly responsible for the success of the program?

It is very important that the principal have a clear understanding of a proposed project before it is to be implemented in his building. Be sure that all the details of the planned project have been worked out and that he approves. Solicit his ideas and suggestions from the very start so that he feels an integral part of the program. If you are writing a proposal for federal funds, ask him to help. He may refuse but still be pleased that he was asked. When all of the plans are made, be sure he has a copy for his files. Never plan inservice meetings or planning sessions without consulting him about the time and place. Then send him a copy of all written memos regarding the project.

Every person hired to work in the program should have a written job description. This includes you. If ever there are questions or misunderstandings pertaining to the specific roles and responsibilities of project participants, you can refer to the official job description for guidance. This is probably one of the most important steps you can take, for most disagreements arise over who has the authority to make important decisions. (Rarely does a problem arise over who is to do the work.) Consider the following approaches:

1. Study the principal's personality traits and background. Find out what his interests and concerns are. Capitalize on these when the opportunity arises.
2. Handle all data from the needs assessment and evaluation very carefully so that no teacher, parent, or principal will receive bad publicity as a result.
3. Take care to use the term "we" instead of "I" when discussing project plans and successes.
4. Never ignore the principal when bringing visitors or inspectors to see the project. Introduce them and make an effort to mention the principal's contribution to the program.
5. Discuss every phase of work with him.
6. Send him a copy of every memo written to teachers, parents, or students.
7. Take time to chat with him occasionally. Always have a smile and a friendly "good morning" to let him know he is certainly worthy of recognition.
8. Talk with him about the school's problems. Ask his opinion on various subjects, especially your project. Be gracious in accepting or rejecting suggestions he may have made. Give him the credit for any work he has done or ideas he has had.
9. If he has an area of expertise you can tap, by all means do so. Elicit his advice on materials, teaching methods, testing and locating materials. Let him know you respect his opinion and remember to tell him when his suggestions are being used. In short, make him feel important as a senior member of the team.

Situation

You have just received a call from a board member who has had numerous complaints from parents about Mrs. White's ability to teach reading. This teacher is the direct responsibility of the building principal. She has a master's degree and three years of teaching experience. How do you find out if she truly needs help without threatening the teacher or infringing upon the principal's territory while identifying the problem and attempting to solve it? (You must maintain the confidentiality of the board member.)

Reaction

First, if you have access to personnel records, get Mrs. White's personnel file and search for information concerning her professional training, experience and recommendations. From the school office, obtain additional information on the number and type of students she is teaching as well as the instructional materials and diagnostic tools she is using. Does she have an adequate supply of instructional materials?

If the principal is open to suggestions and readily accepts help, go to him and frankly discuss the complaints with him. Probably, he can shed some light on the situation and you will begin to plan some strategies toward solving the problem cooperatively. The administrator may know the parents who are complaining and have an entirely different perspective.

When you have obtained as much information about Mrs. White's background as possible and have consulted with the principal concerning the parents, the class, and the availability of instructional materials, it is time to discuss the situation with the classroom teacher. Now we need to determine whether the teacher is aware of the problem. She has a right to know about the complaints, whether or not they are justified.

Assuming there appear to be justifiable reasons for the criticism, make an appointment to discuss the situation with Mrs. White. Since you have a great deal of information already, use it wisely to put Mrs. White at ease and to convince her that you are there in her behalf. Teachers must feel that administrators are on their side. They share common goals, thus they must help each other. Do not allow a barrier of mistrust to threaten the success of your goal. Persuade the teacher through your actions that her success is your success and that you, too, have experienced a similar problem. Be armed with ideas for classroom management, diagnosis, practical instructional strategies and various means of evaluation. Also, keep in mind some professional books, pamphlets, and inservice meetings which she might find helpful.

Never allow yourself to assume that all teachers who have some classroom experience and a master's degree are good reading teachers. It simply is not true. However, every teacher has some positive points to compliment. Find them and build on them. Approach every problem diagnostically:

1. Maintain an awareness of what a good teacher knows and can do.
2. Find out what particular skills or knowledge Mrs. White needs to improve her classroom instruction.
3. Plan a program of remediation based on your findings. Prescribe ways the teacher can improve her knowledge, teaching strategies, methods of reporting to parents, and interaction with students. Take care not to intimidate her. Consider observation of other teacher inservice meetings, informal talks, professional readings, and university courses.
4. Provide support, encouragement, and know-how.
5. Be sure that your mannerisms do not portray an air of superiority but one of respect and honesty.
6. Do not leave it here. If needed, demonstrate diagnostic teaching techniques, creative use of materials, record keeping, etc.
7. Observe and assist with reading instruction a number of times if possible. Go back and give honest praise for a job well done.
8. Promote a climate of mutual respect; this makes it possible to really help a teacher. Encourage her when the signs of progress are evident.
9. Always maintain a sense of humor and display common courtesy.

Self-evaluation. When you have finished this task, analyze your results. Were you successful? What mistakes did you make? How will you proceed the next time? Did you gain the respect and gratitude of a teacher, a principal, and board member?

Situation

Many reading problems have environmental correlates such as illiterate parents or guardians, poor attitude toward education, or unhealthy mental and/or physical home en-

vironment. In what ways could you and the social worker co-operate to facilitate reading improvement?

Reaction

It seems that there certainly is a large percentage of children with reading problems among those whom the social worker serves. Generally, the families who need the services of a social worker over an extended period of time will need the services of a reading specialist for at least one (probably more) of the children. If parents can't get along, it disturbs the children; if children are hungry and poorly clothed, they can't concentrate on learning. Emotional, social, and physical problems cause distractions which hinder learning to read. So you see, you and the social worker do, indeed, have a common concern.

You would find it helpful to plan with the social worker some means of providing mutual services for those who need them. She may have discovered through home visits that some of your students are not well, have vision or hearing problems, are experiencing emotional stress, or are being neglected. Any of these conditions may be significant factors to consider when diagnosing and treating reading difficulties. The social worker has many agencies at her disposal and can assist in remedying many of these conditions. She may have access to funds to buy glasses, clothing, medical help, and perhaps housing.

The two of you should exchange important information you may have gathered. Your teaching will be more effective if the children are motivated; they will be easier to motivate if they are not experiencing difficulties at home.

If the social worker schedules regular counseling sessions, she may be invaluable in motivating individual children to learn to read. In other words, "She can make them want to read, and you can teach them how to read." You may be able to shed some light on a problem she is working with by observing a child and watching for signs or symptoms of problems. The two of you, along with other involved persons, will be able to deal more effectively with the problem than any one person could.

Some schools plan evening meetings on "How Parents Can Help Their Children at Home." The parents are invited by the social worker to attend. These meetings can take different approaches such as the following:

1. Plan a series of meetings on "the home life that promotes successful learning at school" or "things children need in order to read well."
2. Have a session or two demonstrating ways parents can teach their children at home before and after they start school.
3. Prepare videotaped films of parents at home. Show the "right" and "wrong" way to handle a situation.
4. Prepare helpful handouts and brochures and discuss how they can be used at home.
5. Have a "get acquainted night" and work to put parents and children at ease. By your words and mannerisms show them that you care. "They won't care what you know until they know that you care." Show common courtesy and friendliness at all times.

In summary, there are many causal factors in reading disabilities which are environmental in nature. An alert social worker can provide great assistance in helping to solve some of these problems. Don't hesitate to take advantage of these services.

Situation

The school psychometrist, Mr. Young, tests children and makes reports and recommendations that wield a great deal of influence in placing children in special programs. In what ways can the reading consultants work cooperatively with the school psychologist to effect the most appropriate placement solution for children having great difficulty in school?

Reaction

Some teachers perceive the work of psychometrists as if it were some mystical, magical field of study which only psychometrists can understand. Some teachers seem to believe that there is little or no room for error in their judgment and that one must not question it. This is simply not true. Psychometrists have a very specialized field of study, but they do not claim to be infallible. Learn what you can about their work. This will help you to dispel any feelings of inferiority you may have had.

Get personally acquainted with the psychometrist and ask him to explain his tests, methods of diagnosis, the collection of important data, and the writing of recommendations. Find out how your work dovetails with his. This might be a very profitable way to use some inservice time. Perhaps all of your reading teachers could profit from these meetings.

Get a list of special terms and their definitions and study them carefully so that you can converse easily with good understanding. If you have access to rooms with one-way mirrors, ask him to test a child while you and your colleagues watch. When the sessions are finished, use your inservice meetings to discuss his findings. Note his alert observation skills and how cautious he is about reading too much into some test results.

If, as is the truth in many cases, Mr. Young's written reports are not easily understood by teachers, discuss ways to help him write the reports in terms more easily understood. Also, assist your teachers in gaining a better grasp of the terminology, concepts, ideas, and recommendations presented in these reports.

Once you have demonstrated genuine interest in gaining insight into Mr. Young's work, he will, most likely, have developed a keener interest in yours. For instance, he may be having difficulty making practical suggestions to classroom teachers or special teachers for remedial reading. Since this is where you are most comfortable, discuss this at length. You can help him to suggest the most appropriate teaching methods and specific materials to use which are available in your school.

You might also find it mutually beneficial to discuss your methods of diagnosing reading problems, the tests you use and your recommendations for instruction. Occasionally, you will find that both of you are using similar methods of discovering a problem. You will be invaluable in transferring his diagnosis into a blueprint for remedial instruction.

Mr. Young may not have a very adequate means of determining the extent of a reading problem; thus, he will probably refer many such cases to you. However, you can suggest that he administer parts of some of your tests to get some general information about reading level. Instruments such as an Informal Reading Inventory, the Woodcock Reading Test and the Slosson Intelligence Test may be very helpful to him. At the very least he will want to understand your work.

Remember your areas of expertise differ. Mr. Young is a testing expert; you are a curriculum specialist. The more widely each of you spreads your expertise, the more children you can serve.

A very competent psychometrist stated that she sincerely believed that 80 to 90 percent of the learning problems she deals with are due to a mismatch between the child's developmental level and the instructional level. Be sure to take advantage of the psychometrist's diagnostic skills. Let him know what information will be helpful to you. Ask very specific questions about information you will need in order to prescribe the most appropriate instruction.

Of course it is imperative that you keep Mr. Young apprised of your various programs and the student entry requirements. Then, he can consider them among the various options as he writes his recommendations. Ask Mr. Young to visit your reading projects so that he will have first-hand knowledge of them.

Encourage staff meetings where all concerned, knowledgeable personnel can have input into pupil placement. Always display a spirit of friendliness and honesty. Determine to learn all you can and be willing to share what you know.

Situation

You have spent a number of years writing a five year reading plan which includes special resource rooms for reading instruction. New federal guidelines for special education are causing large numbers of children to be placed in special education programs labeled "learning disabilities." All available rooms have been taken and, as more children are identified, additional space will be needed. Your special remedial reading programs do not take precedence over this ever-expanding program; hence, you are in danger of having them displaced by learning disabilities classes. (You are not in total agreement with the criteria used for identification of the children for the instructional procedures in the classes.) Is there any way to resolve your problem? What are the alternatives?

Reaction

Obtain a copy of the federal law which mandates these special education programs and study it carefully. Also, search the professional journals for articles which interpret and discuss the law. Learn all you can about the law and gather as much reliable information as you can from every available source. You may learn of new information which will help you to establish the direction you should take.

Of course, you understand the necessity for these programs and must make this fact understood to those persons teaching and supervising them. The question is, must they displace your programs? Discuss this situation with knowledgeable administrators and solicit their assistance. Try to ascertain whether the intent of this law is being followed carefully. Contact officials from the State Department of Public Instruction and get their official interpretation of this law. You may also want to plan a meeting with other school administrators in surrounding districts to discuss mutual concerns and possible solutions. From this group of administrators (representing various school districts) you might wish to draft a letter or petition stating your concerns and making some precise recommendations to the SDPI or the congress. Talk with university professors. They will usually be delighted to help you.

It is imperative that you explain this critical situation to your superintendent (and perhaps the school board) objectively and thoroughly, for without this support you will gain nothing. In the meantime, make every effort to assist the special education director in finding appropriate rooms (other than yours) to house the newly established classes. How about a vacant house? Are there basement rooms that could be fixed up adequately? Could the students be bussed to a nearby school where there are extra rooms?

It is possible that your educational philosophy concerning these special education classes is not in agreement with that of the federal mandate. In such an event, it is wise to consider very carefully every move you make. You could, possibly, have the entire special education department angry with you. Remember, everyone is defensive about his own programs and resents an outsider treading on his "sacred ground." If, in fact, your concern is that students are being placed in learning disabilities programs because they have a reading disability, you could discuss this with the psychometrist and others who make the recommendation for special placement. Usually, they are open to new ideas and will listen to good suggestions. After all, they are interested in helping the children. If your reading program appears to be the best solution for some of these children, it will most likely be recommended. Prepare brochures describing your services for children and be sure copies are circulated.

If you are still distressed about this problem, discuss it further with officials at the state, regional, and/or national reading meetings. Try to establish whether you are in an either/or situation.

In summary, consider the following suggestions:

1. Have an open discussion early in the year with the school principal, special education director, and others involved in the mutual conflict of time, space and materials. If both parties are aware of both sides of the problem, it is easier to resolve disagreements and prevent hard feelings.
2. Consider possible compromises such as sharing materials and equipment on a type of advance sign-up or alternating basis.
3. Space problems might be resolved by bringing in yet another party such as the principal or the superintendent. Perhaps the same room could be used by both classes as a resource room. One might meet in the morning and the other in the afternoon. Perhaps the entire staff could be called together to try to develop a feasible solution to the space problem. Is there a lounge, stage, or auditorium that could be utilized?
4. If there is a conflict in teaching methods it might be dealt with by promoting the sharing of ideas among teachers.

Different teachers could be assigned to make short presentations each month on important phases of their projects. Also, schedule time for classroom observation periodically. Having combined inservice sessions on topics of mutual interest will help to develop a climate of teamwork.

Reading Consultant's Relationship with Students, Faculty, Administration, and Community: Establishing Credibility

Overview

The reading consultant is responsible for the establishment of his own credibility in the school community. The consultant may be met with varying degrees of skepticism or acceptance by the community and still he must view the establishment of long term credibility as a paramount objective. This objective is important because the degree to which a consultant is believed has a direct bearing on the press coverage given to the school's reading program, the understanding the community has of the reading program, the financial support the community gives the program, and the community's acceptance of the ideas and the program offered by the consultant.

The reading consultant establishes credibility by accurately perceiving the needs of the school community, by accurately ascertaining his ability to meet those needs, and by his ability to recognize and deal with the vulnerable areas inherent in the consultant's role. A consultant is more likely to perceive the needs of the community accurately if he has a broad and deep understanding of the reading process as it affects the lives of the people in the school community. That is, if the consultant perceives reading as being an intricate part of development, learning, and values of the entire community, then he realizes that the community's attitudes toward reading have direct bearing on that community's view of the school's reading program. The consultant will then see the need to work toward establishing an atitude within the community that is compatible with the nature of the program. A thorough self-understanding is necessary because the consultant should rely on his strengths in order to help ensure success in what is attempted. For example, a consultant who teaches well should take advantage of that strength and model teaching whenever possible in order to demonstrate a point. Finally, all consultants, by the nature of the job, are vulnerable in certain areas. Knowledge of these vulnerable areas will help protect the consultant from them. For example, some people in the school community may feel that a person aspires to be a consultant because he is not able to "take" the classroom, others may believe the reading consultant is hungry for power, and others may feel threatened by the knowledge the reading consultant has. The consultant seeking credibility, then, will make a conscientious effort to know the community, to know himself, and to protect himself in those areas where vulnerability may exist.

Situation

Your job as a reading consultant was created by people other than your principal. In other words, you were "dumped" on him and he really doesn't know what to do with you. How do you find your niche in this rather ambiguous situation?

Reaction

This problem is not at all unusual. In many school districts, reading specialists at the school level are a new breed. Theoretically, principals are the instructional leaders of the school. More often than not, the reading consultant becomes the instructional leader. As a result, it is very possible that a school principal may feel a bit threatened by the consultant's role.

So, the consultant's task is a complex, but not insoluble, one. First, the consultant must be very clear in her own mind about what she wants to do and what services she believes she could best provide the school. Obviously, if a traditional role is chosen, such as developing a lab for students to visit, the consultant's dealings with the principal are easier because she can show him many other examples of this sort of program. But if a less traditional role is chosen, like being a resource teacher for other teachers, the task is much more difficult.

Whatever role is decided upon it must then be communicated to the principal. Here are a few suggestions as to how this might be done:

1. Believe in the principal as a reader. Give him any literature you can find that supports the chosen role, the program, and your understanding of the reading process.
2. Ask him for advice. Make certain that whenever you ask for advice that you are willing to take it or at least be able to develop a good rationale for not taking it.
3. Report in writing, on a regular basis, all the things you are doing. Repeat the most important activities to him verbally, asking for feedback and evaluation.
4. Involve as many teachers in the program as possible. Help them develop and implement their good ideas. Then make sure the principal knows.
5. Finally, don't be afraid to admit your failures, fears, and disappointments. Initiate a sense of teamwork with the principal. Your attitude will do much to help him accept you and your contributions.

Situation

As a reading consultant, you are having a problem with your job description. The people (administrators, teachers, and students) seem to believe that your primary purpose is to work with the students who have a "reading problem." You, on the other hand, believe you should be a resource to all teachers and to all students. What can be done to change their perception of your role in the school?

Reaction

This dilemma is common to many specialists and consultants around the country. The solution lies in two areas: 1) the specialist's security in her own role and 2) the education of those people in the school.

The first part of the solution—security in one's own description—is fundamental to getting people to change their view of the consultant's job. Individuals in the consultant position have a good deal more power than they sometimes give themselves credit for. People will generally treat one as one expects. Thus, the consultant's first task is to clearly decide what role she desires to play and why. This takes clear thinking about the reading process, a sound understanding of one's own strengths and weaknesses, and a thorough understanding of why the program being established is necessary. Once a consultant is secure in these three factors, she is capable of being a flexible leader. Being a flexible leader means that she can make decisions concerning how far to compromise on which issues, which issues to remain firm on, and which issues to let slide for awhile. This decision making ability will facilitate the consultant's ability to plan a program for educating the people in the school.

Next, the consultant should begin to educate the teachers, administrators, and students concerning those most important issues. No stone should be left unturned. The consultant should talk to anyone who will listen as to why the established program should be as it is. The consultant should also use many types of media to present the program. Examples of what can be done are these: 1) posters can be made and hung all over the school; 2) announcements can be made in the school bulletin; 3) noon hour seminars can be held; 4) a newsletter can be printed; 5) TV and radio can be utilized—the list goes on and on, depending on the resources of the school.

In conclusion, these points are very important: educating the people in the school is of little value if the consultant doesn't know 1) the purpose for the educating, 2) how to articulate the purpose, and 3) how to "sell" the program. A good consultant is, after all, a good teacher with the school as her classroom.

Situation

You have just been hired as a reading specialist in a community that you don't know very well, so you decide to attend the local school board meeting in order to find out more about the board's opinions concerning the reading process. You get a chance to talk to most of the members and find that they basically believe that reading is just a "sounding out words" process. As you leave the meeting all you can hear is phonics, phonics, phonics. You can barely remember three phonics generalizations! What are you going to do?

Reaction

This is a dilemma. If the consultant behaves less than positively toward phonics, the school board members are likely to put little credence in what the consultant says about reading generally. Careful thinking and planning must go into this problem as many school boards have a great deal of power that could make or break a reading program.

The consultant must collect a good deal more information before anything else is done regarding this problem. Additional information that needs to be gathered is the following:

1. Historically, how much involvement has the board had concerning the reading program?

2. What has happened that the board members have such a narrow definition of the reading process? Have their opinions been influenced by a certain person? By a certain group?

3. How do other educators in the community deal with the attitude of the board?

4. What can you find out about the board members? Who is most approachable (most open-minded)? Who has been on the board the longest? Who is the newest member? Who is the most influential?

5. What sorts of information do they expect concerning children's reading progress? How sophisticated is the board with regard to testing and measurement?

The reading consultant should be able to solve this particular dilemma once the above questions are answered. While it is impossible here to map out the various approaches a consultant might use, given all the combinations of answers to the above questions, there are a few principles to be kept in mind:

1. Approach the problem from at least two directions at once—on a personal level with the most approachable member and by making sure that data collection on the children's progress encompasses your understanding of the reading process.

2. Listen carefully to what a board member says, always push for clarification so that you know as well as possible what is being said, respect members' opinions while trying to get those with differing views to understand and respect yours.

3. Remember that people are not going to change their opinions and attitudes overnight; rather they will have to go through a series of experiences, which you as the consultant are in a position to facilitate, in order to understand the reading process in a broader sense.

Situation

As a reading consultant, you have parents who want to help their sons and daughters do better in reading; but you are concerned that the parents may be too pushy and overbearing. You fear that their attitudes may do more to discourage their children's reading than encourage it.

Reaction

This dilemma can be a sticky one. Often, on the surface, it seems very logical that parents should be encouraged to help their children; yet, there are examples of parental involvement that are destructive rather than constructive. However, parents should be involved in their children's learning; therefore, unless very sound evidence exists to the contrary, the reading consultant should work with the parents so that their involvement with their children's reading will be constructive.

One of the most positive things a consultant could do is to have a workshop for those parents who have indicated an interest in helping their children. Certain principles such as the following should be emphasized in the workshop:

1. Parents should invite their child to read aloud something that the child has enjoyed reading silently.
2. Parents should read to their child as a natural family event.
3. Parents should read silently in front of their child and show their emotional response to the reading.
4. Parents should read aloud to the family those things that strike the parents as interesting, informative, and fun.

5. The parents should be led to understand that reading is a form of the communication process; that is, the understanding of what is read is dependent upon what has been written and what the reader brings to the reading as well as what the reader takes from the reading.
6. Parents should realize that their major role can be that of a model—showing their children how to unlock new and unfamiliar words (whether by context, structure, sounding out, or by going to a dictionary) and modeling their love for reading.
7. Parents could be introduced to some of the new children's literature being published as well as some of the tried and true children's classics.
8. Parents should be reminded that sometimes reading is a very private matter and that not all things read are meant to be shared (a good example would be some of Judy Blume's literature).
9. Parents should be reminded that there are individual differences in children's interests and abilities to read, and they should be encouraged to allow their children those differences.
10. Parents should be given ways to support their children's efforts in school.

Situation

Your school's reading program has changed—new materials have been adopted and the teachers are utilizing some different methods. You believe that the parents should know something of this new program. The problem is how to go about doing it.

Reaction

Parents should be informed about what the reading program is and be aware of what is going on in their children's classrooms. A reading specialist with credibility prepares for questions that are likely to arise should parents become misinformed, or if they should become worried or distressed. Also, especially with a new program, some teachers may be somewhat insecure and react defensively to parents' questioning. Whatever you as the specialist can do to avoid this sort of situation is prudent.

The reading consultant can come up with many ideas for explaining the reading program to the community at large and to the parents of the children in the school, if the task is thought of in terms of good teaching. That is, simply consider the community to be the boundaries of the classroom rather than the four walls that most teachers find themselves bounded by. Basically, what this means is that the specialist should use every available means by which to reach people in the community—just as a good classroom teacher provides every experience possible for the children when teaching a new concept or a new skill.

Here are some specific suggestions:

1. Send a letter home with the children—well written and interesting—that explains that some new reading materials are being used in the school.

2. Get a newspaper reporter to interview you and to write an article about the program.

3. Allow the children to take books home and show them to their parents.

4. Take advantage of the PTA and other organizations to introduce the program. Perhaps you could have the parents role-play being children and then go through a typical reading lesson. Another idea is to invite children to a meeting to be your "model class."

5. Utilize local talk shows on the radio or TV to explain your program, or to present your model class.

6. Invite parents to observe one of your master teachers using the program in the classroom.

Generally, the reading consultant should keep the following three points in mind:

1. Do not try to make reading specialists of the parents. Each parent has a concept of the reading process; build from where the parents are.

2. Make yourself truly available to the community. It is easy in many communities for the consultants to become invisible. As a curriculum leader in the school community, the consultant should be highly visible and accessible.

3. Be careful not to be too hard on the old program; rather, be very positive about the new one.